Oskar Fischinger

Oskar Fischinger 1900–1967

EYE Filmmuseum
Center for Visual Music

Experiments in Cinematic Abstraction

Edited by Cindy Keefer and Jaap Guldemond

Contents

6 Sandra den Hamer
Preface

8 Cindy Keefer
Introduction and Acknowledgements

10 Jaap Guldemond, Marente Bloemheuvel, Cindy Keefer
Oskar Fischinger An Introduction

13 Oskar Fischinger
Autobiography

15 **Images I**

Oskar Fischinger and the International Avant-Garde

33 Jean-Michel Bouhours
Oskar Fischinger and the European Artistic Context

40 **Wax Slicing Machine**

42 Jeanpaul Goergen
Oskar Fischinger in Germany 1900 to 1936

50 Ilene Susan Fort
Oskar Fischinger, Modernist Painter

61 **Images II**

Oskar Fischinger and Hollywood

89 Esther Leslie
Oskar Fischinger / Wassily Kandinsky
Where Abstraction and Comics Collide

Texts, Letters and Documents by Oskar Fischinger

96 Oskar Fischinger
The Composer of the Future and the Absolute Sound Film

98 **Images from Ornament Sound Experiments**

106 Author unknown
A Timetable and Music
A Visit to Oskar Fischinger's Color-Sound Animated Film Studio

109 Cindy Keefer
Fischinger's Early Color Experimentation

112 Oskar Fischinger
My Statements are in My Work

114 Oskar Fischinger
About "Motion Painting Nr. 1"

115 **Images** **III**

Oskar Fischinger and Music

135 Jörg Jewanski
The Visions of Oskar Fischinger and Alexander Lászlo in 1935/36 about a New Way of Visualizing Music

140 Richard H. Brown
The Spirit inside Each Object
John Cage & Oskar Fischinger

145 Joseph Hyde
Oskar Fischinger's Synthetic Sound Machine

148 Joseph Hyde
Fischinger's Scores
New Perspectives on His Approach to Music

152 James Tobias
Essay without Words
Motion Painting No. 1, Insight, and the Ornament

Oskar Fischinger and Visual Music

161 Paul Hertz
Fischinger Misconstrued
Visual Music Does Not Equal Synesthesia

164 Cindy Keefer
Optical Expression: Oskar Fischinger, William Moritz and Visual Music
An Edited Guide to the Key Concerns

167 **Images** **IV**

Oskar Fischinger and the Lumigraph

193 An Interview with Barbara Fischinger by Cindy Keefer
The Lumigraph
Dancing with Your Hands

201 **Images** **V**

216 Cindy Keefer
Oskar Fischinger's *Raumlichtkunst*

Testimonials 219 Various Authors

Appendices
227 Filmography
229 Selected Chronological Bibliography
232 Sources for Fischinger's Films
233 Images
238 Contributors to this Publication

Preface

Sandra den Hamer

We at EYE, the new film museum in Amsterdam, are hugely proud to be bringing our inaugural year to a close with a new exhibition entitled *Oskar Fischinger (1900–1967). Experiments in Cinematic Abstraction*. It is devoted entirely to the spellbinding work of the master artist Oskar Fischinger. The exhibition was realized in close collaboration with Cindy Keefer, the Center for Visual Music (CVM), and the Fischinger Trust, to whom we owe a great debt of gratitude.

EYE is dedicated to safeguarding and stimulating film art and culture in the Netherlands. We collect, preserve, present and celebrate cinema, from its very earliest beginnings to the newest work by contemporary filmmakers and visual artists.

All exhibitions at EYE focus on one of four topics: the work of great filmmakers (such as our summer 2012 exhibition on Stanley Kubrick); filmic themes (such as EYE's opening *Found Footage* exhibition); crossovers between film and visual arts (such as *Expanded Cinema*); and important movements and innovative developments in experimental and mainstream cinema. In fact, this Oskar Fischinger exhibition encompasses all the areas covered by our exhibition policy. It presents an overview of the work of a unique artist and a great filmmaker whose innovative experimental work organically merges music, visual art, and cinema, and has influenced generations of visual artists and filmmakers to this day.

EYE holds several Fischinger films in its collection, because in the past the Dutch Film League distributed and screened them here in the Netherlands. Fischinger himself came here in 1931 to present his films in Amsterdam. But it is only now, in our new premises, that we can proudly present his work in its full glory.

Together with CVM, we have been working hard in the Netherlands and the US making new digitized copies of Fischinger's work. And now they are ready at last to be viewed, re-viewed, and viewed again.

In addition to the work presented in the exhibition space, there will be series of noteworthy film programs, as well as events such as Fischinger Classics, curated by Cindy Keefer, and the Lumigraph performance by Barbara Fischinger. Joost Rekveld has curated a program of avant-garde films by past and present Dutch filmmakers who have clearly been inspired by Oskar Fischinger. There will also be seminars, public debates, lectures, guided tours, cinema concerts, educational activities for the very young ones, and exciting shows. So all in all it's the packed exhibition program that we have dreamed of making for years, but we could only make that dream come true in our new museum.

We are grateful to all the people involved in making this exhibition possible, first and foremost to Cindy Keefer, whose passionate commitment was indispensable, and to Jaap Guldemond, whose idea it was to set up this exhibition, and who curated it in collaboration with Cindy Keefer. This catalogue could never have been realized without the infinite energy and passion of Marente Bloemheuvel. Thanks also to Mark-Paul Meyer and Simona Monizza who carried out important work on the processes of digitizing the films of Oskar Fischinger in the exhibition. The generous support of the VSBfonds and Goethe-Institut Nederland means we are now able to show that, nearly a century after his first films, Fischinger's work has lost nothing of its power. It remains to this day innovative, controversial, and supremely enchanting, and is still an endless source of inspiration for the makers of today and tomorrow.

Amsterdam, November 2012

Introduction and Acknowledgements

Cindy Keefer

It's finally time for Oskar Fischinger to receive the much-deserved attention denied during his lifetime. Fischinger's work seems fresh to many discovering it today, perhaps because for the past eight decades it has exerted great influence on the development of today's media and digital culture. This renewed and new attention occurs at a point in time when the histories of the avant-garde, animated cinema, computational audiovisual media, musical media, expanded cinema, and time-based media are being reexamined and are intersecting in a new context, transformed by digital culture and its access and production processes.

At this writing, Center for Visual Music (CVM) has an Oskar Fischinger exhibition at the Whitney Museum, New York ("Oskar Fischinger: Space Light Art, A Film Environment," a.k.a. *Raumlichtkunst*); an installation of *Raumlichtkunst* (until May 2013) at Tate Modern, London; an upcoming exhibition at EYE in Amsterdam; a travelling 35mm film retrospective screening at venues worldwide; a Fischinger DVD distributed to seven continents (including a copy donated to an Antarctica research center); and forthcoming *Raumlichtkunst* installations in major museums in Europe and North America. Fischinger has just received excellent press in *The New York Times* and *Artforum*—it truly is the season of Oskar Fischinger. We are so very pleased to have continued Elfriede Fischinger and William Moritz's mission to preserve and promote Fischinger's films and work.

I first met Elfriede and Bill in 1997, a life-changing experience. Elfriede took me into her garage and began showing the treasures in the estate of her husband Oskar: equipment, machines, paintings, drawings, file cabinets full of papers and periodicals, boxes full of stencils, artifacts, and paint tubes; even some film prints and nitrate animation cels were still stored there. It was overflowing, and never-ending. And it all needed rehousing and proper storage, just for a start! We soon removed the nitrate, film prints, and paintings from the garage, but the work hasn't stopped since.

That year I also began processing and inventorying Moritz's books, papers, films, videotapes, artifacts, and other materials, a thirty-year collection of his research on visual music and Fischinger. Moritz introduced many of us to the little-seen films, and to the history of visual music. I'm indebted to him for six years of intensive visual music education, while working closely with him. Moritz was a founder of CVM, and his original research collection resides in our archives.

Those papers from Elfriede's garage, animation drawings and other materials from her house and various storage vaults, form the core of CVM's Fischinger collection now. In those papers were correspondence from Lang, DeMille, Rebay, Ruttmann, Richter, Belson, Cage, Bertoia, and so many more, plus numerous charts, diagrams, graphs, plans for unmade films, unfiled patent drawings, and many more discoveries. The Fischinger Trust began donating Fischinger's papers and animation material to CVM in 2009, and it is from this collection that material for this book and exhibition has been drawn. Both serve as a good introduction to the vast holdings of our archive.

Center for Visual Music has been restoring Fischinger's films for the past nine years (and those by artists he influenced), and we gratefully extend our thanks to the funders and donors who have supported this work: The National Film Preservation Foundation; The Avant-Garde Masters Program, funded by The Film Foundation, administered by The National Film Preservation Foundation (for the photochemical restoration of *Raumlichtkunst*); The Fischinger Trust; Centre Georges Pompidou; and private donors. We thank those who have supported our digitization of the films, including EYE, Scott Bradbury and Westwind Media (Burbank CA); and Timothy Finn. We thank CVM's other funders, including The Judith McBean Foundation, The Lefkowitz Family Foundation, The NASA Art Program (for Jordan Belson's *Epilogue*), and private donors.

CVM extends thanks to those whose past projects have preserved some of the films: The Academy Film Archive (with support from Sony and The Film Foundation, in 1999 and 2000), Nederlands Filmmuseum in past decades (now called EYE), The Fischinger Trust, Cinémathèque québécoise, and, always, to Elfriede Fischinger and William Moritz for their decades of duplicating, distributing and promoting the films. We thank EYE (Mark-Paul Meyer, Simona Monizza, and Annike Kross) for the current digitization of some of the films, and support for our current co-preservation project for *Studie Nr. 5*.

For this publication we chose to present all new scholarship, instead of reprinting Moritz's work. His book *Optical Poetry* remains an essential resource (cited by nearly all of our authors), and some of his best articles are available on CVM's website. A good deal of new research has begun at CVM with our Fischinger collection and some is presented here, including some of the music-related research of Joseph Hyde and Richard Brown. We present a sampling of Fischinger's texts, diagrams, and sketches, most of them newly discovered in the archive. A very significant new result is the correction of the release date for the film *Kreise* (*Circles*), as per the research of Jeanpaul Goergen indicating 1934, rather than Moritz's 1933 date.

I cannot thank Barbara Fischinger enough, for without her support CVM could not have achieved its successes today. Her never-wavering support for my work, CVM, and all of our Fischinger projects has been a source of great strength and inspiration over the years. The first of several interviews with Ms. Fischinger is presented in this volume.

I thank James Tobias for his help with this book, with the Fischinger collection, and for his generosity and expertise as a board member with aspects of shaping and guiding CVM.

Many have helped to bring Fischinger the attention he deserves today, and for their work over recent decades, we must thank Angelica Fischinger, John Canemaker, yann beauvais, Jean-Michel Bouhours, Michael Friend, Cecile Starr, Jörg Jewanski, Ilene Susan Fort, Leonard Maltin, Eva Mason, Arthur and Corinne Cantrill, Ingo Petzke, David Curtis, Gary Schwartz, Amy Halpern, Marco de Blois, Pacific Film Archive (Berkeley), Goethe Institut (Los Angeles), Light Cone (Paris), Deutsches Filmmuseum (Frankfurt), and all of our authors in this book.

For recent exhibitions and attention to Fischinger, we thank Chrissie Iles and The Whitney Museum (New York), Stuart Comer and Tate Modern (London), Suzanne Buchan, Kerry Brougher, Marcella Lista, Ken Johnson, Jonathan Rosenbaum, William Poundstone, Dave Kehr, Michael Sporn, Holly Willis, John Schaefer and Peyton-Wright Fine Arts (Santa Fe). For support for this publication and related exhibition, we thank EYE Filmmuseum.

Thanks are extended to our film laboratories: Film Technology Co., Hollywood (especially the late Alan Stark); Cinema Arts, Cinetech, Triage/Eque and Cineric; plus Chace Audio by Deluxe, Audio Mechanics, Technicolor, Point 360, FotoKem, and Hollywood Vaults.

Very special thanks must be given to the CVM Founder's Circle (especially Stephen Beck, Susan Bolles, Barbara Fischinger, Lawrence Janss, and Ed and Laura Lantz), and all of our other donors. We thank the CVM Members who support our programs and work, and contribute their expertise, especially Xarene Eskandar, Jack Ox, Steve Roden, Scott and Isabel Draves, Heike Sperling, Maura McDonnell, Scott Snibbe, Joseph Hyde, Barry Spinello, Joost Rekveld, Liza Simone, Greg Leeper, Bruce Lane, Steve Cheatham, Suzanne Perkins, Rol Murrow, Mark Rowan-Hull, Cameron Gainer, and during our founding period, Richard Baily and Jules Engel.

Finally, we must thank Oskar Fischinger for making such exquisite work, and Elfriede for saving everything related to it, making possible the books and exhibitions of today and the future.

Los Angeles, October 2012

Oskar Fischinger An Introduction

Jaap Guldemond
Marente Bloemheuvel
Cindy Keefer

In December 2012 the new EYE Filmmuseum in collaboration with the Center for Visual Music, Los Angeles, presents a major exhibition dedicated to one of the foremost pioneers of animation and abstraction in cinema, Oskar Fischinger (1900–67). Fischinger created a new abstract film language that parallels and interacts with musical qualities such as harmony and dissonance, polyphony and timbre.

In 1920 Fischinger started developing a unique oeuvre of more than fifty films, experimenting with numerous technically advanced methods of producing his highly artistic abstract films, animations and special effects. Fischinger constantly invented new devices and techniques to realize his visions. These ranged from his very early wax slicing animation machine, to his radical manipulation of synthetic sound in order to extract sound from images, and to live performances using his Lumigraph color-light instrument.

Fischinger was a true virtuoso in the way he created highly complex patterns that develop dynamic rhythms, harmonies, and counterpoints. Fischinger played an important and influential role in the development of early abstraction in film during the interwar period, amid artistic movements such as Orphism (Kupka, Delaunay), Neo-Plasticism (Mondriaan, Van Doesburg), Suprematism (Malevich), and Futurism (Marinetti, Boccioni). In 1926 Fischinger began working with multiple projector cinema performances, creating some of the earliest cinematic immersive environments, precursors to expanded cinema.

Visual Music

"This art emphasizes the effect of music. It is to music what wings are to birds." (Fischinger, c. 1948)

Emerging from the Absolute film movement in Berlin in the 1920s, Fischinger's abstract film experiments exploring time, motion, and music resulted in a groundbreaking series of black and white Studies synchronized to music (1929–34), which were screened in first-run theaters worldwide. Using music to give his abstractions a more accessible compositional structure, he paved the way for an art form that came to be known as Visual Music. Rather than being direct expressions or illustrations of music, his sound films explore various relationships between image and sound.

Fischinger was known in Berlin as the "Wizard of Friedrichstrasse" because of his expertise with special effects and his many inventions. They included the Wax Slicing Machine, an animation device that cut thin slivers of wax and recorded this process using a stop motion technique. Walter Ruttmann, who had inspired Fischinger with his own work, licensed one of these Wax Slicing Machines to create effects for Lotte Reiniger's *Adventures of Prince Achmed*. Fischinger's special effects were used in several films, including Fritz Lang's classic *Frau im Mond* (*Woman in the Moon*, 1929).

From 1933 onwards Fischinger created the abstract color films *Kreise* (*Circles*, 1933–34), *Quadrate* (*Squares*, 1934) and *Komposition in Blau* (*Composition in Blue*, 1935) in which he explored the interplay of abstract shapes and color using the new Gasparcolor three-color process. In the same period Fischinger made some remarkable advertising films including *Muratti Greift Ein* (*Muratti Gets in the Act*, 1934).

Oskar Fischinger's Berlin years (1927–36) were highly successful, with respect to both his art and its appreciation. Fischinger's films were screened by Moholy-Nagy at the Bauhaus, and most of his black and white Studies and color films were distributed throughout Europe, the US, South America and even in Asia. In the Netherlands, his work became known to a wider public from 1931 onwards, through screenings in various film houses including De Uitkijk in Amsterdam. The Dutch Film League was responsible for introducing Fischinger's work to the Netherlands, where it struck a chord with critics and audiences alike. The Dutch avant-garde documentary filmmaker Joris Ivens was a great admirer of Fischinger's work, and he even organized screenings of Fischinger's films in Moscow.

Hollywood

The Nazi rise to power and condemnation of "degenerate art" made it increasingly difficult for Fischinger to continue work on his abstract films, and in 1936 the celebrated German émigré film director Ernst Lubitsch invited Oskar Fischinger to Hollywood. Fischinger's *Studie Nr. 5* (*Study No. 5*, 1930) had already been released successfully in the US—Universal Pictures distributed it in their newsreels screening before feature films.

In his first years in California, Fischinger worked for various major Hollywood studios, including designing an animation sequence for Disney's *Fantasia*. However, he soon terminated his job with Disney due to the creative limitations he encountered. The restrictions of the Hollywood studio system conflicted with his artistic freedom. Despite his projects with Paramount Pictures, MGM, and Orson Welles' Mercury Productions, his relationship with the major Hollywood studios remained strained.

Fischinger made a number of films in the US, including *An Optical Poem*, *Radio Dynamics*, *Allegretto*, and *An American March*. All are beautiful and complex abstract film works that demonstrate Fischinger's talent and artistry.

His last major film, *Motion Painting No.1* (1947), was made with the support of the Museum of Non-Objective Painting (now the Guggenheim Museum). It is a film of and about painting. Fischinger photographed a painting as he created it, over the course of nine months. Each time he applied a new brushstroke he shot a single frame, thus recording the entire process.

Ultimately, he found no success in Hollywood and was finally forced to give up filmmaking due to lack of support. Fischinger spent the last twenty years of his life painting and working on various small-scale tests and inventions. In the late 1940s he developed the Lumigraph color-light instrument, and in the 1950s he experimented with 3D film and his Stereo paintings, and planned various film projects that were never made due to lack of funding.

In a letter he wrote in 1949 to the curator of the Museum of Non-Objective Painting, Baroness Hilla von Rebay, Fischinger describes how he found the artistic climate in the US to be so lamentable that he had decided to move to the Netherlands. He had received an offer from the Netherlands extending support to make more films, and for distribution of his existing films. The following is a transcription from the original letter to Rebay:

> It is much nicer to hunger and starf with the hungry people over there then to see your own children starf in a place so rich that it could not be richer. It is much more bitter to be hungry between rich people. This is just one reason for going back to Europe.
>
> The other is that here there is not the least bit of under-standing of anything I do my work is of no value here. The people need more Iceboxes more Television sets more cars, more gadgets of all kind. Art is not only not necessary it is not wanted not appreciated.
>
> Any Artist here is just out of place. Europe so poor it is has still a feeling for Art. In Holland the people like my work so why should I not go to this country?[1]

1
Letter from Fischinger to Hilla Rebay (March 19, 1949), Photocopy in Collection of Center for Visual Music, Los Angeles.

In the end, however, Fischinger remained in Los Angeles, partly because his family did not want to move to the Netherlands. His European relatives warned him of the continuing economic difficulties in Europe.

Over the course of the 1940s and 50s, interest did gradually grow in his films and his paintings. The Museum of Modern Art in New York screened his films, his paintings were shown in gallery and museum exhibitions, and in the late 1940s the San Francisco Museum of Art began a series of Art in Cinema screenings that prominently featured Fischinger's work. Due to this, a new generation of artists became acquainted with the films, and they, much like the earlier generation in 1930s Europe, were inspired by Fischinger's work to engage in abstract film. Fischinger's studio in Hollywood was a mecca for the burgeoning avant-garde film community, and Jordan Belson, Harry Smith, John and James Whitney, Maya Deren, and many others paid visits.

Fischinger's work continues to influence today. An example of his multiple projector film performances, *Raumlichtkunst* (c. 1926/2012) has recently been restored and re-created in high definition video by Center for Visual Music, and is currently being exhibited at various museums. This work not only gives an insight into one of the earliest multimedia works, but also confirms Oskar Fischinger's importance to the history of cinema.

Amsterdam, November 2012

Autobiography of Oskar Fischinger, c. 1952

Editor's note: Many of the dates are not the official release dates. Elfriede Fischinger dated this document in pencil at top.

probably ca. 1952

Oskar Fischinger

Account of artistic creations:

a.) absolute graphic films;
produced in Munchen, Germany;

1919-1920	One reel	experimental films	35mm	black	&	white
1920-1922	Second "	"	"	"	"	"
1923-1926	Third "	"	"	"	"	"

b.) absolute graphic films perfectly synchronized to music (first films made this way);
produced in Berlin, Germany.

Film Study Nr 1	made 1927-28	35mm	Black	&	White-music
" " 2	" 1928	"	"	"	"
" " 3	" 1928	"	"	"	"
" " 4	" 1928	"	"	"	"

These 4 films were synchronized to music on records only.

c.) absolute graphic films to music - soundfilm;
produced in Berlin, Germany and distributed all over the world. To name the countries where these films were sold: Germany, Belgium, Holland, France, Switzerland, Italy, Spain, Portugal (South America - Argentina, Brasil, Uruguay, Chile) (North America- U.S.A., Canada), England, Ireland, Norway, Denmark, Sweden, Finland, Poland, Hungary, Japan, and Czlechoslovakia.
The films:

Study Nr. 5,	1929	Soundfilm	Black	&	White	35mm	and	16mm
" " 6,	"	"	"	"	"	"	"	"
" " 7,	"	"	"	"	"	"	"	"
" " 8,	1930	"	"	"	"	"	"	"
" " 9,	1931	"	"	"	"	" only	---	
" " 10,	1931	"	"	"	"	" only	---	
" " 11,	1931	"	"	"	"	"	and	16mm
" " 12,	1932	"	"	"	"	" only	---	
Koloraturen	1931	"	"	"	"	"	and	16mm

Synthetic Sound-Painted Sound 2 reels 1931 35mm only
These experiments in Sound were shown in 1931 at the Kaiser-Wilhelm Institute, Berlin, and to the Verein Deutscher Ingenieure and was not released to the public in spite of a tremendous world-wide publicity these experiments got through the press.

d.) Color films 1932 "Kreise" (Circles) Soundfilm 35mm and 16mm
Composition in Blue color - Soundfilm 35mm and 16mm
Besides these Films, I made during 1932 and 1933-34, a number of Advertising films. The best known is probably a cigarette film, "Muratti greift ein" (color) 1933, where the marching cigarettes walked for the first time over the screen. This film was copied here in this country through the Lucky Strike television advertising extensively.

c.) After coming to the United States of America in February, 1936, I produced through Paramount Motion Picture Corporation.

Oskar Fischinger - 2

In 1936
The Colorfilm "Allegretto" Soundfilm, 35mm and 16mm.
In 1937
The colorfilm "Optical Poem" to the second Hungarian Rapsody by Franz Liszt - released worldwide through M.G.M. and now available through the "Teaching Film Custodian", New York.

In 1938-39
I was engaged through the Walt Disney Corp. to lay out and plan the work on the first part of "Fantasia", the Toccata and Fugue by Bach section. After working one year with that studio I left it, dissatisfied with the way my ideas were broken down by a whole staff of other Disney artists and I never claimed any credit on that work. My previous films were shown many times to all the artists in the Disney Studio and my direct work nevertheless influenced these artists and the whole studio.

In 1939-40
I produced the colorfilm "An American March", 35mm and 16mm; then in 1946-47 I made the Color-Soundfilm "Motion Painting Number One", first released in 1948. This film was awarded the Grand Prix at the International Art and Film Festival at Bruesseles, Belgium, in 1949; 35mm and 16mm.

f.) Since all my films are graphic paintings in motion, and painting was always the most significant part in these films, I made a great number of Paintings in Oil during all these years. I had many Exhibitions of Paintings alone and many Exhibitions where the Paintings and the films were shown together. For example, the present October one-man show at the Frank Perls Gallery, Beverly Hills, California. I enclose the Poster I made for that show and some recent articles from Los Angeles newspapers.

Paintings were shown alone and sometimes together with the films, at:
The San Francisco Museum of Art (repeatedly).
Los Angeles County Museum (repeatedly).
Non-objective Museum, N.Y., which has a collection of most of my films, plus about 9000 water colors on Celluloid and some Oil paintings.
Chicago Museum of Art.
Cleveland Museum, Pomona College, Long Beach Art Association, Westwood Art Association, Los Angeles Art Association, College of the Immaculate Heart, Caltec Institute of Technology, Pasadena, Art Center School, Los Angeles, repeatedly, probably 12 times. Karl Nierendorf Gallery, N.Y., Ph. Boyer Gallery, N.Y., Stendahl Gallery, Los Angeles, Chaffey College, Ontario; University of Southern California, Berkeley University, U.C.L.A. to name only a few.
Many Museums in Europe like the Museum in Copenhagen, The London Museum, Academy in Paris. The Luzern Film Museum has some of my films and Paintings in their collection.
Paintings are in many private collections as are many of my films.

I

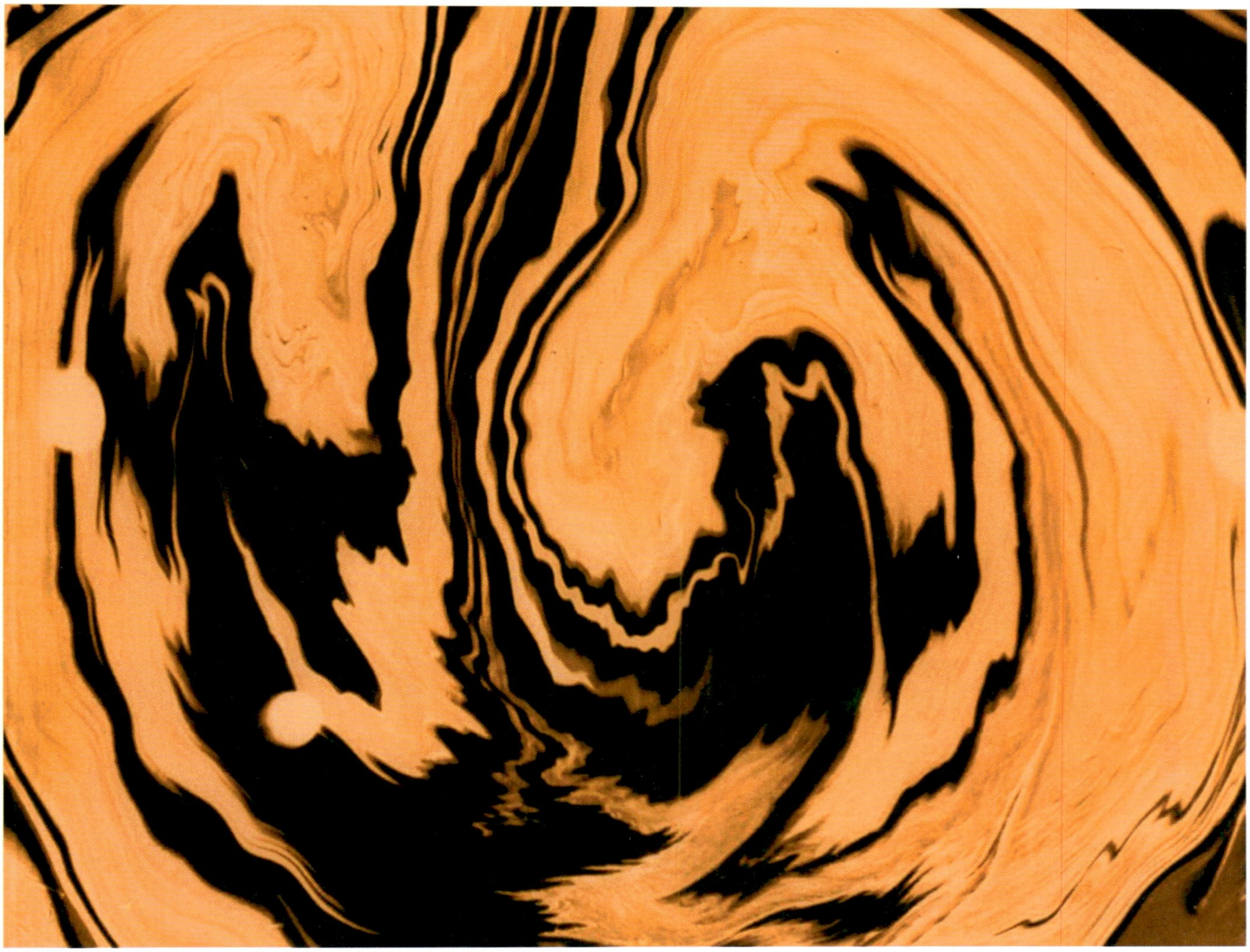

Film still from Oskar Fischinger's very early tinted liquid experiments, c. 1920
35mm, tinted

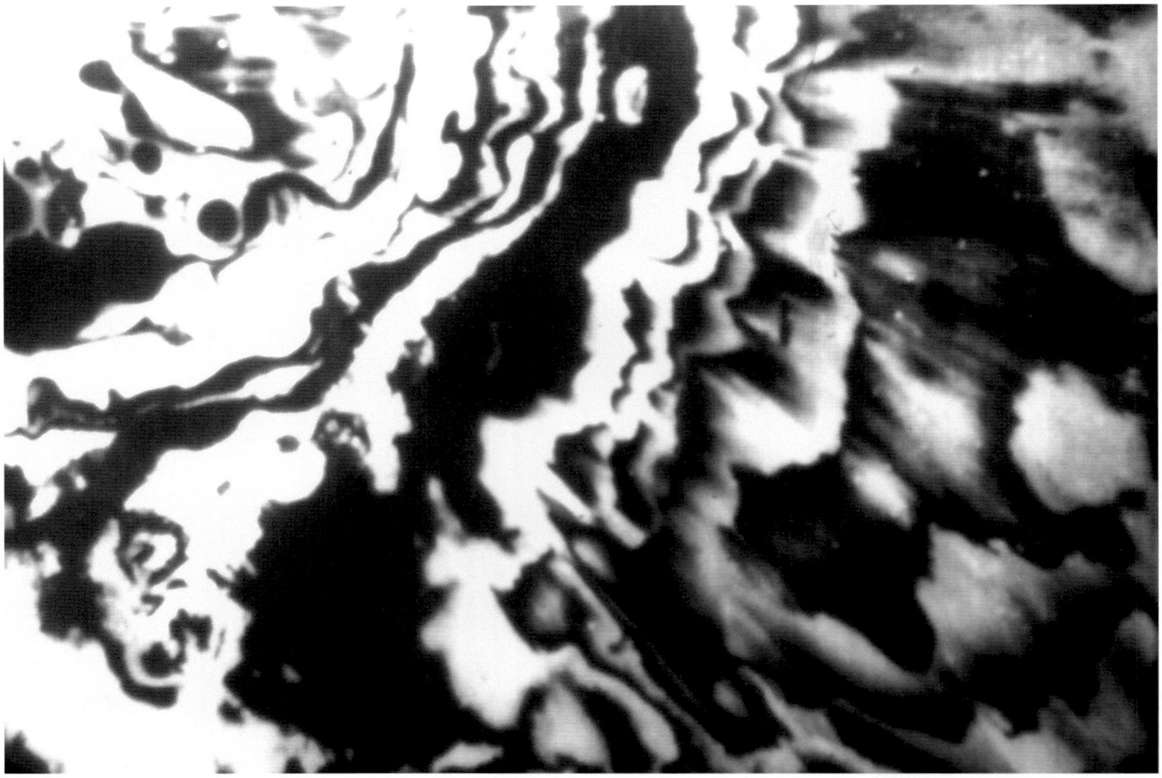

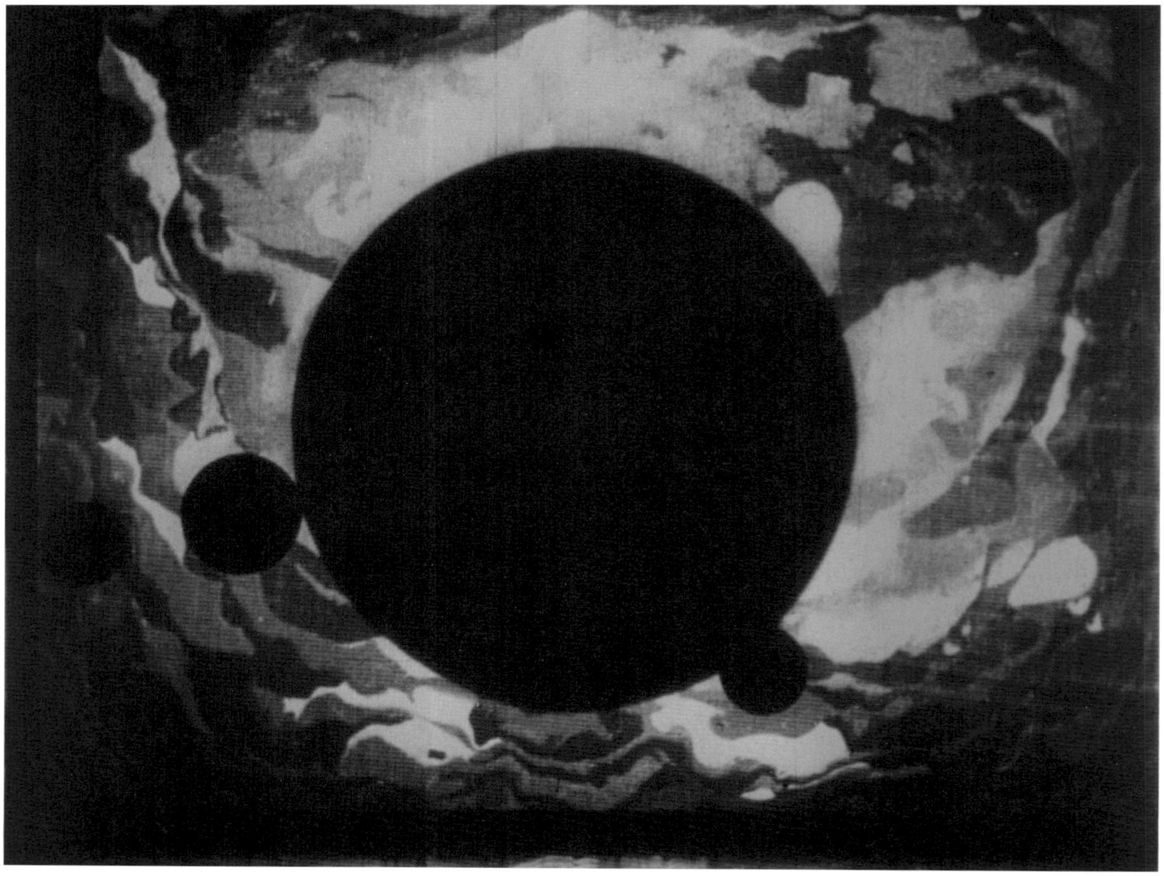

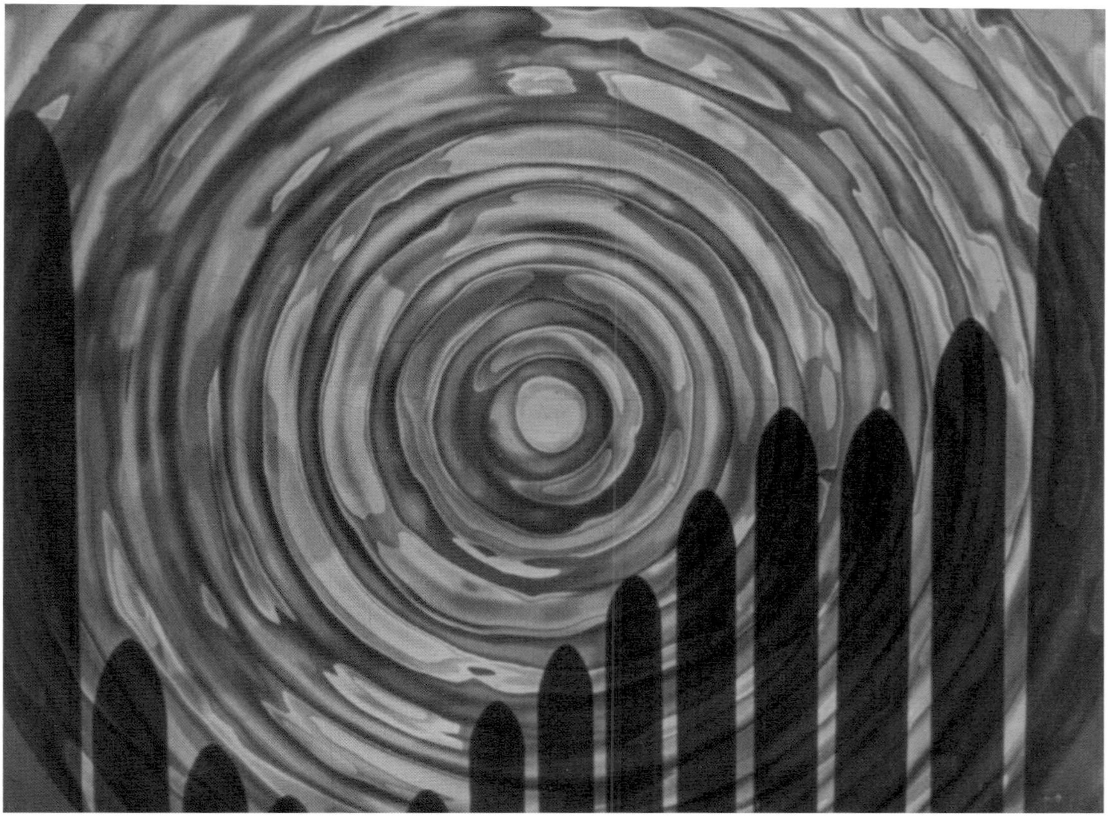

↑
Example of Oskar Fischinger's very early film experiments, film still, c. 1923
35mm, b/w, silent
Collection Center for Visual Music
←
Stills from *Wachsexperimente* (*Wax Experiments*), 1921–26
35mm, b/w and tinted, silent

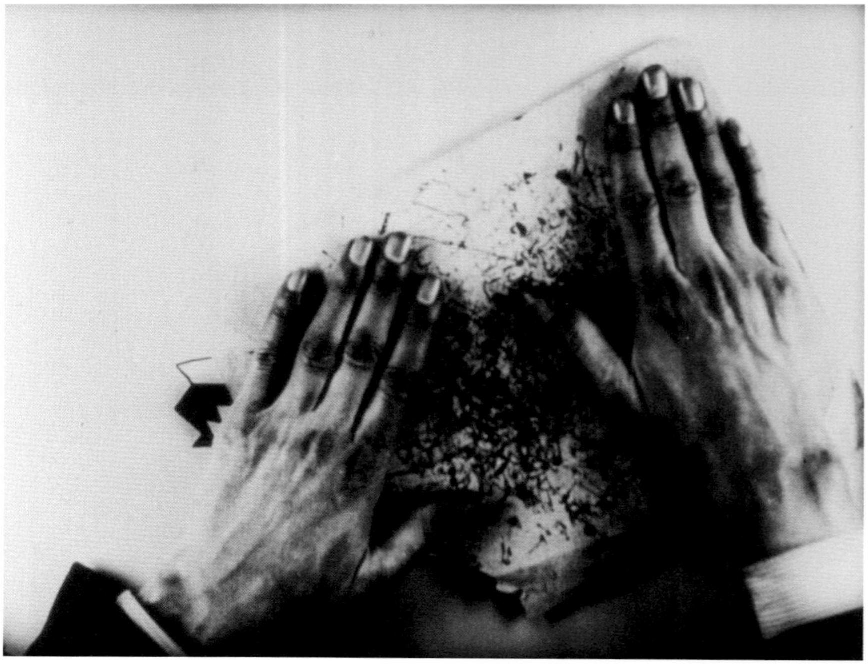

↑
Stills from *Pierrette 1* (from *Münchener Bilderbogen* series), 1924–26
35mm, b/w, silent
→
Early animation drawings, c. 1920–21
Charcoal on paper, 8.8 x 11.2 in. / 22.5 x 28.5 cm
Collection Center for Visual Music

Stills from *Spiralen* (*Spirals*), c. 1926
35mm, b/w, silent

Stills from *Spiralen* (*Spirals*), c. 1926
35mm, b/w, silent

Example of Oskar Fischinger's early film experiments,
film still, early 1930s
35mm, b/w, silent
Collection Center for Visual Music

Still from *Seelische Konstruktionen* (*Spiritual Constructions*), c. 1927
35mm, b/w, silent

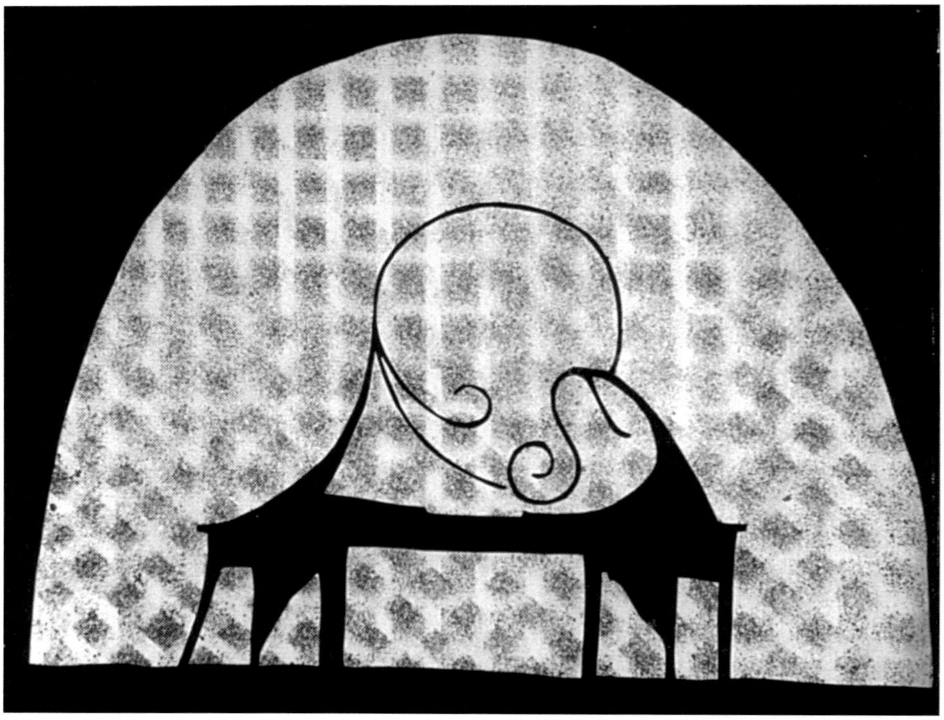

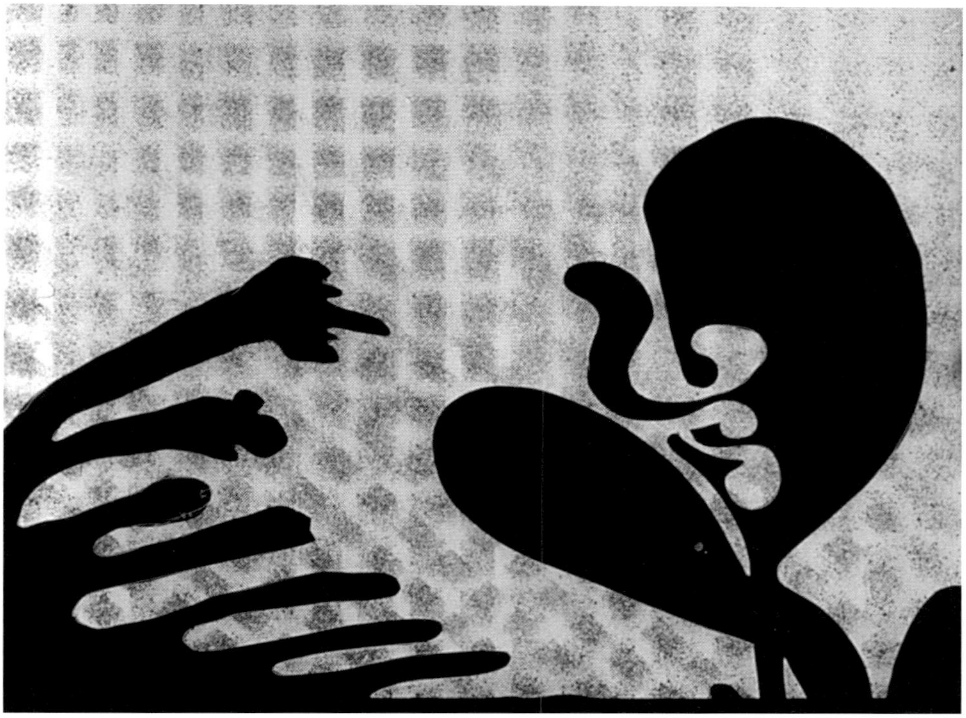

Stills from *Seelische Konstruktionen* (*Spiritual Constructions*), c. 1927
35mm, b/w, silent

Stills from *München–Berlin Wanderung* (*Walking from Munich to Berlin*), 1927
35mm, b/w, silent

Oskar Fischinger and the International Avant-Garde

Oskar Fischinger and the European Artistic Context

Jean-Michel Bouhours

With Walter Ruttmann, Viking Eggeling, and Hans Richter, Oskar Fischinger shares a similar cinematographic approach, using animation techniques to produce abstract paintings in motion. The historical importance of these four major figures of European avant-garde cinema in the 1920s is reason enough to acknowledge the existence of a "German School" of abstract film which had no equivalent in France or any other European country. The presence of Wassily Kandinsky and Franz Marc in Munich, the creation of the Bauhaus in Weimar in 1919, the influence of the prominent painters and theoreticians Kandinsky and Paul Klee, and the proximity of the De Stijl group, all account for the flowering of abstract cinema in Germany.

However, in spite of being recognized by the German press (Fischinger's Studies were awarded the critics' prize by the newspaper *Der Deutsche*), in spite of an extremely wide international distribution—in Amsterdam, London, Moscow, Leningrad, but also more unlikely countries such as Japan, Syria, Palestine, and even Uruguay[1]—the films of Fischinger remain strangely absent from the film programs of the main avant-garde film theatres in Paris, which was after all the hub of global cinephilia. In fact, this observation applies equally to Eggeling and Ruttmann: it was the whole of abstract cinema that met with little response in the French capital.

Fischinger's embracement of a non-photographic cinema that totally contradicted the impressionist French cinema and theories of pure cinema, which favored the "photogenic," as represented by such great figures as Jean Epstein, Germaine Dulac, Alberto Cavalcanti, and even Henri Chomette. The second reason, in my opinion, is the dominant position and intellectual authority in Paris of Surrealism, which lasted from the mid-1920s until World War II. The Surrealists mocked the "little squares and lozenges" of abstract art in general and of cinema in particular, preferring humor and the absurd in the form of the not so pure figures of slapstick cinema embodied by Harry Langdon and Buster Keaton.

However, Oskar Fischinger's films, particularly *Kreise* (*Circles*) and *Komposition In Blau* (*Composition in Blue*), the high points of his European career prior to his emigration to the United States, have clear formal links with French abstract painting, particularly Orphism, a movement championed by the poet Guillaume Apollinaire. The concentric or superposed circles, the use of pure colors of the visible spectrum, the references to the laws of optics, and to the disks of Newton and Philipp Otto Runge's color sphere, are all found in both Orphism and Fischinger's cinema.

1
William Moritz, *Optical Poetry. The Life and Work of Oskar Fischinger* (London, UK: John Libbey Publishing, 2004), 37.

The mythical project *Colored Rhythm*, a never to be realized prophetic project for a new art conceived by the painter Léopold Survage before World War I, prefigures abstract cinema (fig. 1). Although Fischinger's first films were shot in black and white, and Survage's water colors were painted in an "Orphist" color palette, they display closely related forms: images of star matter winding around an epicenter, and of nebulae and galaxies. However, because Léopold Survage's project remained unrealized when the producer Gaumont refused to provide the necessary funds in the summer of 1914, Oskar Fischinger came to be seen as the direct heir to this first Orphist avant-garde and its dreams of a new non-figurative visual art.

Fischinger could have adopted the term "nonobjective art" that his sponsor Hilla Rebay used for her collection of abstract art which laid the foundation for the first Guggenheim Museum in New York. Instead, he chose the term "absolute film." Wagner had used the term "absolute music" to qualify Beethoven's *Ninth Symphony* and he would return to it in his essay "The Artwork of the Future" to designate a language freed from the language of words. The film program *Der Absolute Film*, organized at the UFA theatre in Berlin in May 1925, introduced this terminology into the domain of abstract cinema, in spite of the fact that, as Rune Kreutz pointed out, the extremely heterogeneous contents of the program, including figurative films in the spirit of Dada, did not represent a clearly defined cinematographic field.[2]

In his famous text "Avant-Garde and Kitsch," Clement Greenberg argues that the avant-garde search for a high-level "absolute" art free from all relativities and constraints resulted from its detachment from revolutionary political thought:

> It has been in search of the absolute that the avant-garde has arrived at "abstract" or "nonobjective" art—and poetry, too. The avant-garde poet or artist tries in effect to imitate God by creating something valid solely on its own terms, in the way nature itself is valid, in the way a landscape—not its picture—is aesthetically valid; something given, increate, independent of meanings, similars or originals. Content is to be dissolved so completely into form that the work of art or literature cannot be reduced in whole or in part to anything not itself.[3]

In 1935, Mary Ellen Bute described this as follows: "We view an Absolute film as a stimulant by its own inherent powers of sensation, without the encumbrance of literary meaning,

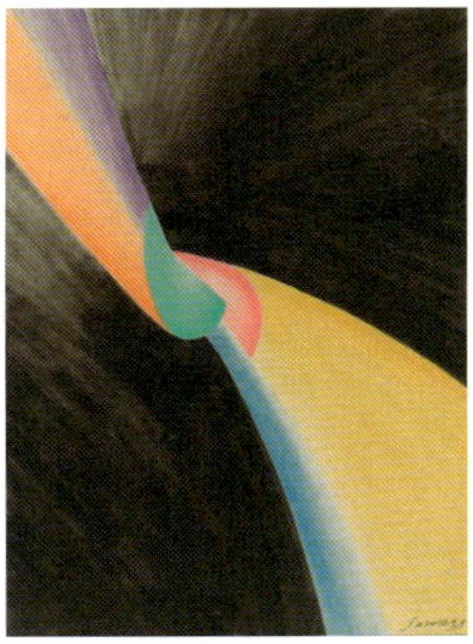

Figure 1 / Léopold Survage, *Colored Rhythm: Study for the Film*, 1913
Watercolor and ink on paper on paper-faced board, 14.2 x 10.5 in. / 36 x 26.6 cm
Collection Museum of Modern Art, New York

Figure 2 / Still from *Spiralen (Spirals)*, c. 1926
35mm, b/w, silent

Figure 3 / Example of Gasparcolor tests, 1933
35mm, silent
Collection of Center for Visual Music

photographic imitation, or symbolism."[4] In Fischinger's view there is a fundamental opposition between a "photographic" or realist cinema aiming to reproduce, and a mode of expression that takes into account a "deep and absolute creative force,"[5] an inner necessity defined by Kandinsky in his work *Concerning the Spiritual in Art*. According to Fischinger, thereby confirming Greenberg's analysis, this absolute creativity can only be the work of an isolated being, without any bounds or constraints whatsoever.

Fischinger's central concern, which he shared with Survage, Viking Eggeling and Hans Richter, was the primacy of motion. Motion defines a new art that transcends the old static painting. Louis-Bertrand Castel's ocular harpsichord, which was developed around 1725, already had its origins in a reflection on the static nature of painting: "[H]armony essentially consists of diversity in motion."[6] According to Survage, the abstract revolution would result in the birth of "kinetic" painting: "[Painting] must rid itself of its last and crucial fetter, immobility, in order to become a means of expressing our emotions that is as rich and flexible as music."[7] Under the influence of the eighteenth-century philosopher Alexander Gottlieb Baumgarten, who determined sensible experience in terms of "vitalistic" notions, the science of sensible knowledge opposes the notions of vivacity and liveliness (*Lebhaftigkeit*) to those of order and composition inherited from academic thought, while in the thought of Henri Bergson, the concepts of intensity and force are substituted with that of harmony. We must also mention the spiritualist approach of the poet and philosopher Ricciotto Canudo, who, with extraordinary foresight, defined a sixth art: cinematographic art. He stressed the advantages of the cinematic medium over the color organs in the domain of abstract imagery: "Velocity possesses the potential for a great series of combinations, of interlocking activities, combining to create a spectacle that is a series of visions and images tied together in a vibrant agglomeration, similar to a living organism."[8] Because the abstract form is motion, it is far better suited to represent the living world than any figurative image.

When Léopold Survage conceived his project *Colored Rhythm*, he could not imagine it without colors, although in 1914 film was still primarily black and white: "Instead of just being an accessory of the objects, [color] becomes the content, the very soul of the abstract form."[9] Fischinger took a more wait-and-see attitude towards color: "Then came color film. Of course, the temptation was great to work in color, and I made thereafter a number of absolute color films. But I soon found out that the simplicity of my own black-and-white films could never be surpassed."[10] (fig. 2)

These words might lead us to think that during his entire first period (until 1932), that of the Studies, Fischinger promoted the objective study of color and its sensuality, remaining rather impervious to the Dionysian conceptions of Orphism as defended and illustrated by Robert and Sonia Delaunay or even Frantisek Kupka. Fischinger appears to be more "minimal," if I may use the term, investigating what he calls "simplicity," which, however, conceals more complex concepts such as "fundamental motion" or "genesis of form" developed by Paul Klee at the Bauhaus.[11] By not using the technique of "direct" film (painting directly onto the film footage, like the Corradini brothers or Len Lye), Fischinger was confronted with the limits of the technology of his days. He would have to wait until he met the brothers Bela and Imre Gaspar, inventors of a color process (Gasparcolor) based on three-color printing, making it possible to reconstitute the color spectrum in film. Immediately following a number of tests with the Gasparcolor process (fig. 3), which enabled him to construct a chromatic language of "strong" primary colors far removed from any naturalistic concept, Fischinger made *Kreise* (*Circles*) and *Quadrate* (*Squares*). In these two films, he uses the process of chromatic separation to his advantage by offsetting and multiplying the number of patterns and their chromatic variations. This resulted in concentric or off-center circles in *Kreise* (*Circles*), intermingled squares in *Quadrate* (*Squares*), and multiple superimpositions. When Len Lye first used Gasparcolor in *Rainbow Dance* in 1936 (fig. 4, p. 36), after making a number of films which were painted

2
Cf. Rune Kreutz, "The Absolute Film and the Role of Abstraction," in *First Light*, ed. Robert A. Haller (New York: Anthology Film Archives, 1998), 70.

3
Clement Greenberg, "Avant-Garde and Kitsch," in *Art and Culture: Critical Essays* (Boston: Beacon Press, 1961), 5–6.

4
Mary Ellen Bute, "Statement II," in *Articulated Light – The Emergence of Abstract Film in America*, eds. Gerald O'Grady and Bruce Posner (Boston: Harvard Film Archive, 1995), 8.

5
Oskar Fischinger, "My Statements are in My Work," in *Art in Cinema*, ed. Frank Stauffacher (San Francisco: Art in Cinema Society-San Francisco Museum of Art, 1947). Reprinted in William Moritz, *Optical Poetry*, 174. Included in this volume, pp. 112–13.

6
Cf. Louis-Bertrand Castel, *Journal de Trévoux*, vol. 139 (August 1735), 1480; and vol. 141 (December 1735), 2685.

7
Léopold Survage, "La couleur, le mouvement, le rythme," text contained in the sealed envelope deposited at the Académie des Sciences de Paris on June 29, 1914. Reprinted in Léopold Survage, *Rythmes colorés 1912–13* (Saint-Etienne/Les Sables-d'Olonnes, Musée d'art et d'industrie/Musée de l'abbaye Sainte-Croix, 1973).

8
Ricciotto Canudo, "The Birth of a Sixth Art," in *French Film Theory and Criticism. A History/Anthology 1907–1939*, vol. 1, ed. Richard Abel (Princeton: Princeton University Press, 1988), 59.

9
Léopold Survage, "La couleur, le mouvement…," no pagination.

10
Oskar Fischinger, "My Statements…," in *Optical Poetry*, 174.

11
Paul Klee, *Notebooks I: The Thinking Eye*, ed. Jürg Stiller (London: Lund Humphries, 1961), 18.

directly onto the film stock, he attempted, like Fischinger, to make color autonomous, somehow realizing what Guillaume Apollinaire had once said about pure painting:

> The first painting was just a line surrounding the shadow of a man cast by the sun onto the ground. But now we are far removed from these "simulacra" with our contemporary means; we have light (light colors, dark colors, their complements, intervals, and simultaneity) and every kind of color that arises from the intellect to create harmony. [12]

Fischinger and Len Lye cultivated the same tropism in relation to Gasparcolor, severing the age-old connection between drawing and color in the visual arts. They proceeded to separate the line (representing the subject) from "filling in the form," which here is pure color. Len Lye spoke of subjects that were "subdivided into echoes."[13] As a result, for example in *Kreise* (*Circles*), Fischinger was able to create colored disks as a tribute to the color disks of Newton and/or as an allusion to the disks in "simultaneous motion" in the paintings of the Delaunays.[14]

The Gasparcolor process of trichromatic separation enabled Fischinger to explore the intermingling of forms as a visual equivalent of the polyphonic structure in music, in the same way that Paul Klee's *Fugue in Red* (fig. 6) repeated and intermingled different motifs in the manner of a chronophotograph (pitchers, circles, rectangles, and so on). Kurt Schwerdtfeger and Ludwig Hirschfeld-Mack's *Reflektorische Farblichtspiel* (*Reflecting Color-Light-Play*), made at the Bauhaus, was inspired by an observation made during a shadow play of the way in which different light sources tend to multiply the shadows of a form.

However, Fischinger believed that his investigations of color only came to full fruition in *Motion Painting No. 1* (1947):

> The color film proved itself to be an entirely new artform with its own artistic problems, as far removed from black-and-white film as music itself—as an art medium—is removed from painting. Searching for the last thirteen years, to find the ideal solution to this problem, I truly believe I have found it now, and my new, forthcoming work will show it.[15]

In this film, Fischinger resorted to the technique of painting on a Plexiglass plate in front of the camera lens, like Henri-

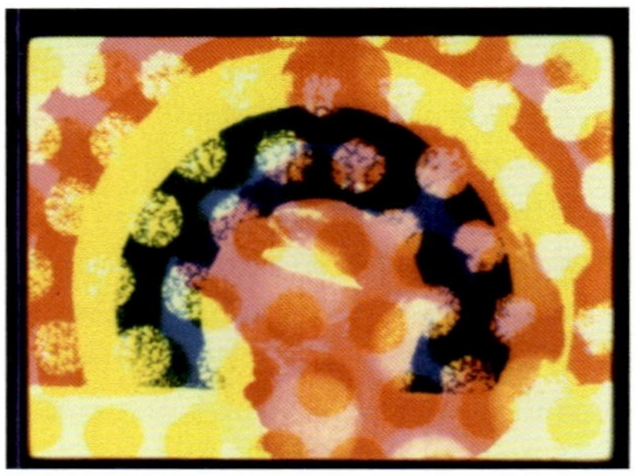

Figure 4 / Len Lye, stills from *Rainbow Dance*, 1936
35mm, color, sound; Gasparcolor

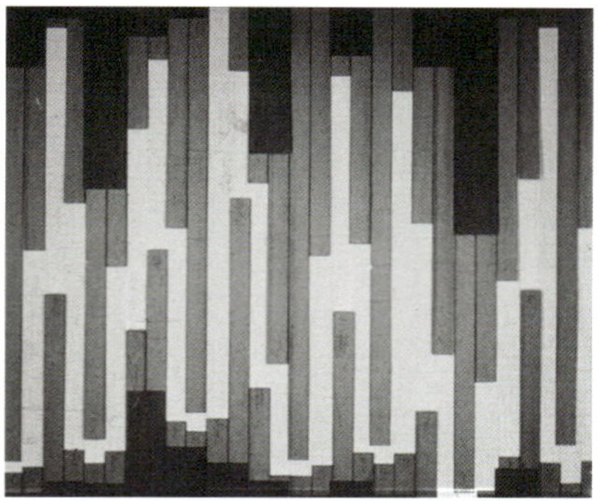

Figure 5 / Still from *Staffs*, 1923–27
35mm, b/w and tinted, silent

Figure 6 / Paul Klee, *Fugue in Red*, 1921
Watercolor and pencil on paper on board, 9.65 x 12.4 in. / 24,5 x 31.5 cm
Private collection Switzerland, deposit at Zentrum Paul Klee, Bern (Switzerland)

Figure 7 / Still from *Radio Dynamics*, 1942
35mm, color, silent

Georges Clouzot in *The Mystery of Picasso*. The technique is that of pixilation: the first, pointillist part of the film reminds us of the texture and modeling of images shot with the pinscreen technique by Alexandre Alexieff and Claire Parker in *Night on Bald Mountain* (1933). A point draws forms that evolve in time in the same way as in Viking Eggeling's *Diagonal Symphony*. Fischinger uses the overabundance of spirals that roll up one by one until they fill the entire screen and that are in turn "wiped out" by colored rectangles and a play of lines along the edges of the screen.

According to William Moritz, Fischinger had a great admiration for Paul Klee. In his *Staffs* (fig. 5) experiments (1923–27), Fischinger creates a rudimentary language of small, vertically juxtaposed cardboard strips in a wide range of grey shades. This "grammar" is closely related to that which Hans Richter used in *Rhythmus 21*. Richter used simple geometric forms: squares and rectangles which grew or shrank within the space of the image, creating the impression of an approaching or receding motion in the depth of the visual field. For *Staffs* Oskar Fischinger invented modular forms resembling juxtaposed, growing or shrinking "organ pipes." These forms are musical in an iconographic sense, and seem to replicate a succession of musical notes of different height. The "pipes" create lateral, sinusoidal movements that behave like the crest of a wave. The film is a perfect response to the reflections of Paul Klee on the creation of an artificial order reproducing movement and countermovement—these are Klee's terms—between light and dark in nature, illustrated in the painting *Separation in the Evening*, a water color from 1922. Paul Klee's graphs reproduce intermediate gradations, the counterpoint of the blackness in the heart of the light, in a crenellated form which recalls the abstract structure of the images in *Staffs*. The dynamics of light and dark in *Staffs* represent natural light phenomena without any recourse to mimesis, but simply through the elaboration of a language of elementary forms, realizing an almost word for word translation onto film of the method developed by Klee in the graphic arts. *Komposition In Blau* (*Composition in Blue*), with its fine grid of horizontal lines against a yellow background in between which blue, green, yellow or red squares appear, evokes Klee's more specifically musical research. In *Radio Dynamics* (fig. 7), the small squares, stacked much in the same way as a chess table, form a grid that closely resembles that in Klee's *Polyphony* (1932).

12
Guillaume Apollinaire, "Réalité, Peinture pure," in Robert Delaunay, *Du cubisme à l'art abstrait*, ed. Pierre Francastel (Paris: S.E.V.P.E.N, 1957), 156.

13
Len Lye, "Experiment in Colour," *World Film News* (December 1936), 33.

14
Robert Delaunay, *Du cubisme à l'art abstrait*, 125.

15
Oskar Fischinger, "My Statements ...," in *Optical Poetry*, 174.

It would be equally interesting to compare Klee's lessons at the Bauhaus with Fischinger's Studies. By moving, the point draws a line, materializing "fundamental motion." The surface itself is the result of the shifting motion of the line and the volume is the result of the movement of the surface. He shares with Kandinsky[16] a conception of geometry which is radically different from the principles of Euclidian geometry, and is nourished by the principles of Einstein's special theory of relativity. Each image in a Fischinger film is in itself a painting. He took a very early interest in the possibilities of creating the illusion of a third dimension—a virtual third dimension.[17] Using spiral forms, he created graphic mandalas with honeycomb textures reminiscent of the skeletons of radiolarians in nature. These moving forms revolve around their center, producing hallucinatory optical effects, powerful black and white contrasts and moiré patterns which prefigure the experiments of kinetic art in the 1950s and 1960s. The gaze is absorbed by a meshed structure and drawn towards a point of absolute light or a central black hole. These depth effects closely resemble what Marcel Duchamp achieved by spinning his spiral-shaped Rotoreliefs in front of the camera lens for his 1925 film *Anemic Cinema*. In *Studie Nr. 7* (*Study No. 7*), set to Brahms' *Hungarian Dance No. 5*, deformed rectangles represent a transition into the third dimension, while circles become cylinders following more classical line drawings based on the rules of perspective (fig. 8). The curved forms, which are used by Fischinger in this film for the first time, reappear in *Studie Nr. 8* (*Study No. 8*), in which curling surfaces also suggest a virtual three-dimensional form.

The filmmaker went one step further in *Komposition In Blau* (*Composition in Blue*), which is based on a three-dimensional space placed in front of the camera lens in which cylinders or tetrahedrons move or are deformed. (fig. 9)

In Frankfurt, Fischinger joined the circle of Dr. Herzfeld, the Vereinigung von Freunden der Literatur (Friends of Literature club) where he met the eminent theatre critic Bernhardt Diebold. According to William Moritz, Diebold's 1916 article "Expressionismus und Kino," in which he called for a visual music based on a synthesis between art, music, dance, and cinema, made a lasting impression on the young Fischinger. It was also Diebold who took Fischinger to a "sneak preview" of Walter Ruttmann's film *Lichtspiel Opus I* on April 1, 1921. In 1927, the professor of psychology Georg Anschütz, a specialist of music, art and synesthesia, who was already familiar with Fischinger's Studies, organized a Kongress für Farbe-Ton-Forschung (Congress for Color-Sound

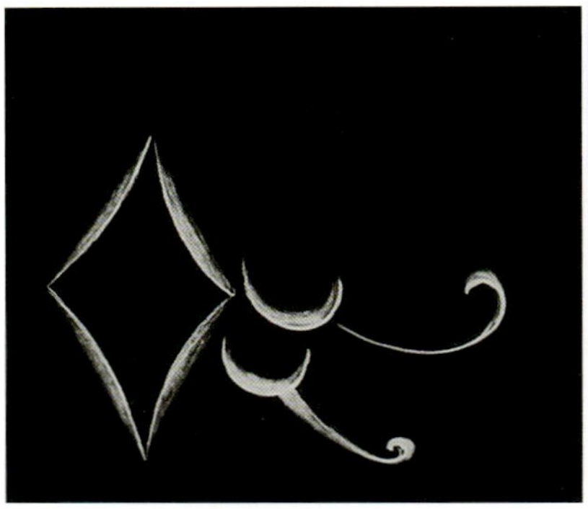

Figure 8 / Still from *Studie Nr. 7* (*Study No. 7*), 1931
35mm, b/w, sound

Figure 9 / Still from *Komposition In Blau* (*Composition in Blue*), 1935
35mm, color, sound

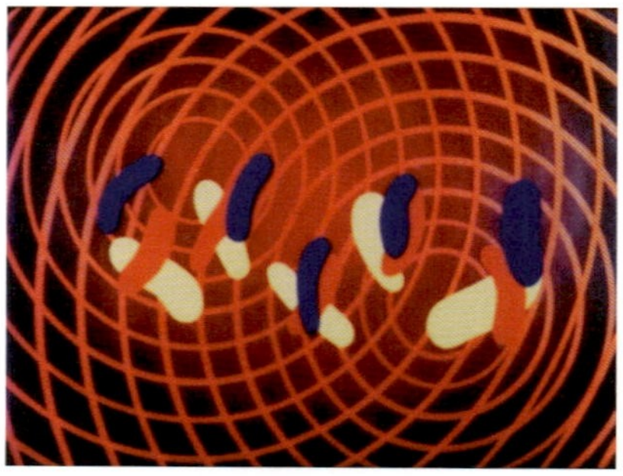

Figure 10 / Still from *Allegretto*, 1936–43
35mm, color, sound

Research) in Hamburg, followed by a second one in October 1930.

Fischinger, who was a trained musician, saw sound as an advancement and an opportunity to develop his work. Although he used existing music for the Studies, Fischinger did not adopt an illustrative approach, but instead was inspired by symbolism, using music to generate "correspondences," models for spatial movements inspired by instrumental movements. However, the presence of music in his sound films also served to defer the natural apprehension of an audience which is confronted with images that have no clear meaning. Music heightens sensation: "The flood of feeling created through music intensified the sensation and the effectiveness of this graphic cinematic expression, and helped to make the absolute film understandable."[18] It works as a stimulant, removing the spectator's inhibitions by immersing him in a familiar acoustic universe of pure emotions. Fischinger draws a meaningful parallel between his art and dance. Moreover, films such as *Studie Nr. 5* (*Study No. 5*), *Studie Nr. 7* (*Study No. 7*), set to Brahms' "Hungarian Rhapsody," *Studie Nr. 12* (*Study No. 12*), and even *Allegretto* (fig. 10), contain a large number of movements based on recognizable choreographic figures.

Although Fischinger rejected any constraint imposed by society on the contents of his absolute films, he nevertheless nurtured a utopian project for universal harmony, reaching back to the myth of the *lingua adamica*, the Romantic project for a total art. According to William Moritz, Fischinger's theory implies that images which produce pleasure and wonderment leave a lasting, precious impression in our understanding, while if the result troubled and perturbed the subject, the intrinsic ideas of the work would be perceived as disagreeable and would soon be forgotten.[19] This was confirmed by Elfriede Fischinger: "Oskar and I always believed that balanced and beautiful objects tend to create a meditative state of mind, and wild and turbulent ones make one rebel and stimulate violence."[20]

Abstract artists turn their back on the project for the "representation of the visible world." However, they do not turn their back on the world or on nature as such, but look for its essence, the monad, whether it would be given by the knowledge of astrophysics, the physics of matter, biology, or by different beliefs or theosophical systems. In the sixteenth century, Giordano Bruno defined the monad as an invisible entity constituting the minimal element of material and spiritual things. The monad—which corresponds with the point in mathematics, the atom in physics, or the unicellular organism—is a primitive being, physically and spiritually imperishable, which engenders the life of the world through reciprocal relations. It is a microcosm, an aspect of infinite essence (the macrocosm). Kandinsky evoked a fundamental difference between the immaterial "geometric" point, which corresponds with the zero in arithmetic, and the pictorial point or the point as it is found in matter (cosmos, atoms, cells, nucleus...), whose variable form and dimensions have different "sonorities." The points in the Studies films, which have the density of small balls shooting across the screen and look like fingerprints that leave a light trace as they move, have a metonymic relationship with the grain of the photochemical film image. The grain of the image is itself a point in space that recreates a form in association with other grains. Like Ruttmann in *Lichtspiel Opus I*, Fischinger's approach involves a re-examination of the elements of language of the medium under formalized conditions. In Italy in 1908, the Corradini brothers thought about a new pictorial art form based on similar monads, colored forms that "do not represent any image." They were steeped in theosophy and sought to paint the abstract states of the soul: "Forms expressing joy and pessimism" (1911), drawings inspired by the thought-forms of Annie Besant and Charles Webster Leadbeater, two leading members of the British Theosophical Society.

The thought-form is conceived as an exteriorization in the shape of the vibratory intensity of the "mental body": flows of spiral-shaped threads, trajectories of projectiles, streams, zigzags, splashes are typical thought-forms linked to psychological states described by their creators; the thought-form circles and hovers over its creator.[21] Like the points and disks in *Studie Nr. 6* (*Study No. 6*), the ectoplasmic forms in *Opus I*, in a syncretic sense, match both the thought-forms of theosophy and the elementary form which is everywhere in the universe. Like Kupka and many other artists of his generation, Fischinger was convinced that the general law of the universe would become accessible thanks to the unification of knowledge and belief.

16
Cf. Wassily Kandinsky, *Point and Line to Plane* (New York: Solomon R. Guggenheim Foundation, 1947); and Paul Klee, *Notebooks I: The Thinking Eye*, ed. Jürg Stiller (London: Lund Humphries, 1961).

17
Fischinger started making stereoscopic paintings in the early 1950s.

18
Oskar Fischinger, "My Statements...," in *Optical Poetry*, 173.

19
William Moritz, *Optical Poetry*, 29.

20
Elfriede Fischinger "Remembrances," in *A Retrospective of Paintings and Films by Oskar Fischinger 1900–1967* (Denver: Gallery 609, 1980).

21
Cf. Annie Besant and Charles Webster Leadbeater, *Thought Forms* (Wheaton: Theological Publishing House, 1997).

Dear Mr Fischinger,

Thank you for both your letters telling me about your invention. May I offer my congratulations—it seems to me an excellent idea and without doubt very promising.

I wonder if you could explain one or two points.

For instance, how is it possible to depict planes in such a way that on one hand they are sharply defined, yet on the other hand gradually dissolve? This seems to me a rather difficult thing to achieve; it is also of the <u>greatest</u> importance to my own work. When you were in Munich you talked of the possibility of depicting cloud-like formations in motion. For that to happen, it would be absolutely essential that the half-tones merge into each other.

In addition, I do not quite understand how you will make somewhat more complicated linear forms appear. This point is also extremely important because of the crucial question as to whether your invention applies to the entire area of the drawn animation. The difficulties of modeling, for instance, a face that changes its shape, seem to me so immense as to cast doubt on this whole area.

A third point that concerns me is the precious nature of the material. I am not sure of the price of kaolin, but presumably it is very expensive; if, therefore, it were not possible to use the same material several times (by grinding it down), then it would be worth trying to replace the kaolin with a less expensive substance.

However, these concerns by no means lessen my joy at your invention. I thank you for your trust in me and hope to hear more from you soon.

With best regards,
Yours,
Walther Ruttmann

By the way, roughly how much is pared off in each rotation? If it is very little, it could be very difficult to model very precisely or to create quick movements!

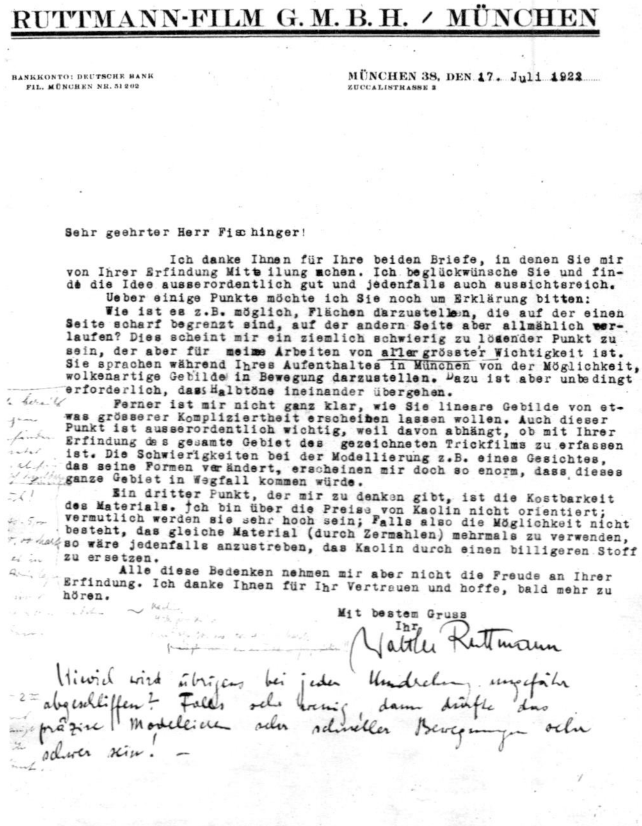

RUTTMANN-FILM G. M. B. H. / MÜNCHEN

BANKKONTO: DEUTSCHE BANK
FIL. MÜNCHEN NR. 51202

MÜNCHEN 38, DEN 17. Juli 1922
ZUCCALISTRASSE 3

Sehr geehrter Herr Fischinger!

Ich danke Ihnen für Ihre beiden Briefe, in denen Sie mir von Ihrer Erfindung Mitteilung machen. Ich beglückwünsche Sie und finde die Idee ausserordentlich gut und jedenfalls auch aussichtsreich.

Ueber einige Punkte möchte ich Sie noch um Erklärung bitten:

Wie ist es z.B. möglich, Flächen darzustellen, die auf der einen Seite scharf begrenzt sind, auf der andern Seite aber allmählich verlaufen? Dies scheint mir ein ziemlich schwierig zu lösender Punkt zu sein, der aber für meine Arbeiten von allergrösster Wichtigkeit ist. Sie sprachen während Ihres Aufenthaltes in München von der Möglichkeit, wolkenartige Gebilde in Bewegung darzustellen. Dazu ist aber unbedingt erforderlich, dass Halbtöne ineinander übergehen.

Ferner ist mir nicht ganz klar, wie Sie lineare Gebilde von etwas grösserer Kompliziertheit erscheinen lassen wollen. Auch dieser Punkt ist ausserordentlich wichtig, weil davon abhängt, ob mit Ihrer Erfindung das gesamte Gebiet des gezeichneten Trickfilms zu erfassen ist. Die Schwierigkeiten bei der Modellierung z.B. eines Gesichtes, das seine Formen verändert, erscheinen mir doch so enorm, dass dieses ganze Gebiet in Wegfall kommen würde.

Ein dritter Punkt, der mir zu denken gibt, ist die Kostbarkeit des Materials. Ich bin über die Preise von Kaolin nicht orientiert; vermutlich werden sie sehr hoch sein; Falls also die Möglichkeit nicht besteht, das gleiche Material (durch Zermahlen) mehrmals zu verwenden, so wäre jedenfalls anzustreben, das Kaolin durch einen billigeren Stoff zu ersetzen.

Alle diese Bedenken nehmen mir aber nicht die Freude an Ihrer Erfindung. Ich danke Ihnen für Ihr Vertrauen und hoffe, bald mehr zu hören.

Mit bestem Gruss
Ihr
Walter Ruttmann

Wieviel wird übrigens bei jeder Umdrehung ungefähr abgeschliffen? Falls sehr wenig, dann dürfte das präzise Modellieren oder schneller Bewegungen sehr schwer sein! –

Letter written by Walter Ruttman to Oskar Fischinger, 1922
Thermal copy in Collection Center for Visual Music

Wax Slicing Machine

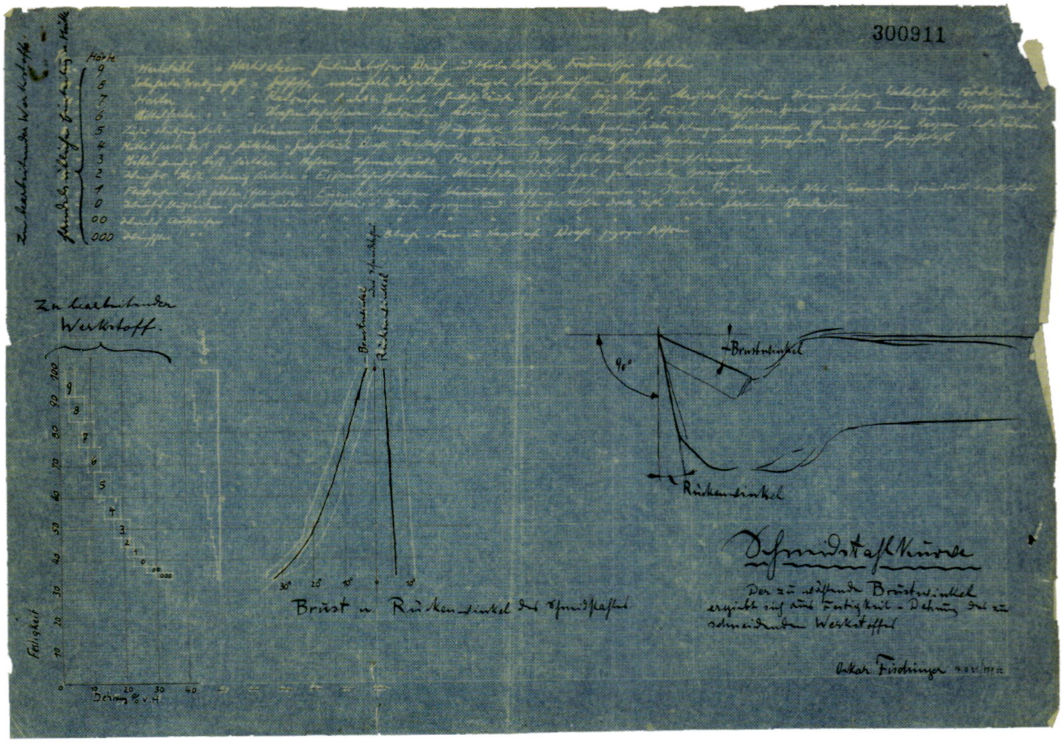

Technical drawing related to the Wax Slicing Machine,
likely prepared for a patent application, 1921
Collection Center for Visual Music

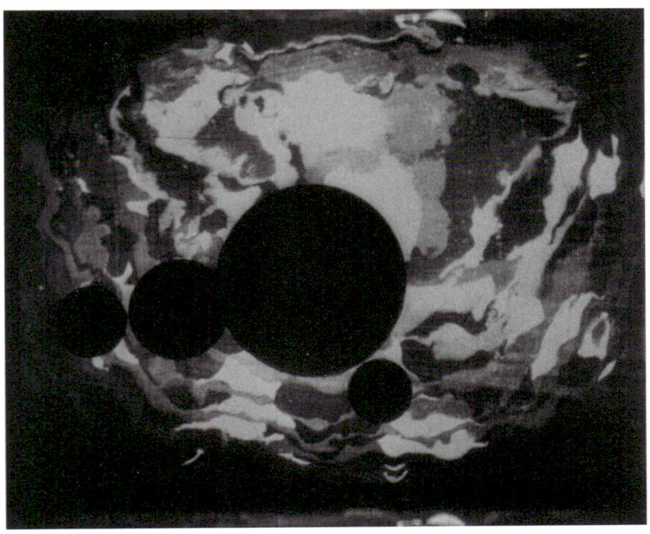

Still from *Wachsexperimente* (*Wax Experiments*), 1921–26
35mm, b/w and tinted, silent
→
Wax Slicing Machine by Oskar Fischinger, c. 1922
Collection Center for Visual Music

Oskar Fischinger in Germany 1900 to 1936

Jeanpaul Goergen

Chronological overview of the reception of the work of Oskar Fischinger in Germany in the context of the avant-garde. This timeline lists Fischinger's most important works and documented screenings. For more detailed information on his life and work, see William Moritz's *Optical Poetry. The Life and Work of Oskar Fischinger*[1] and the Fischinger section of the website of the Center for Visual Music, Los Angeles.[2]

[The running times and the lengths given in meters are from original German censor records, and differ in many cases from extant films. Also, several versions exist of some films. Some films exist only in fragments today.]

22 June 1900: Oskar Fischinger is born in Gelnhausen near Frankfurt am Main. He takes violin lessons while at school, and has an apprenticeship with an organ builder.

February 1916: The Fischingers move to Frankfurt am Main. Apprenticeship as a draftsman and toolmaker; further qualification in engineering (1922).

April 1916: The actor Paul Wegener envisions a reform in cinematography through abstract-ornamental animations.

14–16 September 1916: In a three-part series in the *Neue Zürcher Zeitung* on "Expressionismus und Kino," the critic Bernhard Diebold presents the case for "films painted by artists."

1919–21: Fischinger becomes acquainted with Bernhard Diebold at the Vereinigung von Freunden der Literatur (Association of Friends of Literature).

1920: In Munich the painter Walter Ruttmann founds a company producing "drawn films." On June 27, 1920, Ruttmann patents his animation stand for making cinematographic images.

Early April 1921: At a private screening of Ruttmann's *Lichtspiel Opus 1* (*Lightplay Opus I*) in Frankfurt, Bernhard Diebold introduces Fischinger to Ruttmann. Fischinger tells him of his idea for a labor-saving animation machine: thin slices are pared off a prepared wax block and filmed as a stop-motion animation, so that the finished film portrays a progressive cross-section of motifs in the wax block.

27 April 1921: Premiere of Walter Ruttmann's *Lichtspiel Opus 1* (*Lightplay Opus I*) in Berlin. Colored in a variety of hues and

with accompanying music by Max Butting, it is the very first screening of an abstract animated film. At the screening, the film images and the music alternated. First there was a musical introduction, then the first part of the film with the corresponding music, then again a musical section without film, and so on.

1922: At the Bauhaus in Weimar, Ludwig Hirschfeld-Mack and Kurt Schwertfeger develop their Reflektorische Lichtspiele (Reflecting Light Play), a color-light projection machine coordinated with music. In 1923 they go their separate ways; Hirschfeld-Mack starts to present his Farbenlichtspiele (Color-Light Play) throughout Germany and Austria.

Late 1922: Fischinger moves to Munich.

November 1922: Ruttmann signs a licensing agreement for one of Fischinger's wax-slicing machines.

March 1924: Fischinger starts work on films for the animated series *Münchener Bilderbogen* for a company founded by the American draftsman Louis Seel. From now on he becomes known for his special effects for feature films.

5 November 1924: Premiere of Viking Eggeling's abstract animated film *Symphonie Diagonale* in Berlin. For Eggeling film is a purely visual art that can hold its own without music.

3 May 1925: Film matinee *Der absolute Film* in Berlin. First overview presentation of German and French avant-garde films. Ludwig Hirschfeld-Mack's *Dreiteilige Farbensonatine* (*Three-Part Color Sonatina*) is performed, as well as films by René Clair, Fernand Léger, Viking Eggeling, Hans Richter, and Walter Ruttmann.

19 May 1925: Death of Viking Eggeling in Berlin.

Early 1926: Fischinger collaborates with the Hungarian composer Alexander László, whose Farblichtklavier color-organ system performs music with colored light projections. At László's presentations in several cities Fischinger shows abstract films, some made using his wax-slicing machine.

1 July 1926: Premiere of *Die Abenteuer des Prinzen Achmed* (*The Adventures of Prince Achmed*) by Lotte Reiniger. Walter Ruttmann uses Oskar Fischinger's Wax Slicing Machine to create magical effects.

12 July 1926: Rudolf Schneider reports on films by Fischinger that he has seen during a performance by Alexander László and Fischinger at the Residenztheater cinema in Munich. He explains the principle of the Wax Slicing Machine and continues: "No longer, as in the past, does the artist making an absolute film have to laboriously paint every single stage of the movement, for now this new artist—for whom we as yet have no designation—models in a malleable material … he makes a kind of 'temporal body' which enacts the desired movement. A very simple thing, once you have found how to do it. Of course this art, which Fischinger has provisionally called Raumlichtkunst (I would consider 'form play' more appropriate), has little to do with films for ordinary viewing. … At this presentation, Fischinger's fragments with their scurrying snakes, mists, with spheres, rings, and fantastic masses that rush into view from infinitely far away—only to dissipate, to change, and to be swept aside—were met with the greatest appreciation. Although these are only early days as yet, it is a beginning that promises great things to come. Fischinger is currently working on a film for multiple projection devices … and his intention is that it should be an innovative, fully rounded, independent work of art."[3]

1926: Fischinger presents multimedia performances of *Raumlichtmusik* (*Space Light Music*), with tinted abstract films and colored images projected side-by-side on three screens. In an unpublished typescript, he comments: "Of this Art everything is new and yet ancient in its laws and forms. Plastic—Dance—Painting—Music become one. The Master of the new Art forms poetical work in four dimensions. … Cinema was its beginning … Raumlichtmusik will be its completion."[4] [The name of these performances is soon changed to *Raumlichtkunst* (*Space Light Art*). Fischinger is no longer working with László on these performances with these names]

15 January 1927: Walter Jerven reports on Oskar Fischinger's work with his Wax Slicing Machine: "Fischinger is his own poet, director, architect, and operator. He models his 'themes' in wax. The whole film is made from a kneaded substance. ... His images play out in lyrical and dramatic oscillations, in all nuances from black to white. The wax he uses covers all the various shades of gray and allows him to create a differentiated spectrum of half-tones. He also uses colored modeling substances. ... He creates a detailed model of the body to be filmed (be it a cloud formation, or be it the sun) and embeds this in the modeling substance, which now

1
London, UK: John Libbey Publishing; Bloomington, IN: Indiana University Press, 2004.

2
www.centerforvisualmusic.org/Fischinger.

3
"Formspiel durch Kino," *Frankfurter Zeitung* (July 12, 1926).

4
"Raumlichtmusik," unpublished typescript, n.d., Fischinger Collection, Center for Visual Music, Los Angeles.

encloses it in a right-angled block. By means of a simple cutting machine, with blades that can cut the thinnest of slivers, cross-sections are successively removed from the block. Shots of these cross-sections are taken by a camera that has previously been put in position. In his studio Fischinger also has a rotation machine that cuts the block at exactly the same speed as the individual frames are later projected. There is a similarity here with working at an animation stand. Human figures only appear fleetingly, as silhouettes kneaded onto the glass of the animation stand—lit from below and filmed from above. One of the themes of the films Fischinger is currently working on is 'power.' Another is 'fever.' Another theme, 'vacuum,' is already finished and almost ready for public presentation. [These were names for his multiple projector shows, which included *Wachsexperimente* (*Wax Experiments*) footage and other films.] The title of the film that I can see him working on at the moment is *Der Vortrag* [*The Lecture*]. I can see silhouettes of the heads of audience members; I see the speaker who will later transmute into a flame = symbolizing what has been said."[5]

Summer 1927: Fischinger journeys on foot from Munich to Berlin. He documents his three-and-a-half-week walk with a 35 mm camera, in extremely short shots. This film is only distributed after his death, as *München–Berlin Wanderung* (*Walking from Munich to Berlin*, 78 m = 3'45" at 18 frames per second).

1927–35: Fischinger establishes himself in Berlin as a specialist for animated cartoons and as a provider of special effects for art films, advertising campaigns, and feature films, including Fritz Lang's *Frau im Mond* (*Woman in the Moon*, 1929).

1929: *Studie Nr. 1* (*Study No. 1*)[6] is screened, undocumented as yet, at the Berlin art house cinema Kamera.

May 1930: In Berlin the Deutsche Liga für den unabhängigen Film (German League for Independent Film) is founded. The board includes Hans Richter, Werner Graeff, Herbert Ihering, Mies van der Rohe, Asta Nielsen, Lotte Reiniger, and Walter Ruttmann.

17 January 1930: German premiere of *The Barn Dance*, the first Mickey Mouse movie screened in Germany.

8 August 1930: Premiere of the sound-on-disc film *Tanzende Linien* (*Dancing Lines*, 61 m = 2'14" at 24 frames per second)[7] at the Kamera, synchronized with the gramophone record "Vaya, Veronica" (Electrola EG 1663). This film, then publicized as a "play of lines" and now known as *Studie Nr. 2*, meets with an enthusiastic response from film journalists: "Skilled transposition of two kinds of poetry: music into dance. ... It was made like all drawn animations (the film in question, which was sixty meters in length, required 2880 individual drawings). However, after years of trial and error, the artist has also developed a new technique of his own, which allows his line-figures to move in a completely rhythmical —never stuttering—manner. ... New possibilities in the art of film: self-contained, perfect forming in the moving image —a most wonderful film."[8]

22 August 1930: Premiere of the sound-on-disc film *Studie Nr. 3* (88 m = 2'14") at the Kamera. Given the name *Vinka* in the pre-screening publicity, the film is synchronized with the gramophone recording of the foxtrot of the same name (Electrola EG 1530). As an experiment, *Studie Nr. 3* is screened again on 22 September 1930 in Berlin at the Ufa-Theater Kurfürstendamm. "Like bacilla and spirilla lines leap and dance to fiery music; they come from all sides, linear and curvilinear materializations of impressions of music, springing hither and thither, replicating like protozoa, multiplying like thread algae, with saxophone breaks shooting across the screen like jellyfish, with timpani welling up from below, shimmering drum, and the ever elegant melody dancing its way through the luxuriant accompaniment that embraces and entwines it. 'Hot' style for the eyes: recreating music (an American foxtrot) purely through forms in motion."[9]

1–5 October 1930: Hamburg. Second Kongress für Farbe-Ton-Forschung (Congress for Color- Sound Research). Screening of Oskar Fischinger's *Filmstudie Nr. 5* (now titled *Studie Nr. 5*).

3 October 1930: Fischinger talks of his next work: "This time it will not, as hitherto, be music that is transposed into pictorial form; that was just the beginning, a makeshift effort. Now I am going to start exploring in greater depth the mathematical and optical laws of the absolute image. Since these laws are also in keeping with the laws of acoustics, the result will be a kind of space-music. The process—set out in a precise timetable—will involve tracing musical values and curves on graph paper. Then, at every phase of the work,

I will play the relevant phrase. It is my aim to make absolute film theater-worthy. For I am firmly convinced that there is still much that is new and beautiful to be discovered in this area."[10]

17 October 1930: Public premiere of *R. 5—Ein Spiel in Linien* (now titled *Studie Nr. 5*, 89 m = 3′15″) at the Titania-Palast in Berlin-Steglitz. Synchronized with the foxtrot "I've Never Seen a Smile Like Yours" by Johnson and Frazer.

14 November 1930: Premiere of *Studie Nr. 6* (58 m = 2′07″) in a program of ten sound-shorts at the Theater am Nollendorfplatz in Berlin. Synchronized with the fandango "Los Verderones" by Jacinto Guerrero.

Late January 1931: Oskar Fischinger visits the Netherlands on the invitation of the Dutch Film League. Screenings of *Filmstudie Nr. 5, 6, 7, 8*, and 9. "There were presentations in Amsterdam and The Hague. The press had provided excellent advance publicity so the response was not lacking. ... Abstract film is the closest we can get to the true nature of film. Richter and Ruttmann have got stuck in technicalities; I have now found my own path. ... Of course I am nowhere near my goal, there is still much to be done honing my craft, but the more perfect the craft the greater the ensuing artistic values."[11]

Late February 1931: *Studie Nr. 7* (73 m = 2′40). Music: "Hungarian Dance No. 5" by Johannes Brahms. Shown at the Capitol in Berlin as a short before *Ariane* by Paul Czinner. *Studie Nr. 7* is distributed by Star-Film. "This could be the first abstract film to be included in the regular list of a commercial distribution company."[12]

16 March 1931: At a special event at the Kamera, Degeto (Deutsche Gesellschaft für Ton und Film, German Association for Sound and Film) shows *Studies Nr. 5, 6* and *7*.

1931: Paul Hindemith challenges his students at the Hochschule für Musik in Berlin to compose new music for *Filmstudie Nr. 6*, as an exercise for teaching purposes. None were used by Fischinger for his films.

8 August 1931: *Film-Kurier* reports on Oskar Fischinger's *Studie Nr. 8* and on works by Hans Fischinger. "The Eighth Study uses *The Sorcerer's Apprentice* by Paul Dukas. The 'dancing lines' are joined by planes, geometric-figural forms, expanding and shrinking shapes in full light and half shadow. There is no mistaking the progress in artistic sensitivity in these latest works by Oskar Fischinger. And there is also a substantial improvement in the techniques used in these studies. The movements of these drawn figures are softer and more flowing; recorded discs have been replaced by coordinated light and sound. (Sound-on-film system by Tobis.) ... Hans Fischinger's first work, *Studie Nr. 9*, to Brahms's *Hungarian Dance No. 6*, has a certain individuality and—despite still being dependent on forms as such—holds out promise for the future."[13] [*Studie Nr. 9* was made under Oskar's direction. As in the preceding extract, it is often incorrectly credited solely to Hans Fischinger].

16 October 1931: Premiere of Oskar Fischinger's *Studie Nr. 8* (126 m = 4′36″) at the Kamera. Music: *The Sorcerer's Apprentice* by Paul Dukas.

22 October 1931: In the supporting program at the Ufa-Theater Kurfürstendamm in Berlin, *Studie Nr. 9* is shown, made with the assistance of Hans Fischinger and registered on September 9, 1931, under the title *Schule Oskar Fischinger, 9. Studie, gezeichnet von Hans Fischinger* (School of Oskar Fischinger, 9, Study, drawn by Hans Fischinger, 81 m = 2′58″). Music: "Hungarian Dance No. 6" by Johannes Brahms. In early 1932, UFA adds *Studie Nr. 9* to its distribution list.[14]

26 November 1931: Fischinger's *Studie Nr. 8* is included in the inaugural program of Die Kurbel, a new avant-garde cinema in Frankfurt.

1931: The Dutch author Simon Koster writes of Oskar Fischinger:

"He is concerned not with elementary mental movement, but with the purely subjective response of the mind to music. Fischinger's films are, then, also sound films.

5
Walter Jerven, "Bei Fischinger in München," *Film-Kurier* (January 15, 1927).

6
No translation is provided for further mentions in this timeline of the original German titles of Fischinger's various Studies.

7
The following running times are all based on 24 frames per second.

8
"Neue Formen der Filmkunst. Spiel der Linien von Oskar Fischinger," *Film-Kurier* (August 6, 1930).

9
"Die Ufa zeigt: Oskar Fischingers neuer Kurzfilm. Hot-Stil wird optisch. Belauschte Traumbilder," *Film-Kurier* (September 23, 1930).

10
"Absoluter Film nach musikalischen Gesetzen. Gespräch mit Oskar Fischinger," *Film-Kurier* (October 3, 1930).

11
"Paradies Holland. Ein deutscher Avantgardist berichtet," *Film-Kurier* (February 9, 1931).

12
"Starfilm übernimmt Fischinger," *Film-Kurier* (March 5, 1931).

13
"Studie VIII. von Oscar Fischinger," *Film-Kurier* (August 8, 1931).

14
Film-Kurier (February 20, 1932).

The goal of the cineaste is to represent optically the mental impressions excited by music. He endeavors to achieve his goal through the powerfully rhythmical movement of fine and heavier straight and curved lines and complexes of lines that emerge and glide past, undulating and vibrating, coming together in new groups, shattering, shooting forward, and then chased by yet other figures. The rhythm of this interplay of lines is so forceful that at times it seems as if the music is being directed by the film images. But here the abstract film has largely lost its 'absolute' character, becoming illustrative rather than elementary."[15]

1932: *Studie Nr. 10* (110 m = 4'01").

1932: Oskar Fischinger's team at his studio now includes his brother Hans, his cousin (and later his wife) Elfriede, and three employees.

February 1932: Joris Ivens takes films by Fischinger to Moscow and Leningrad.

1932: In Munich, Rudolf Pfenninger (1899–1976) is experimenting with "drawn sounds." The jagged patterns of an optical soundtrack are painted on long rolls of paper, which are then transferred into the soundtrack area of the film strip. Pfenninger realizes four short films with synthetic sound and presents a detailed account of this process in the documentary film *Tönende Handschrift, das Wunder des gezeichnetes Tones. (Sounding Handwriting, the Wonder of Hand-Drawn Sound)*.

10 January 1932: The Film Society in London shows "Musical Abstracts" (1931) by Oskar Fischinger.

4 April 1932: Fischinger creates the trailer *Koloraturen* (*Coloratura*, 122 m = 4'28") for the feature film *Gitta Entdeckt ihr Herz* (*Gitta Finds her Heart*) by Carl Froelich.

27 May 1932 (approx.): Premiere of *Studie Nr. 12* at the Kamera. Registered as *Schule Oskar Fischinger, 12. Studie: "Lichtertanz," gezeichnet von Hans Fischinger* (School of Oskar Fischinger, 12, Study: "Candle Dance" drawn by Hans Fischinger, 133 m = 4'52). Music: "Lichtertanz der Bräute von Kaschmir" (Candle dance of the Kashmiri brides) from *Feramors* by Anton Rubinstein. "Fischinger is working in a more concentrated manner with fewer forms than before; a few main elements take up the melody, with no hint of playful arabesques. Now a single curve, a moving line, can suffice to fully express a musical passage—and this line now has an air of singularity; this line, and this line alone can interpret the music; it has achieved irrefutable perfection. Thus absolute film—often regarded as an artisanal curiosity—has advanced into new realms. More than just manifestations of artistic skill, the forms in these films are revelations; sound and images have melded into a single, eternal entity."[16]

30 July 1932: *Film-Kurier* reports on Oskar Fischinger's experiments with synthetic sound, created by photographing geometric figures and ornaments to the soundtrack area of the film stock. Fischinger explains: "The composer of the future will no doubt no longer just use musical notation, which he himself can generally not bring to life and has to be left to random reproducers; by contrast, here the musical artist—working exclusively with the most rudimentary foundations of music, that is to say, sound waves and vibrations—can enjoy the greatest freedom."[17] In 1972 a selected compilation of these experiments was assembled by William Moritz for The Fischinger Archive and is now distributed as *Ornament Sound*.

21 October 1932: The Liga für den unabhängigen Film (League for Independent Film) in Munich screens all of Fischinger's twelve Studies at the Marmorhaus. "The cinema was sold out. The audience came from all the various culturally aware circles in Munich, with leading lights from the music world and the visual arts."[18]

4 December 1932: At the Gloria-Palast in Frankfurt am Main, the Bund das neue Frankfurt (New Frankfurt Alliance) film league shows László Moholy-Nagy's program "Die neuen Film-Experimente." This includes Fischinger's *Studie Nr. 7*, *Studie Nr. 12*, and *Tönende Ornamente* (*Ornament Sound*).[19]

1932–33: *Studie Nr. 11* (113 m = 4'08"). Music: "Minuet from Divertimento in D, KV 334" by Wolfgang Amadeus Mozart.

1 January 1933: Fischinger's article "Der absolute Tonfilm" (The Absolute Sound Film) is published in various newspapers:

"I have been able to determine, through repeated experiments, the ways in which ornaments produce complex tones as soon as they are scanned with the light aperture of a photoelectric cell. ... Here lie great possibilities for the truly independent artist, as he shapes not simply images but creative works."[20]

21 May 1933: The Film Society in London shows *Early Experiments in Hand-Drawn Sound* (1931) by Oskar Fischinger. "These patterns, drawn on paper with pen and ink and photographed direct on to the margin of the film reserved for the sound track, were designed by Mr. Fischinger himself. ... Variations in volume are obtained by varying the density of the patterns on the sound track, a soft note being pale grey and louder effects being graded from darker grey to black, the maximum. A chord is played by superimposing on the same portion of track a different pattern for each note."[21] These films are shown again by the Film Society on 10 December 1933; this time the program also includes *A.B.C. In Sound* (1933) by László Moholy-Nagy, who is also experimenting with synthetic sound.

2–9 October 1933: At the third Kongress für Farbe-Ton-Forschung (Congress for Color-Sound Research) in Hamburg, Leonhard Fürst illustrates his lecture "Formprobleme im Film" with, among other things, Fischinger's Studies 5, 7, 8, and *12*. Fischinger's *Tönende Ornamente* (*Ornament Sound*) is also presented, as are the first of his tests using the three-color Gasparcolor process.[22]

25 October 1933: At the 118th meeting of the Deutsche Kinotechnischen Gesellschaft (German Cinetechnology Society) the Hungarian chemist Bela Gaspar presents his Gasparcolor process, which is exclusively used in animated films.

12 February 1934: The colored *Studie Nr. 11A* is registered (53 m = 1′56″). It is shown from 26 February briefly as *Ein Spiel in Farben* (*A Play in Colors*). [Fischinger wasn't satisfied and did not distribute this film.]

Summer 1934: Work on the unfinished *Studie Nr. 13*. Music: Overture to *Coriolan* by Ludwig van Beethoven.

1934 onward: Fischinger is increasingly making abstract commercials using Gasparcolor.

11 April 1934: *Muratti Greift Ein* (*Muratti Gets in the Act*, 72 m = 2′3″) is registered as a Gasparcolor animation advertising Muratti cigarettes. Music: excerpt from *The Doll Fairy* by Josef Bayer.

1–20 August 1934: *Studie Nr. 7*, *Studie Nr. 8*, and *Studie Nr. 9* are shown at the Mostra internazionale d'arte cinematografica di Venezia (Venice Film Festival).

15 August 1934: *Alle Kreise erfasst Tolirag* (*Tolirag reaches all Circles of Society*, 50 m = 1′50″), a commercial for the advertising agency Tolirag, which itself produces commercials, is registered. Color: Gasparcolor; possibly the first film completed in Gasparcolor. Music: the Venusberg ballet music from *Tannhäuser* by Richard Wagner and "Triumphal March" from *Sigurd Jorsalfar* by Edvard Grieg. Fischinger also produces an abstract version titled *Kreise* (*Circles*) with no advertising message. [Though biographer William Moritz used 1933 for the release date of *Kreise*, no proof can be found for any public release in 1933. Upon consultation with the author and original documents, CVM has now amended the date for this film to 1933–34].

1 October 1934: Writing in *Film-Kurier*, Hans Schuhmacher reports on Oskar Fischinger's plans to use color as a fully-fledged, constitutive element in his films. "This series of new, absolute films, in which Fischinger now wants to use color as a means of expression in its own right—like sounding color-light plays—are to mark the beginning of a European production with specifically German standards. ... It is therefore to be hoped that Fischinger's plans will receive the strongest support, all the more so since, besides this new and striking series, he already has plans for a major, feature-length work. This work, a color-light opus, will both break new ground in the realms of absolute film and set a benchmark for future study, it will promote deeper understanding and smooth the path to the art of abstract film. ... Film without language, without actors, film as purely optical expression and abstract forming, as pure music—for every sentient eye, for every ear, intelligible and comprehensible the world over—awaits its birth. It could coincide with the Olympiad of 1936, as Germany's trailblazing, innovative contribution to an art form that has long been dormant, as a symphony of colors and forms, setting out in a new direction, obeying new laws that are created and realized during its own making and that in turn convey new insights: absolute film."[23]

15
Simon Koster, *Duitsche filmkunst* (Rotterdam: Brusse, 1931), 70.

16
Lotte H. Eisner, "Lichtertanz," *Film-Kurier* (June 1, 1932).

17
"Tönende Ornamente. Aus Oskar Fischingers neuer Arbeit," *Film-Kurier* (July 30, 1932).

18
"Erfolgreicher Fischinger-Abend," *Film-Kurier* (October 28, 1932).

19
"Interessante Film-Experimente," *LichtBildBühne* (December 10, 1932).

20
Dortmunder Zeitung (January 1, 1933). A version of this essay is reprinted in this volume, pp. 96–97.

21
The Film Society Programmes 1925–1939 ed. George Amberg (New York: Arno Press, 1972), 259.

22
"Aus der Arbeit des 3. Farbe-Ton-Kongresses in Hamburg," *Film-Kurier* (October 5, 1933); "Vom 3. Farbe-Ton-Kongress" *Film-Kurier* (October 7, 1933); "Gasparcolor-Filme in Hamburg," *LichtBildBühne* (October 10, 1933).

23
Schu. [Hans Schuhmacher], "Fischinger," *Film-Kurier*, October 1, 1934.

Figure 1 / Certificate from Venice Biennale, 1935
Special mention given to Oskar Fischinger (not a juried award), for his "Tontrick Film Atelier" (sound animation film studio). The award is signed "Volpi," for Count Volpi di Misurata, the festival's founder. Many differing accounts of this festival and an unconfirmed award for *Komposition In Blau* (*Composition in Blue*) can be found in articles on Fischinger written over the decades.
Collection Center for Visual Music

3 November 1934: According to reports Rota-Film will add three films from Oskar Fischinger's new Color-Play series to its distribution list, ensuring that "the production of this first regular series of color-sound-plays ... can be taken as read."[24] However, these reports prove not to be true.

25 November 1934: A program of films made using Gasparcolor, presented by the Film Society in London, includes Fischinger's *Kreise* (*Circles*) and *Muratti Greift Ein* (*Muratti Gets in the Act*).

31 December 1935: In the New Year edition of *Film-Kurier* Fischinger writes: "I wish that 1935 may usher in the first, major, feature-length color-film-work—an absolute color-work, born entirely of music, meaningful to all human beings—and—making immense profits for our country! That is what I wish with all my heart!"

2 May 1935: Special screening of *Komposition In Blau* (*Composition in Blue*, registered May 10, 1935, 108 m = 3'57"). Color: Gasparcolor. Music: Overture to *The Merry Wives of Windsor* by Otto Nicolai. "In this new work Fischinger is ... again striking out in a new direction. He always takes new directions, he always seeks out and discovers new things, and his work is growing ever more mature, drawing ever closer to its goal, which is not yet in sight, which we can only sense, as yet. Whether he is really seeking it out, like a scientist, it's impossible to say: perhaps all his creative output has been no more than inspired, artistic playfulness. But this sensuous composition combining color and music, in which Nicolai's composition merges so perfectly with Fischinger's colors, no longer has anything to do with playfulness, even if his earlier works once might have. The two elements combine to create one coherent whole, founded on the artistic idea of the absolute. ... Thus it is our pleasant duty to constantly alert our readers to new things of this kind, which must be allowed to flourish and should be fostered with the greatest vigor."[25] From 5 June onward *Komposition In Blau* (originally also known as *Lichtkonzert Nr. 1*, *Light Concert No. 1*) is screened in the supporting program before Endstation (directed by E. W. Emo) at the Capitol. This occurred on the initiative of Tolirag; the film did not find a distributor in Germany.[26]

July 1935: Fischinger spends some time in Paris, where he licenses *Komposition In Blau* (*Composition in Blue*) to a leading company for distribution. It is also licensed for rental distribution in Czechoslovakia, Italy, Japan, Spain, Belgium, Holland, and Switzerland. *Film-Kurier* comments: "Only the German are slow on the uptake, because—as it would seem —they cannot quite grasp the creativity and innovation of Fischinger's art, although we have been reporting on it for the last five years now."[27]

1935: *Komposition In Blau* (*Composition in Blue*) screens at the Venice Biennale; Fischinger receives a certificate of special mention for his "Tontrick Film-Atelier," or sound animation film studio (fig. 1).

29 October 1935: At the International Film Festival in Brussels *Studie Nr. 7*, *Studie Nr. 8*, and *Komposition In Blau* (*Composition in Blue*) are screened, albeit as non-competing items. The jury singles them out for special mention. The *Film-Kurier* reporter comments: "It is not the first time that Fischinger has received recognition abroad, while it is still withheld from him in Germany. This artist has had to bear the full weight of the lot of the prophet who counts for nothing in his own land. That he is at all able to finance his tireless, ongoing artistic work is really only thanks to the foreign earnings of his films."[28]

27 January 1936: *Film-Kurier* reports that Fischinger has signed a contract with Paramount: "That it should come to this: that a film artist, who is such a true German in his creativity and sensitivities, has been signed by an American studio. As soon as the directors at Paramount saw *Komposition In Blau* (*Composition in Blue*), they ... engaged Fischinger for the next seven years. On 11 February he will set sail for Hollywood. Germany is losing, for the foreseeable future, one of its most inspired artists, who could have been persuaded to stay here if people would only have recognized his unique gift."[29]

Fischinger stays in California for the rest of his life, never returning to Germany.

24 "Rota fördert Fischinger-Studien," *Film-Kurier*, November 3, 1934.

25 Schu. [Hans Schuhmacher], "Der neue Fischinger. Komposition in Blau. Sondervorführung," *Film-Kurier* (May 3, 1935).

26 "Ansichts-Postkarten aus Berlin," *Film-Kurier* (June 14, 1935).

27 "Avantgarde interessiert," *Film-Kurier* (July 9, 1935).

28 "Der Prophet gilt nichts. . . ," *Film-Kurier* (October 30, 1935).

29 "Oskar Fischinger von der Paramount verpflichtet," *Film-Kurier* (January 27, 1936).

Oskar Fischinger, Modernist Painter

Ilene Susan Fort

Oskar Fischinger started painting canvases in 1936 in California (fig. 1). Previously, in Germany, his sketches, drawings and temperas had been part of an elaborate, multi-stage process for making motion pictures (fig. 2). The majority of his oil paintings were independent works, but a number of them did relate to cinema, serving as back-drops (fig. 3) or functioning as initial ideas that were never realized (fig. 4).The canvases and panels that were not specifically linked to a film did still share Fischinger's basic cinema aesthetics: almost all are abstract compositions consisting primarily of geometric shapes, lines and grids, brilliantly hued with little or no reference to the physical world. The essence of his painting was a non-objective, constructivist aesthetic in which color and motion dominated. Because music had been Fischinger's first love, rhythm also played a crucial role.

Most historians insist Fischinger began painting out of necessity: frustrated with commercial movie projects, lacking finances for his personal film experiments, and bored, he began expressing himself in paint.[1] This explanation seems plausible, but oil painting was neither an inexpensive pursuit nor just a hobby for Fischinger. It served as a means for him to continue developing his ideas and solving problems of a formal character, in a manner analogous to his early use of drawings for his films.

Fischinger assumed the sale of his paintings would partly alleviate his difficult financial situation. In this respect he was quite naïve. Although Hollywood was the new capital of the commercial movie industry, the region was only emerging from cultural provincialism. Painters and commercial galleries still promoted Impressionism and representational art. Post Impressionism and Expressionism were deemed modern. During the 1920s, small groups of artists banded together repeatedly to encourage some degree of formal experimentation and to introduce progressive ideas to the public through exhibitions, but most of these organizations were short lived. The Group of Eight was the longest active association exhibiting in Los Angeles throughout the 1920s, and their example did establish the acceptance of experimentation and the analytical and emotional use of color.[2]

Stanton Macdonald-Wright and Lorser Feitelson, the two painters destined to be foremost in the region (both through their own art and as teachers) were modernists. Macdonald-Wright was the only resident artist to have an international reputation, having immersed himself in European avant-garde circles in France and Germany and New York before returning home to California in 1919. Feitelson had been exposed to modernism in New York and through occasional visits to Europe, prior to settling in Los Angeles in 1928. In Paris, Macdonald-Wright developed a personal American version of Cubism and Orphism, based on color and depth relationships, called Synchromism, while Feitelson in Los Angeles rejected his early Cubism to explore a neo-classical version of Surrealism, dubbed by critics Post-Surrealism. By the late 1930s, when Fischinger was first experimenting with oil painting, they both had abandoned in part radical aesthetics to devote much of their energy to supervising various art projects that the federal government was sponsoring during the Depression. Macdonald-Wright directed the Southern California region of the Works Progress Administration / Federal Art Project (WPA/FAP) while Feitelson supervised the mural, painting and sculpture division. Citizenship was required to participate, but Fischinger would in any case not have felt comfortable even if he had been permitted to work on the easel project, since abstraction was discouraged.

Fischinger definitely was one of the most aesthetically sophisticated artists in the region. His new acquaintances had wide-ranging talents. Several were immigrants earlier on—painter Boris Deutsch and architects Rudolph M. Schindler and Richard Neutra, as well as husband-and-wife filmmakers Alexander Hammid and Maya Deren.[3] Dadaist painter and filmmaker Man Ray, who settled in Hollywood in 1940 after leaving Paris, would enjoy discussions with him.[4] Fischinger may have also been acquainted with Elise (a.k.a. Elise Cavanna Seeds), wife of the music impresario Merle Armitage.[5]

Figure 1 / Oskar Fischinger in his Los Angeles studio, c. 1949
Collection Center for Visual Music

Figure 2 / Animation gouache for *Quadrate* (*Squares*), 1934
Gouache on paper, 11.5 x 12 in. / 28 x 30.5 cm
Collection The Fischinger Trust, Long Beach, CA

1
Peter Plagens, *Sunshine Muse: Art on the West Coast, 1945–1970* (Berkeley, University of California Press, 1974), 18; and Marianne Lorenz, "Kandinsky and Regional America," in *Theme & Improvisation: Kandinsky & the American Avant-Garde, 1913–1950*, exh, cat., eds., Gail Levin and Marianne Lorenz (Dayton and Boston: Dayton Art Institute with Bullfinch Press, 1992), 160. Plagens minimized Fischinger's painted output by referring to it as Kandinskyesque abstraction turned "into *light* paintings and remarkable films." (italics the author)

2
Susan M. Anderson, "Modern Spirit: The Group of Eight & Los Angeles Art of the 1920s," in *Clarence Hinkle*, exh, cat., eds., Janet Blake and Susan M. Anderson (Laguna Beach: Laguna Art Museum, 2012), esp. 111–26. The Group of Eight included Mabel Alvarez, Henri De Kruif, Clarence Hinkle, John Hubbard Rich, Donna Schuster, E. Roscoe Shrader and Edouard and Luvenia Vysekal, all of whom painted representationally.

3
Deutsch is best known for his conservative figure paintings, but he occasionally worked in abstract modes (as demonstrated by the drawing of an untitled head in the Scheyer Collection, Norton Simon Museum, Pasadena [Acc.no. P.1953.15]) and also produced one expressionist film, *Lullaby* (1929). Fischinger seems to have met all of these artists and architects through Galka Scheyer.

4
William Moritz, *Optical Poetry: The Life and Work of Oskar Fischinger* (London, UK: John Libbey Publishing, 2004), 90.

5
Fischinger shared several interests with Elise and Merle Armitage: Elise had come to Hollywood as an actress and Armitage was the leading music impresario of Southern California and an art collector.

Her canvases were also spare and geometric, and consequently she shared the same limited recognition. Fischinger established collegial friendships with both Feitelson and Macdonald-Wright. Feitelson presented Fischinger's films to his students at Art Center in Los Angeles and in 1947 invited him to join the California Color Society, and Macdonald-Wright may have discussed his paintings and various versions of his experimental color light machine, the Synchrome Kineidoscope (1969, Collection of the Los Angeles County Museum of Art), which he had worked on for decades. When more emigrés settled in Southern California, Fischinger became part of a large congenial German-speaking network of talented personages, many of whom were in the field of music.

During his first decade in California, Fischinger's friendship with Galka Scheyer was the most beneficial association, expanding his contact not only with local artists, but also with collectors and dealers. A German émigré herself, Scheyer had come to America to promote the group of radicals who became known as The Blue Four: Lyonel Feininger, Alexei Jawlensky, Wassily Kandinsky, and Paul Klee. During the late 1920s and early 1930s she was responsible for the growing reputation of these artists as a result of lectures and exhibitions throughout the country that she organized on her own and with American curators, artists, and commercial dealers, such as William Clapp at the Oakland Museum, Charles Daniel in New York, and Feitelson in Los Angeles. Fischinger, including his growing family, would rank among her closest friends and eventually settled in a house in Hollywood nearby hers. Scheyer's personal collection that decorated the walls of her hilltop home designed by Neutra, as well as the continuing stream of works the Blue Four sent to her for sale, offered the filmmaker a private education in radical German painting. Scheyer introduced Fischinger to the American collectors Walter and Louise Arensberg. They had already amassed in New York City one of the country's finest collections of French modernism (now in the Philadelphia Museum of Art), before settling in 1927 in Los Angeles, where their home became a popular local art salon. The Arensbergs began purchasing Blue Four artists from Scheyer in 1930, and quickly amassed the largest private holding of Klee on the West Coast.[6]

Fischinger had been aware of radical European art before his arrival in the United States. German proponents were amply exhibited in commercial galleries and in official government institutions (until 1933). During the years after World War I, many museum directors throughout Germany were actively committed to acquiring and displaying modern

Figure 3 / *An Optical Poem*, 1938
Oil on plywood, 36 x 25 in. / 91.4 x 63.5 cm
Collection The Fischinger Trust, Long Beach, CA, promised gift to Center for Visual Music
This is part of a background used in the making of the film of the same name.

Figure 4 / *Sound Painting*, 1951
Oil on canvas, 44 x 52 in. / 112 x 132 cm
Collection Center for Visual Music, gift from Dian Iversen

art. In Frankfurt, Munich, and Berlin where Fischinger lived, such art was on view and available for him to study. Dr. Aloïs Schardt, who would settle in Los Angeles in 1939 and become a close friend of Fischinger's, spending many an afternoon discussing art and philosophy with him, served as director of the Städtisches Museum für Kunst und Kuntgewerbe in Halle from 1926 to 1933 and briefly thereafter as the director of the Nationalgalerie in Berlin; for Halle, he organized a 1923 exhibition of Paul Klee and purchased works by Feininger, Klee, and Emile Nolde.[7] In Los Angeles he gave public lectures on topics that would have appealed to Fischinger, such as his 1950 summer talks at the Los Angeles County Museum on how formal elements in art, such as diagonals and circles, corresponded to levels of energy and human emotions.[8] In 1935 Fischinger met the Berlin art dealer Karl Nierendorf and he introduced the filmmaker to various artists and took him to visit Rudolf Bauer's elaborate gallery/studio Das Geistreich (Realm of the Spirit).[9] There he had the opportunity not only to study Bauer's art in depth, but also to examine paintings by Kandinsky and other non-objective artists. Fischinger was able to see compositions in multiple panels which Bauer was fond of creating as triptychs and tetraptychons; the serial nature of these paintings was akin to the effect of motion pictures and surely would have fascinated the filmmaker.

Nierendorf had been involved in early Bauhaus publications, and presented Fischinger with an elaborate book about the innovative art school as a going away present.[10] Fischinger was well acquainted with the Bauhaus, having shared their aesthetic concerns. He probably visited the school, perhaps in the company of his colleague László Moholy-Nagy, who also worked with film and drawn sound experiments, and was also acquainted with at least one other of its teachers, Lyonel Feininger.[11] The Bauhaus was founded in 1919 as a school of design, crafts, and architecture. Fischinger's wife Elfriede may have first encouraged Oskar's interest, for she had studied textiles, weaving and design at the Kunstgewerbeschule (School of Applied Arts) in Offenbach. From the beginning of his painting career, Fischinger utilized the constructivist vocabulary of plane geometry: circles, squares and rectangles. He seems to have echoed the stark simplicity of Bauhaus artists, especially Moholy-Nagy, as well as the Dutch De Stijl of Piet Mondrian and Theo Van Doesberg most during his first decade of painting, composing modest canvases consisting of two or three circles, a tiny one within another quite large circle, which seem to be balanced precariously with a horizontal-oriented rectangle. The potential motion—the orbit of the small circle echoing the circumference of the larger one, or the discs moving in alignment with the bar—also suggests that Fischinger may have known of the *Rotative plaques verre, optique de précision* (Rotary Glass Plates, Precision Optics) kinetic machine that Marcel Duchamp made with the assistance of Man Ray in 1920 in New York. In 1938 Fischinger visited New York for his first showing in the city, actually two solo displays, one at the gallery of his friend Karl Nierendorf , the other at the gallery of Philip Boyer. His *Abstraction* (1936, fig. 6) was sold to Katherine Dreier, an abstract painter who with Marcel Duchamp formed the Société Anonyme (now in Yale University Art Gallery, New Haven) in 1920 to promote modern art in America. It was on this trip he was reacquainted with and began his long association with Hilla Rebay, one of the foremost promoters of non-objective art and film in the United States and the curator of the Solomon R. Guggenheim Foundation; the following year the Foundation would open as the Museum of Non-Objective Painting (now the Solomon R. Guggenheim Museum, New York). Fischinger stayed for several months in New York and at the Connecticut home of Rebay, further studying the works of Kandinsky, Bauer, and others of the avant-garde. In 1940 Rebay would offer Fischinger a grant to make the film *An American March*. She also supplied him with catalogs of the shows at the museum as well as a number of pamphlets on non-objective art that he carefully read and underlined, and in which he made notes and sketches.

6
Naomi Sawelson-Gorse, "Narrow Circles and Uneasy Alliances: Galka Scheyer and American Collectors of the *Blue Four*," in *The Blue Four: Feininger, Jawlensky, Kandinsky and Klee in the New World*, exh. cat., eds. Vivian Endicott Barnett and Josef Helfenstein (Cologne: DuMont, 1997), 56.

7
Schardt's activities in Germany are referenced in several essays and biographical notes throughout *"Degenerate Art": The Fate of the Avant-Garde in Nazi Germany*, exh. cat., ed. Stephanie Barron (New York and Los Angeles: Harry N. Abrams with Los Angeles County Museum of Art, 1991), 104, 107, 109. Schardt was also an early supporter of Feininger's work and remained a lifelong friend of his. According to Barbara Fischinger, the artist's daughter, Schardt owned several Franz Marcs and one decorated his study in Los Angeles.

8
List of topics enclosed in letter announcing the talks, Frances Roberts Nugent (Museum Instructor in Art, Los Angeles County Museum) to "Dear Friend," in Alois J. Schardt file, Oskar Fischinger Collection, Box 5, Center for Visual Music, Los Angeles.

9
Moritz, *Optical Poetry*, 70. The Fischingers knew Nierendorf so well that when he emigrated to the United States, Fischinger's wife, Elfriede, helped the dealer smuggle forty-two paintings out of Germany. Nierendorf stayed briefly with the Fischingers in Hollywood before opening a gallery in New York City.

10
Karl Nierendorf, *Staatliches Bauhaus, Weimar, 1919–1923* (Weimar: Bauhausverlag, 1923).

11
Moritz, *Optical Poetry*, 70; and Lyonel Feininger to Galka Scheyer, April 8, 1936, Galka Scheyer Archives, Norton Simon Museum, Pasadena, California; repr. *Galka Scheyer & The Blue Four: Correspondence, 1924–1945*, ed. Isabel Wünsche (Berne: Benteli Verlag, 2006), 261. Feininger refers to his friend Fischinger in Los Angeles whom he might visit.

Rebay encouraged one aspect of Fischinger's personality that linked him to a sub-current of modernism, both in Europe and the United States: a taste for unconventional spiritual beliefs and a conviction that art was a means to higher truths. Rebay believed that non-objective art would serve as "an initiation to the mystical mission of spiritual realities," thereby helping viewers to attain an elevated state of consciousness.[12] Although Fischinger was not interested in organized religion, he was fascinated by metaphysics since his German days, avidly reading volumes on mystical oriental writings, and subscribing to a Buddhist journal. He probably also read at this time Kandinsky's *Concerning the Spiritual in Art* (1912), a treatise delving into the connections between art, the spiritual, and music. Fischinger would have immediately felt a kinship upon reading:

> A painter who finds no satisfaction in mere representation … cannot but envy the ease with which music, the least material of the arts today, achieves this end. He naturally seeks to apply the means of music to his own art. And from this results that modern desire for rhythm in painting, for mathematical, abstract construction, for repeated notes of color, for setting color in motion, and so on.[13]

Asian philosophy and its modern Western interpretations had a profound impact on California culture beginning at the turn of the twentieth century, due not only to the influx of immigrants from Japan and China, but also to the establishment throughout the state of several religiously oriented, utopian colonies, the Theosophical Lomaland being the largest and best known, established in 1897 at Point Loma near San Diego. Krotona, an offshoot of Lomaland, existed in the hills of Hollywood until 1924 when it moved north to Ojai and became linked with the spiritual leader Jiddu Krishnamurti.[14] Macdonald-Wright's overwhelming love of Asian philosophies and art established a strong foundation for other early California modernists' fascination with Eastern mysticism, and the development of San Francisco as a center of abstract film and beat literature during the 1940s and 1950s also encouraged this trend. By the time of Fischinger's residence, modernist painters Agnes Pelton and Frederick Schwankovsky, ceramicist Beatrice Wood, writer Aldous Huxley, and Beat poet Robert Duncan were California-based followers of these sects. If Fischinger had not yet associated with any of these disciples, the art and people he encountered in New York surely stimulated his return to metaphysical explorations. Through Rudolph Steiner, he studied Theosophy. Rebay, who was a devotee of Edwin J. Dingle (known as Ding Le Mei) arranged for Fischinger to study at his ashram-like temple, The Institute of Mentalphysics, in Los Angeles. He visited the temple two or three times a week and studied Tibetan tantric mysticism there.[15] Ding Le Mei teachings were based on the concept of self-realization, that yoga, meditation, and harmonic breathing exercises awaken understanding of life and the universe.[16] Fischinger also met Krishnamurti, and read books on a variety of topics, including Christian Science and palmistry, a practice that began in the ancient Far East.[17] He would also practice yoga and meditation. His wide-ranging interests in different belief systems would infiltrate various creative activities: his sound experiments (inspired by Buddhism, Fischinger believed that all things in the world had a sound[18]); his frequent mandala forms in film and concentric circles in film and painting (the circle might refer to the Pradakshina, the path around a Hindu temple and the practice of circumambulating the temple after worship); and his explanation of his film on painting abstractly, *Motion Painting No. 1* (1947), included passages from the Hindu Bhagavad Gita.[19]

Fischinger arrived in Hollywood on February 26, 1936, just two days after the Stendahl Art Galleries in Los Angeles opened a Kandinsky exhibition. Although he was probably unaware of the display, he may have wanted to attend. Kandinsky played as seminal a role in American modernism as he had in Europe, his art known through exhibitions and private collections as well as discussed and reproduced in books, articles and reviews, including his own writings *Concerning the Spiritual in Art* (1912) and *Point and Line to Plane* (1926), the latter based on his teachings at the Bauhaus.[20] Although Fischinger occasionally created compositions akin to Kandinsky's early expressionist paintings (which appear similar to his early wax experiments), in general he was averse to their amorphousness. He critiqued them in several satirical collages; using reproductions of Kandinsky paintings from books Rebay had sent him, he added cutouts of the popular Disney characters Mickey and Minnie Mouse, thereby presenting the cartoon figures as if they were running away from an explosion of paint (see p. 90).[21] Fischinger preferred Kandinsky's late, constructivist compositions and the analytical approach to their creation that he presented through text and simple line drawings in *Point and Line to Plane*. Fischinger's emphasis on circles, triangles, rectangular and curved spirals, grids and networks of grids may have been encouraged by Kandinsky's theoretical explanations of what he referred to as the "building materials" of a work of art; through them, he explains the concepts of balance, rhythm, tensions, often relating them to parallels in music and nature. For example, Kandinsky explains that the accumulation of points occurs frequently in the natural realm and illustrates this with a 1921 photograph of a star cluster, concluding that the universe consists of many self-contained cosmic compositions originating from points. During the last decade of his career, Fischinger's circles evolved into more cosmic interpretations, and to underscore his intention, the artist referenced outer space in some titles (fig. 5).

Another Bauhaus-inspired theme may have been Fischinger's Pendulum paintings, which he began in 1942. In each canvas Fischinger drew an organic line upon a dark background. As he drew several on English silk they may originally have been ideas for a film. Kandinsky devoted several pages of his treatise to these "wave-like lines," concluding that they produce "a certain vibration" and caused "a definite loosening-up of the stiff atmosphere of the whole."[22] The idea of vibration as well as Fischinger's

Figure 5 / *Space Abstraction No. 3*, 1966
Oil on canvas, 48 x 35 in. / 122 x 89 cm
Collection The Fischinger Trust, Long Beach, CA

Figure 6 / *Abstraction*, 1936
Gouache and watercolor on paper
17.8 x 11.8 in. / 45.5 x 30 cm
Yale University Art Gallery,
New Haven, Connecticut, gift of
Collection Société Anonyme

12
Rebay wrote this comment in a letter to Harry Bertoia, a designer and sculptor, who, through Rebay, would become a close friend of Fischinger in the late 1940s. Quoted by Joan M. Lukach in her *Hilla Rebay: In Search of the Spirit in Art* (New York: George Braziller, 1983), 150.

13
Wassily Kandinsky, *Concerning the Spiritual in Art and Painting in Particular, 1912* (1914); repr. and trans. in : "The Documents of Modern Art" series, vol. 5 (New York: George Wittenborn, Inc., 1947), 40. If Fischinger had not read the treatise earlier in Germany, he surely would have been encouraged by Rebay to do so. In fact, she edited the first American edition, which was published by the Museum of Non-Objective Painting in 1946.

14
Ilene Susan Fort, "Altered State(s): California Art and the Inner World," in *Reading California: Art, Image, and Identity, 1900–2000*, eds. Stephanie Barron, Sheri Bernstein, and Ilene Susan Fort (Los Angeles: Los Angeles County Museum of Art and University of California Press, 2000), 34–35 ff.

15
William Moritz, "The Films of Oskar Fischinger," *Film Culture*, 58–60 (1974), 53, 68. Ding Le Mei established the institute in Los Angeles in 1927; it was housed near downtown in the International Church of the Holy Trinity; in 1941 a large retreat center was dedicated in Yucca Valley (now Joshua Tree), California, at a location which supposedly has a unique energy vortex. Frank Lloyd Wright designed some of the buildings of the complex.

16
For information about Dingle and the Institute of Mentalphysics, see www.mentalphysics.net (accessed July 20, 2012).

17
Larry Janiak and Dave Daruszka, "Oskar Fischinger. An Interview with Elfriede Fischinger," *Zoetrope*, no. 3 (March 1979), no pagination. Books now in Fischinger Collection, Center for Visual Music, Los Angeles.

18
Moritz, *Optical Poetry*, 78.

19
Moritz, *Optical Poetry*, 78, 184–86.

20
As with *Concerning the Spiritual in Art*, Fischinger may have read *Point and Line to Plane* in Germany or in the United States. The English version was also a Rebay and Museum of Non-Objective Painting project of 1947 (see note 13).

21
Marianne Lorenz, "Kandinsky and Regional America," in *Theme & Improvisation: Kandinsky & the American Avant-Garde, 1912–1950* (Boston: Little, Brown, 1992), 162.

22
Kandinsky, *Point and Line to Plane*, 90–91.

reference to a pendulum in his titles suggests that the artist may have been encouraged by the experimental photograms and photographs of Moholy-Nagy and his fellow Bauhaus colleague (in Europe and Chicago) Gyorgy Kepes. Pursuing the "new vision" of the world, both explored abstract line, Moholy-Nagy sometimes extracting the lines from the silhouettes of his plastic sculpture or from the cast of penlights in darkness.

The art of Kandinsky and Klee would be central to the modernist agenda Nierendorf promoted in his American gallery. Fischinger loved Klee's art, and had ample opportunity to study it, both when he house-sat for Scheyer and visited the Arensbergs and from 1944 to 1946 through the Los Angeles subsidiary of Nierendorf Gallery, International Art in Los Angeles.[23] He admired Klee's draughtsmanship and sometimes followed his example by drawing outlines of geometric shapes in delicate white lines that seem to float over geometric forms. In a number of watercolors that Scheyer eventually acquired, Klee applied his paint with short, staccato precision, so as a group the methodically placed horizontal strokes suggest tesserae of a mosaic. Fischinger utilized such a pointillist handling as early as 1937 (fig. 8), and even referred to several canvases as Mosaic paintings. The small rectangular shapes not only served as the means of applying the pigment but functioned as a compositional device, as Fischinger's *Bird in* Flight (1946, fig. 7) which is similar to Klee's *Memory of a Bird* (1932, fig. 9) that Scheyer had in her possession since 1933.[24] This approach may have also been encouraged by Albert King, a ceramicist who became famous not only for his color glazes but for the innovative patterning of tesserae he created for Macdonald-Wright's large public mural *Re-creations of Long Beach* (1936–38).[25]

During the 1940s, Fischinger created a number of Wave paintings in which he placed the tesserae-like strokes of paint in directional patterns suggesting the movement of water and sound.

> Movement is the basis of all creation. ... When a point becomes movement and therefore a line, it takes time. Similarly, when a line shifts to become a plane. Equally, the movement of planes to become volume. Has a picture ever been created instantaneously? No, it is built up piece by piece.[26]

Klee's comments from one of his lectures could have explained the rationale behind Fischinger creating his 1947 film, *Motion Painting No.1*. Using a series of large (18 x 24 in.)

Figure 7 / *Bird in Flight*, 1946
Oil on canvas, 18 x 24 in. / 46 x 61 cm
Collection Norton Simon Museum of Art, Pasadena, CA

Figure 8 / *Experiment*, 1936
Oil on canvas, 60 x 40 in. / 152.5 x 101.5 cm
The Buck Collection, Laguna Hills, CA

Figure 9 / Paul Klee, *Memory of a Bird*, 1932
Watercolor and pencil on laid paper, 12.4 x 18.9 in. / 31.5 x 48 cm
Collection Norton Simon Museum, The Blue Four Galka Scheyer Collection, Pasadena, CA

Figure 10 / *Circles in Circle* (Stereo painting), 1949
Oil on Masonite, (2x) 12 x 12 in. / (2x) 30.5 x 30.5 cm
Collection The Fischinger Trust, Long Beach, CA

plastic sheets (fig. 12, p. 60), he painted and then filmed stroke after stroke, so multiple layers are seen simultaneously. The entire film is set to two movements of Bach's "Brandenburg Concerto No. 3," but even without the musical accompaniment, a viewer can understand the pace. Fischinger personalized many Bauhaus ideas for the film. It begins with an aggregation of small rectangles (functioning as Kandinsky's points) that change colors and patterns, quickly appearing and disappearing and filling up the two-dimensional space. Then a long section of the film is devoted to spirals in different sizes and colors, dissolving and reconfiguring. Each end of the individual spiral hooks up to its center, and eventually these connect in a wheel-like formation. The spiral movement suggests the Hindu idea of Pradakshia, which is a practice in homage to a deity, performed in a meditative mood. The film thereby functions as a meditative tool. It is a brilliant summation of Fischinger's filmmaking and painting, his interest in color, pure form, movement, and music within each media. Many of the still images are quite similar to the oil paintings that he would create for the next two decades, demonstrating a heightened complexity of imagery.

Fischinger's most unique contribution in painting was his Stereo paintings, unveiled at his 1951 solo exhibition at Frank Perls Gallery in Los Angeles. Two years later, in his first museum solo exhibition of his paintings at the San Francisco Museum of Art, they were prominently featured, hung on the title wall at the gallery's entrance (fig. 11). Each work was a diptych of sorts, some painted on a single support divided in half by a painted line, but framed as a single painting; some juxtaposed next to each other without a dividing demarcation; and others on two separate supports hinged together like a book in the more traditional diptych fashion. The artist experimented with the type of non-objective imagery: in *Mosaic Stereo* (1952), he exploited his fondness for tessellated patterning by covering the entire plane with tiny rectangles arranged in pointed patterns of various colors, while in *Circles in Circle* (1949, fig. 10), *Stereo No. 13* (1949) and most of the others, he presented a variety of larger, geometric shapes against a white or black background.

The two images of each Stereo painting were almost

23
From 1938 on, Nierendorf was the exclusive American representative of Klee, and he was quite successful in selling his work on the West Coast. See Megan M. Fontanella, "'Unity in Diversity': Karl Nierendorf and America, 1937–47," *American Art*, vol. 24, no. 3 (Fall 2010), 117.

24
Vivian Endicott Barnett, *The Blue Four Collection at the Norton Simon Museum* (New Haven and Pasadena: Yale University Press in association with Norton Simon Foundation, 2002), 322.

25
The Southern California branch of the WPA/FAP became famous for its Mosaic Unit, the only one of its kind in the regional projects. Moreover, King wrote a major manual on the subject in the 1930s: Albert King, *Mosaic and Allied Techniques* (Los Angeles: Southern California Works Progress Administration Project, n.d.).

26
Paul Klee, from an unidentified source, quoted by Eberhard Roters in *Painters of the Bauhaus*, trans. Anne Rose Cooper (New York: Frederick A. Praeger, Inc., 1969), 102–3.

Figure 11 / Entrance to Oskar Fischinger exhibition at San Francisco Museum of Art, 1953
Collection Center for Visual Music

identical, their differences primarily based on subtle shifts to the right or left in the placement of the flat forms in the compositions. In this respect, Fischinger followed the principle of stereoscopy, a technique for creating or enhancing the illusion of depth by placing images side-by-side on a two dimensional plane.[27] The painter's extensive work in film surely encouraged his study of different types of perception in terms of binocular vision, and he understood that the parallax provided by the two eyes' different positions on a person's head gave the impression of depth perception. Stereopsis was first discovered in 1838, and after the invention of photography at mid-century it became popular as a form of entertainment. The newly discovered, dramatic landscape vistas of the American frontier were introduced to stay-at-home tourists of the mid-nineteenth century through the display of stereo photographs in specially designed viewers. Perhaps, Fischinger knew of more recent developments, for in 1936, the physicist Theodor V. Ionescu was granted a patent for three-dimensional imaging in cinema. Moreover, in the United States as early as 1931, the company Tru-Vue sold a hand-held version of the stereoscope for film transparencies, and in the 1940s the View-Master was marketed to the general public. By the following decade, plastic viewers with slides of cartoon and fairy tale characters were a favorite of children; Fischinger, the father of five, surely was acquainted with this popular play toy.[28]

Fischinger intended to present more than a painted image in three dimensions, for he wanted to create a new "space reality" (he sometimes referred to the Stereo paintings as "space paintings") by having the viewer manipulate his perception of two images to create the illusion of a third that could be seen, entered and investigated. Perls Gallery issued a statement by the artist in which he explained how to experience the space paintings:

> Stand (or sit) at a comfortable distance, squarely in front of the painting. Eyes horizontal, parallel with the paintings. Look and focus and put all your attention at a nearby point (reading distance) in line with the paintings. …
>
> Adjust the distance … until you have the impression that the two panels of the stereo painting on the wall have moved apart from each other. Then between them a new, a third painting of equal size appears, slightly more brilliant than the images to its right and left.
>
> Now observe with your mind the illusive painting in the middle. This is the space illusion. … then you should actually see and be able to wander around in that space painting and feel the exact location and position of each form and the distance behind them in all sharpness, precision, exactness and perfection. …
>
> New conclusions, ideas, consequences spring out of space paintings.[29]

The renewed popularity of stereoscopic photography, due to the manufacturing of specially designed cameras during the 1950s, did not, however, encourage Fischinger sales. The Stereo paintings remained unsold.

Fischinger continued to exhibit and sell paintings until his death, but largely within a local sphere. It would take a quarter of a century after his demise for his oil paintings to enter the history books beyond a passing reference. Fischinger had been resigned to his isolation. For his last museum exhibition of his paintings, at the Pasadena Art Museum (now the Norton Simon Museum) in late 1956, he wrote a statement of intent. Referring to the difficulties of creating in the new fast-paced world and choosing between cinema or painting, he explained, "So why do I still paint in two or three dimensions after making abstract films since 1919? It is a way out. As Columbus, after discovering America, lived out the rest of his life in misery, so have pioneers in most cases throughout history, after their first achievements, had periods of quietness and solitude, pushed aside by the eager rush of an excited mankind."[30] Forgotten by the commercial film industry, Fischinger found solace for his brilliant creative talents in painting.

27
For a concise discussion of the basic concept of stereoscopy and its history in popular culture, see en.wikipedia.org/wiki/Stereoscopy and en.wikipedia.org/wiki/Stereopsis (accessed August 1, 2012).

28
Moritz notes that before starting to paint the stereo images, Fischinger first analyzed a set of old stereoscopic slides and pairs of photographs he took himself. (Moritz, *Film Culture*, 1974, 72.)

29
Oskar Fischinger, *A Statement about Painting*, leaflet (Los Angeles: Frank Perls Gallery, 1951), no pagination, Fischinger Collection, Center for Visual Music, Los Angeles.

30
Oskar Fischinger, "Oskar Fischinger (Pasadena: Pasadena Art Museum, 1956)," in Oskar Fischinger Curatorial file, Norton Simon Museum, Pasadena; reprinted in Moritz, *Optical Poetry*, 188–89, as "A Document Concerning Painting."

Figure 12 / Oskar Fischinger in his Hollywood studio with panels from *Motion Painting No. 1*, 1949
Collection Center for Visual Music

II

Still from the set of Fritz Lang's *Frau im Mond* (*Woman in the Moon*), showing the special effects rocket by Fischinger, 1929
35mm, b/w, sound
Collection Center for Visual Music

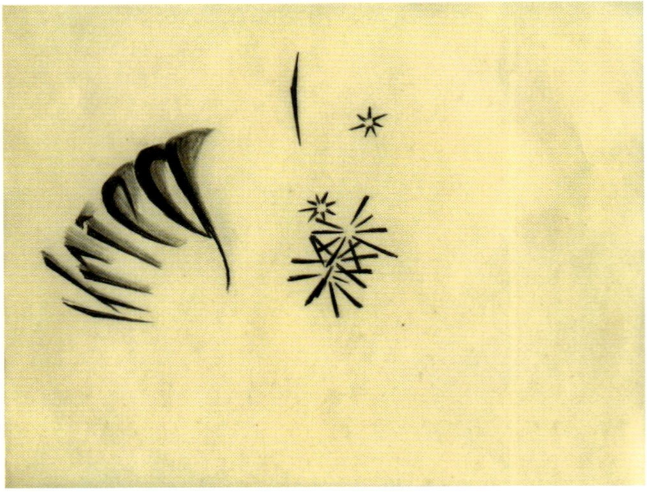

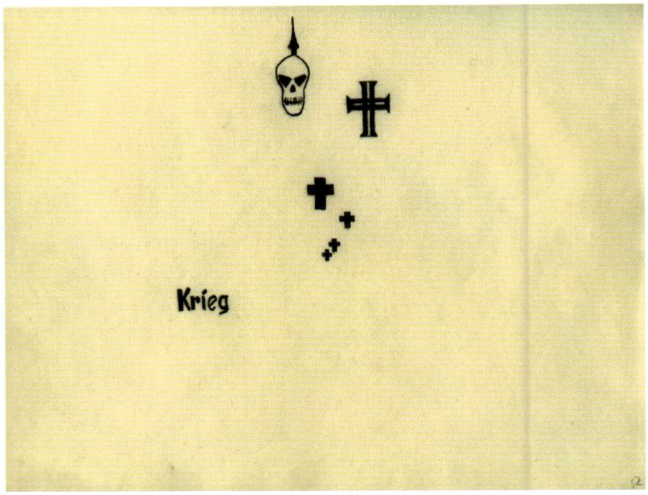

↑
Animation drawing with "Krieg" (War), from a sequence, c. 1927, possibly for a UFA film
Charcoal on paper, 8.8 x 11.2 in. / 22.5 x 28.5 cm
Collection Center for Visual Music
→
Stills from *Studie Nr. 3* (*Study No. 3*), 1930
35mm, b/w, soundtrack lost

(Vinka)
Studie Nr. 3
von
Oskar Fischinger
(Vinka)
Studie Nr. 3
von
Oskar Fischinger

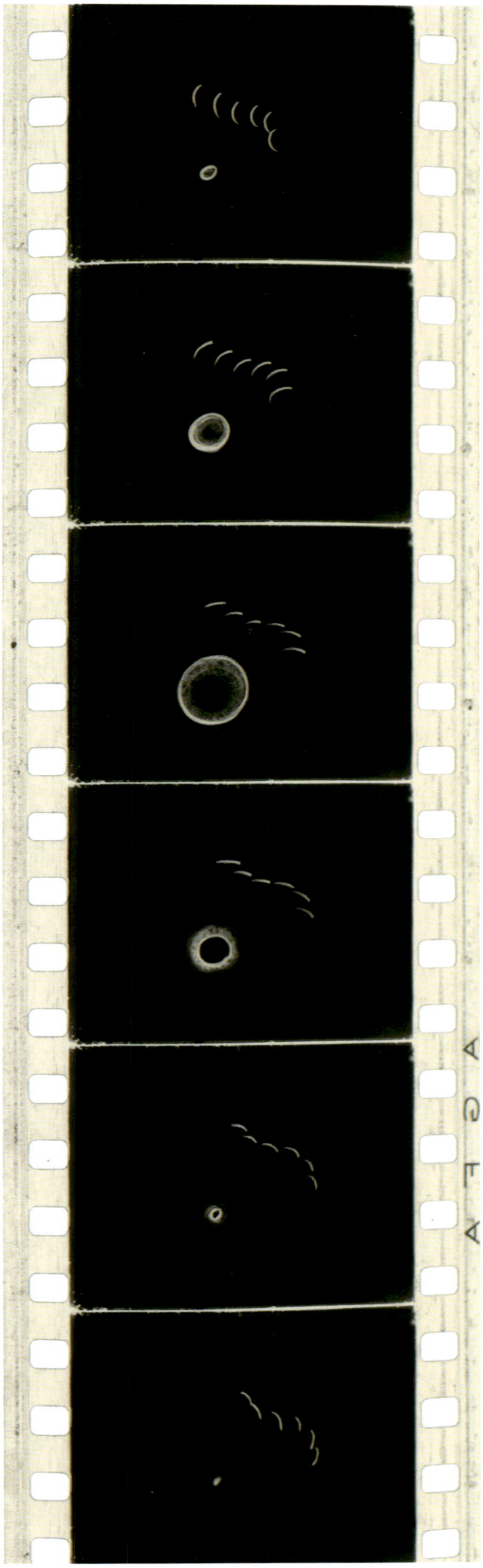

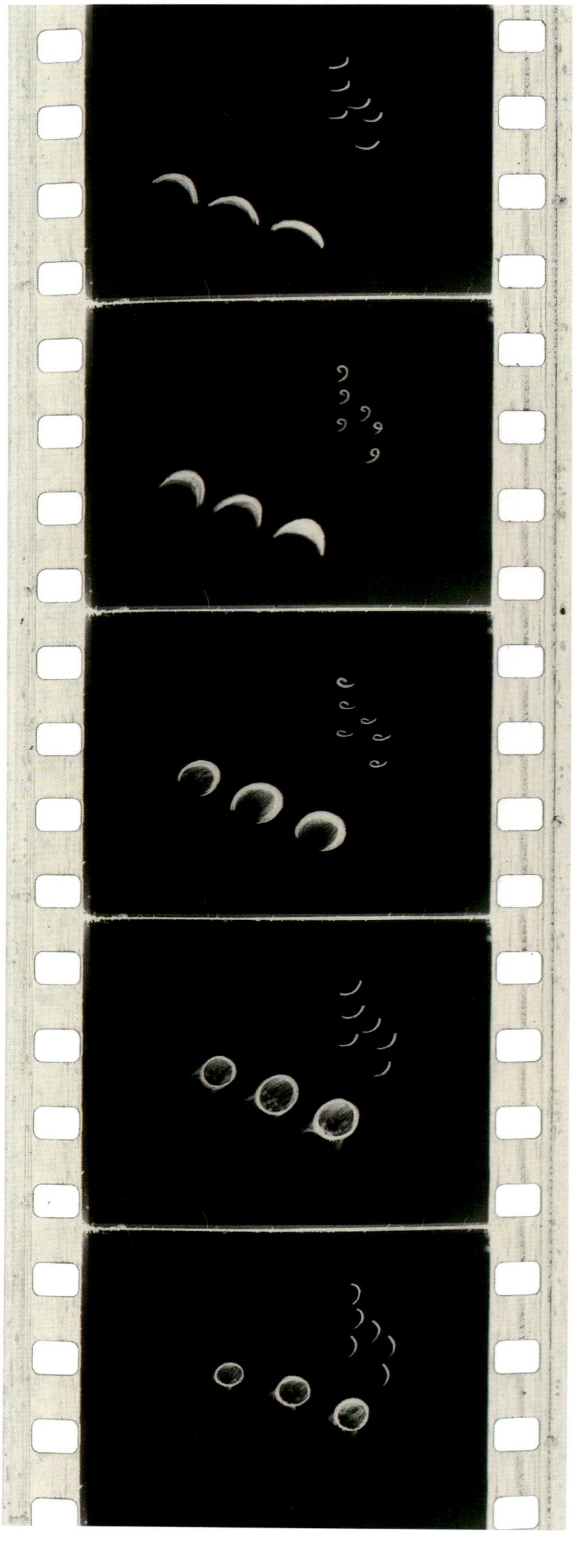

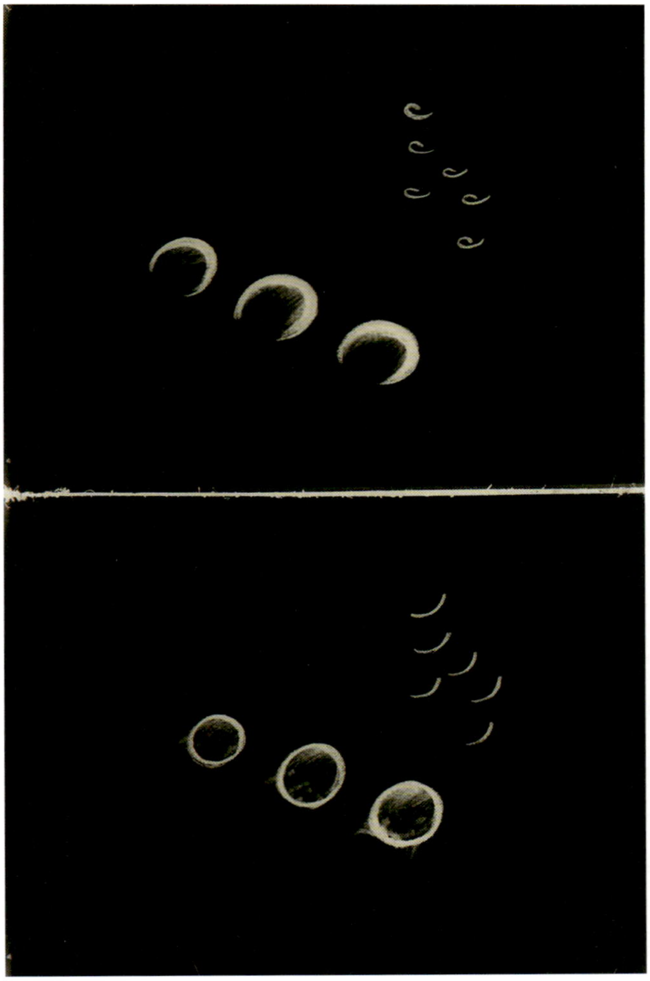

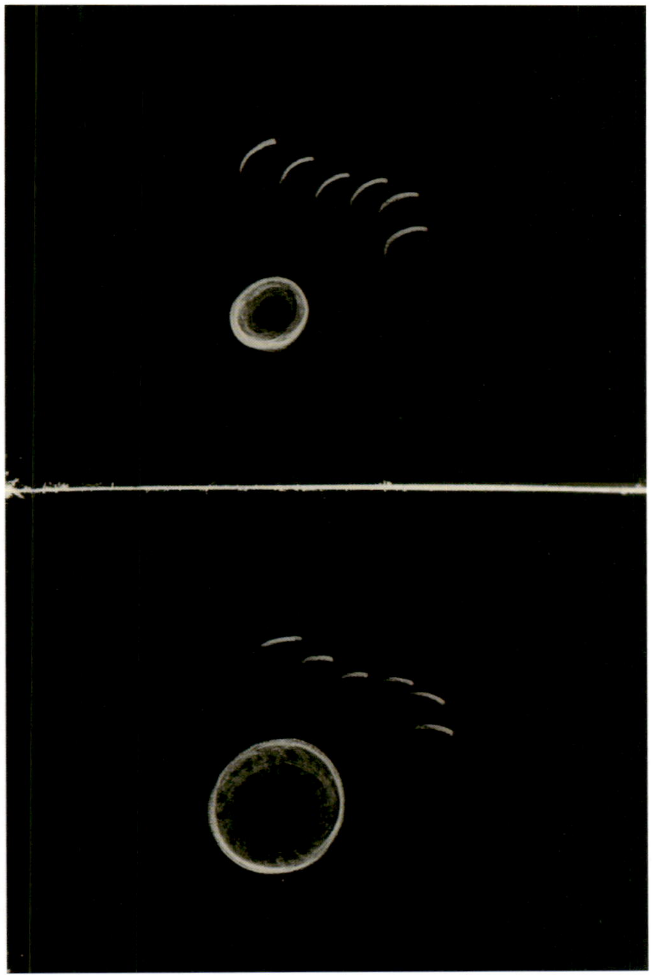

Stills from *Studie Nr. 3* (*Study No. 3*), 1930
35mm, b/w, soundtrack lost

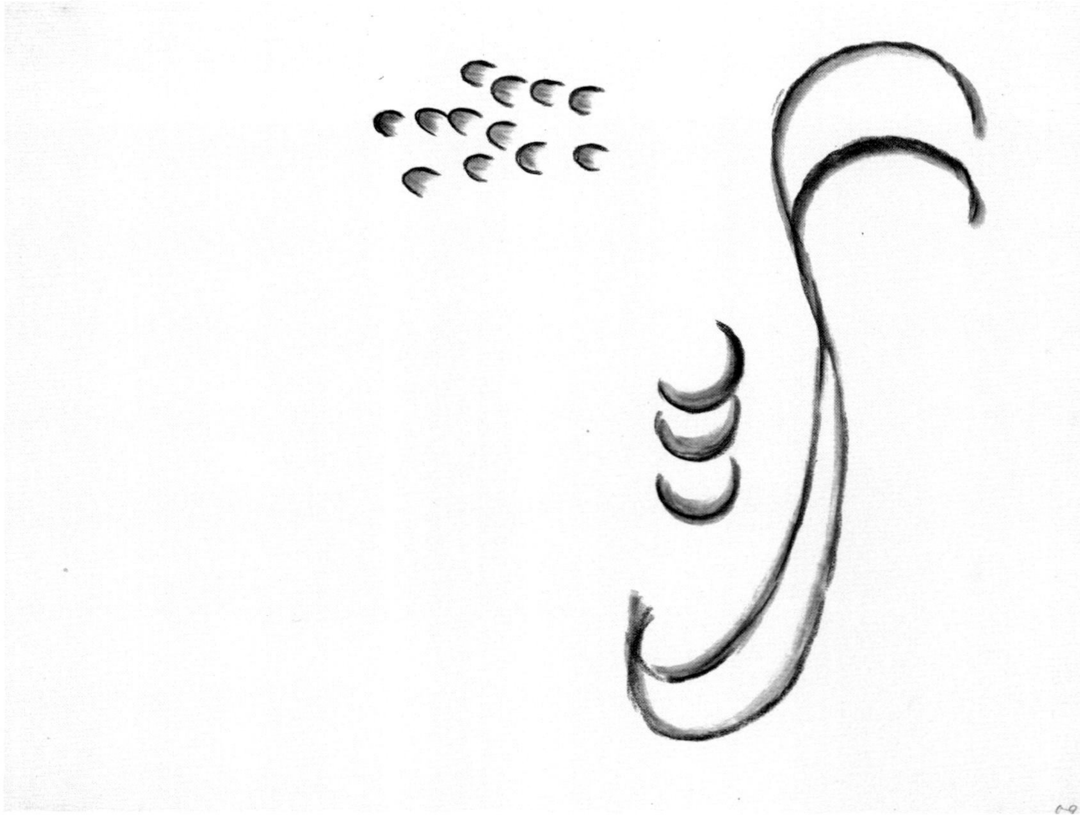

↑
Still from *Studie Nr. 5* (*Study No. 5*), 1930
35mm, b/w, sound
←
Animation drawings for *Studie Nr. 5* (*Study No. 5*), 1930
Charcoal on paper, 8.8 x 11.1 in. / 22.5 x 28 cm
Collection Center for Visual Music

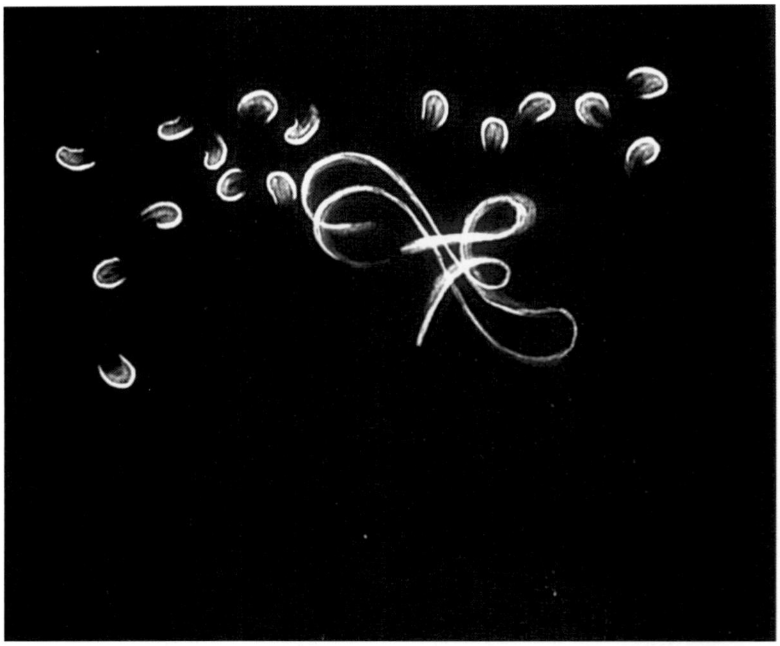

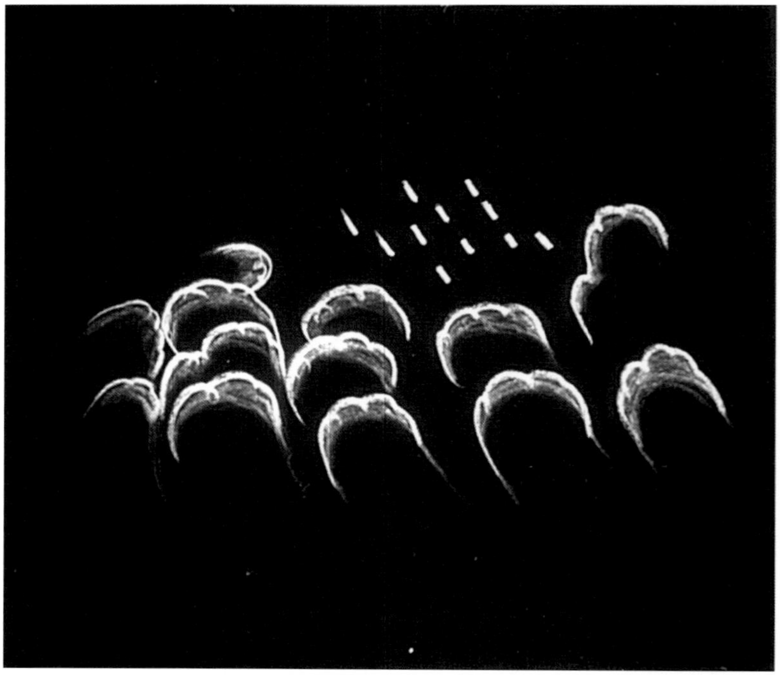

Stills from *Studie Nr. 5* (*Study No. 5*), 1930
35mm, b/w, sound

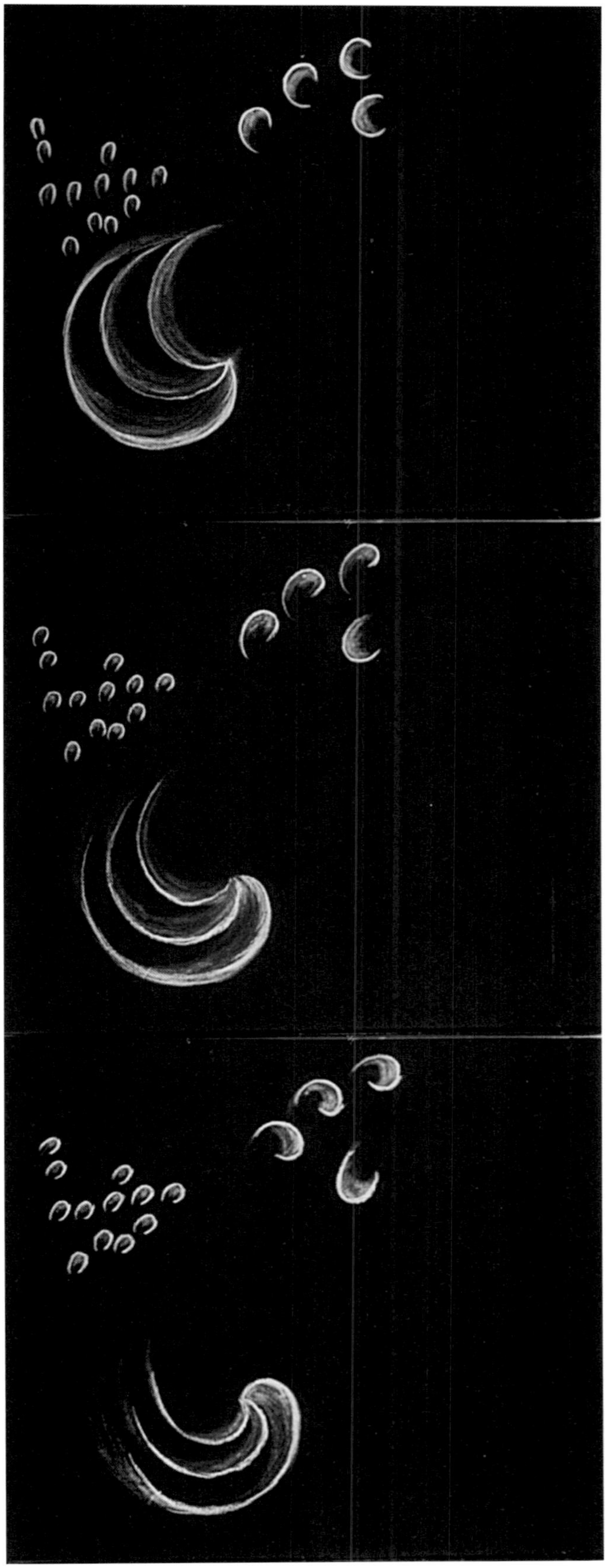

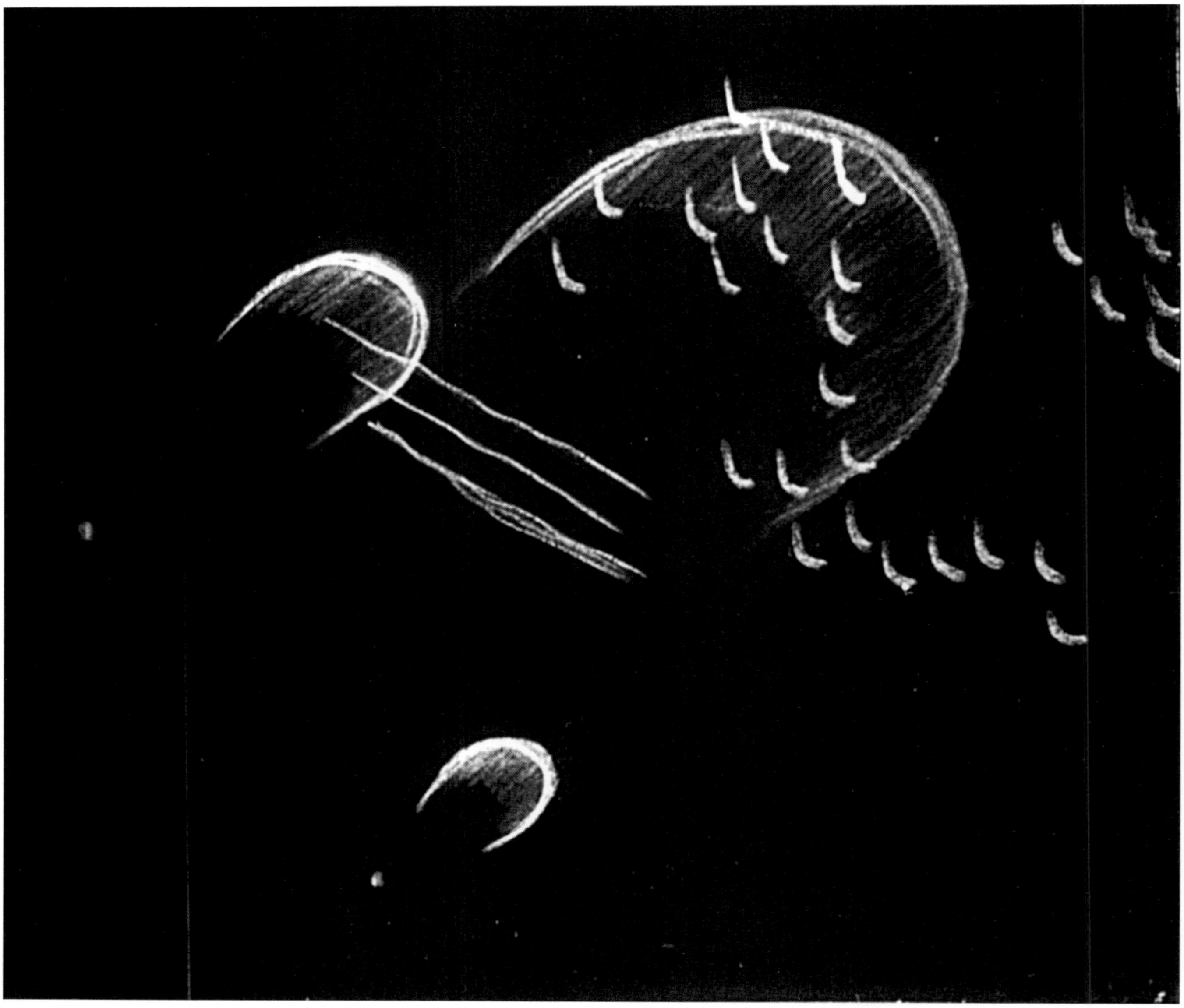

Still from *Studie Nr. 5* (*Study No. 5*), 1930
35mm, b/w, sound

Still from *Studie Nr. 6* (*Study No. 6*), 1930
35mm, b/w, sound

Stills from *Studie Nr. 6* (*Study No. 6*), 1930
35mm, b/w, sound

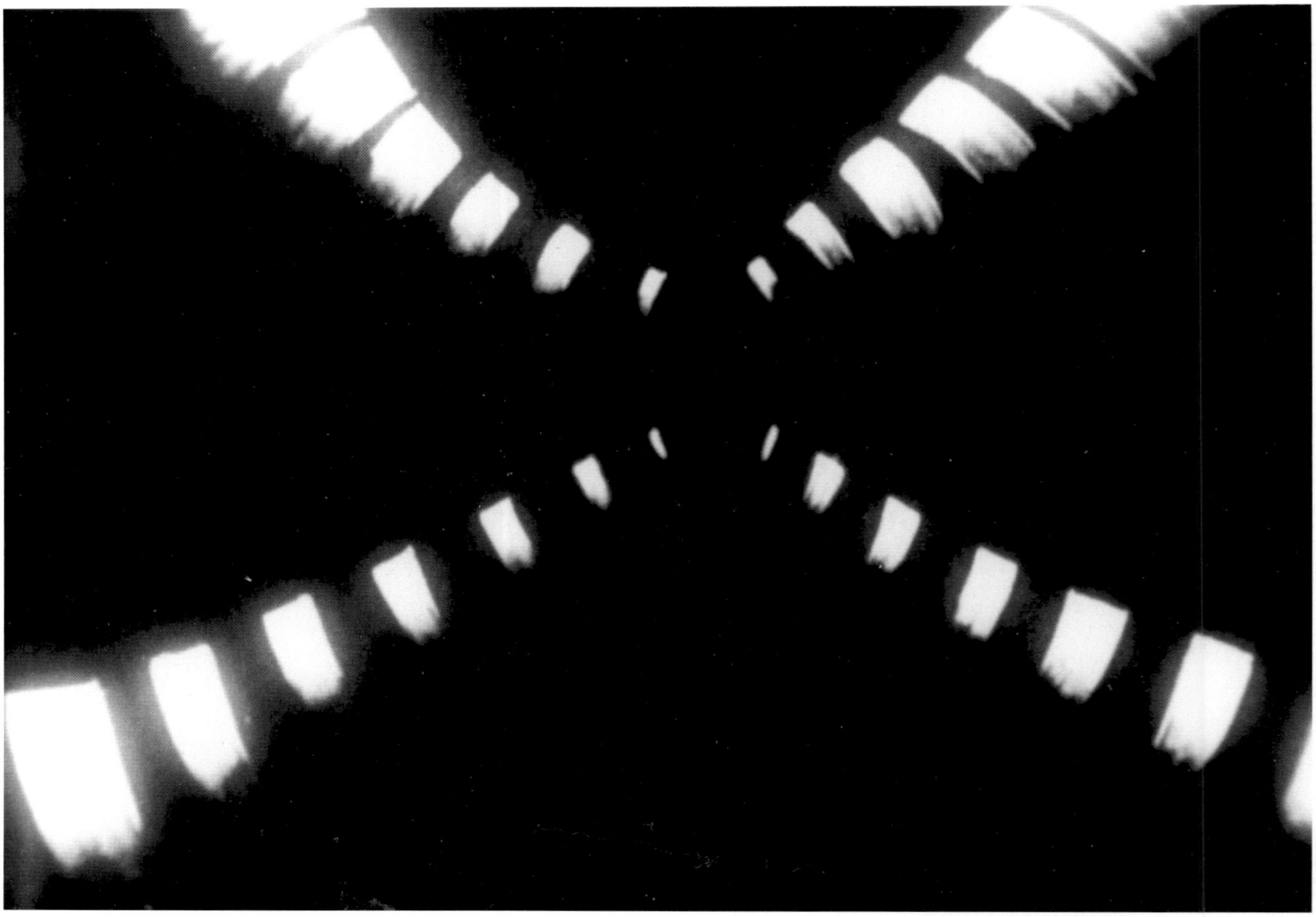

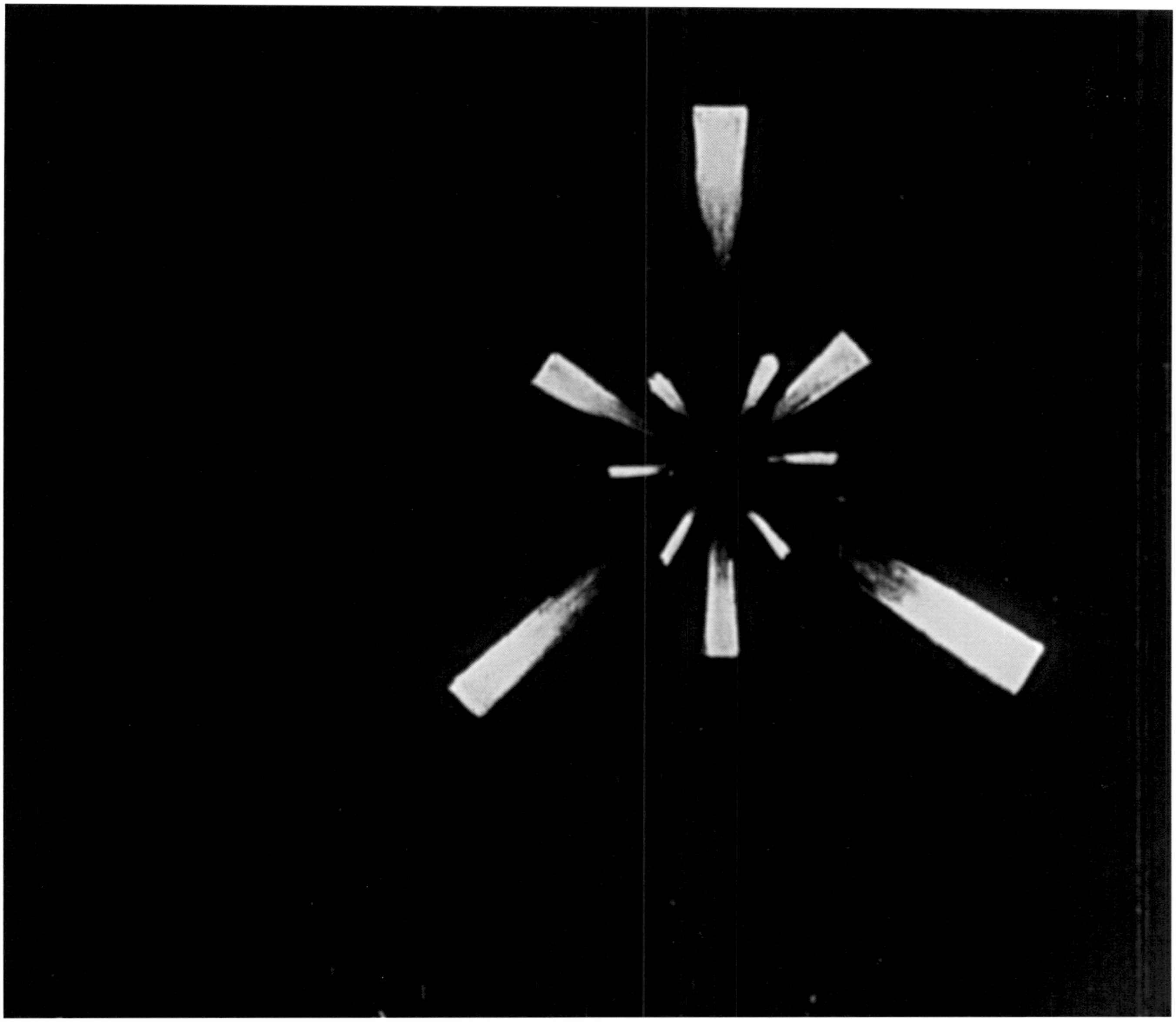

Stills from *Studie Nr. 6* (*Study No. 6*), 1930
35mm, b/w, sound

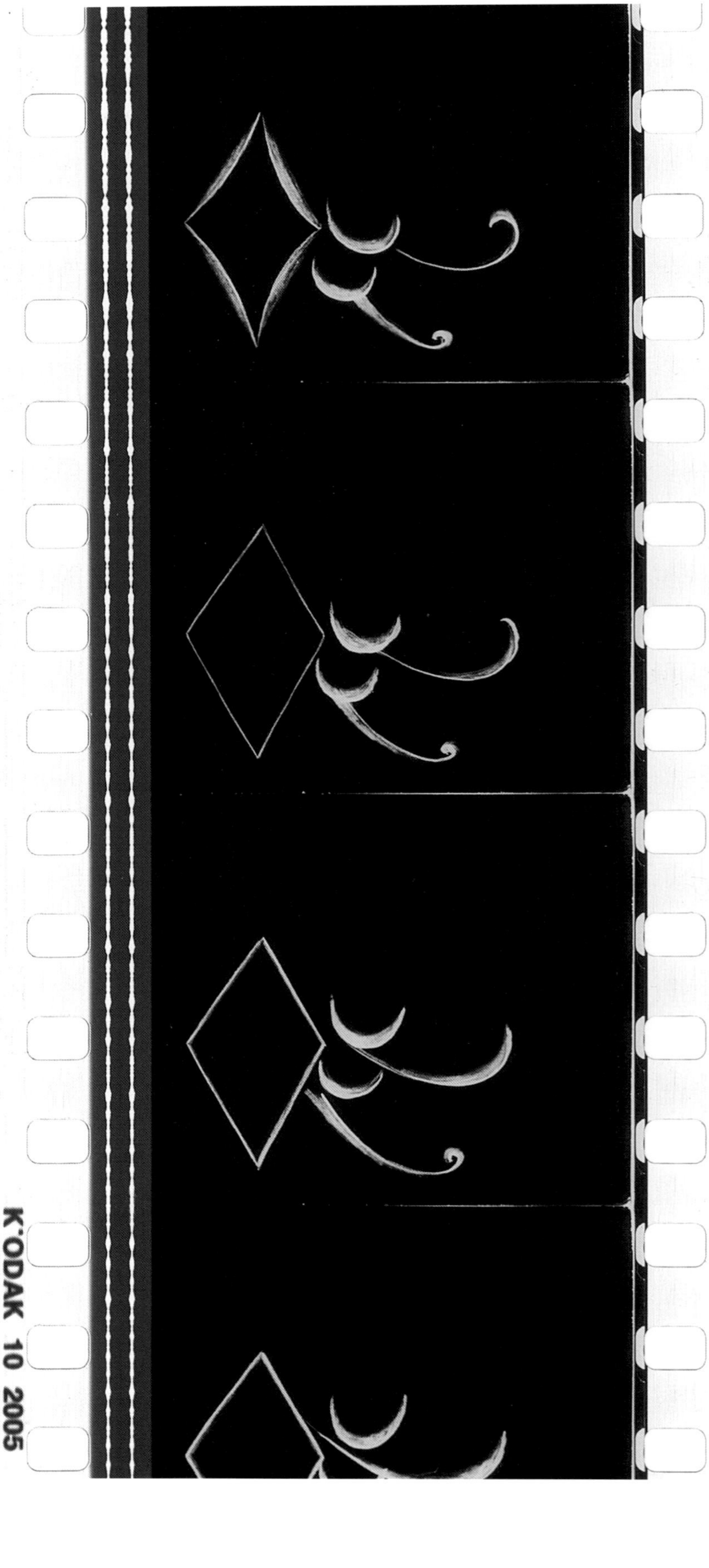
KODAK 10 2005

Stills from *Studie Nr. 7* (*Study No. 7*), 1931
35mm, b/w, sound

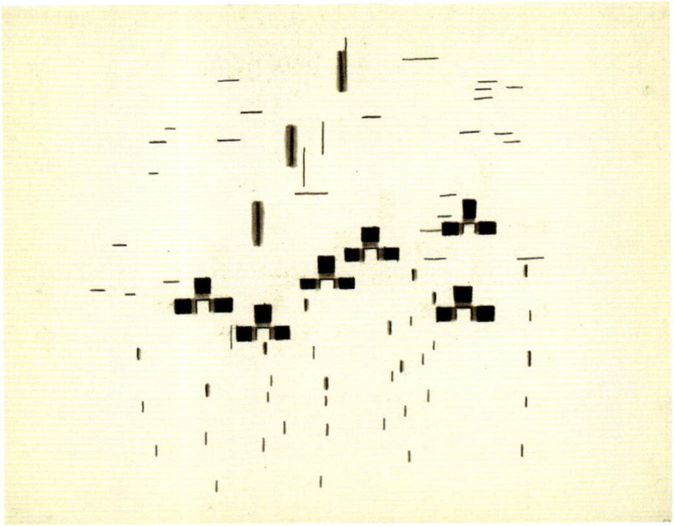

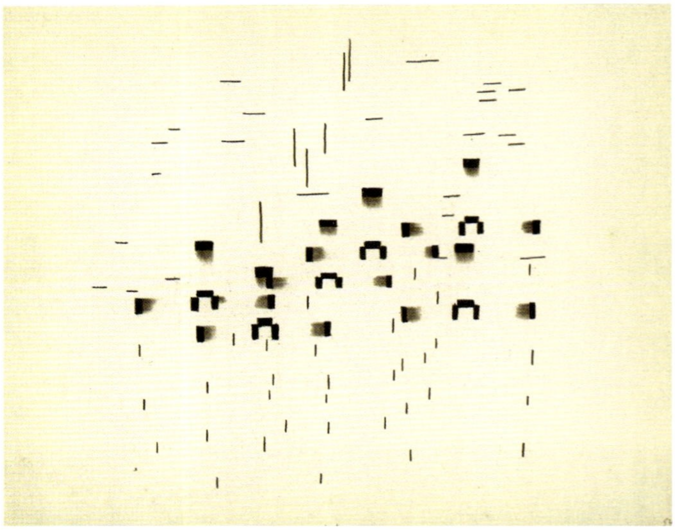

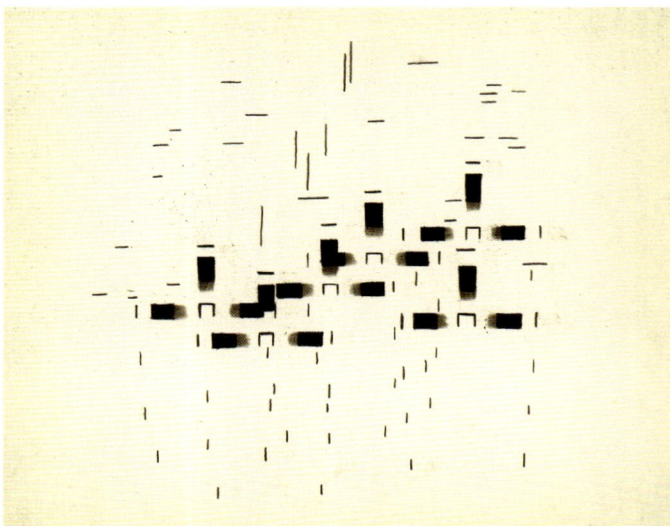

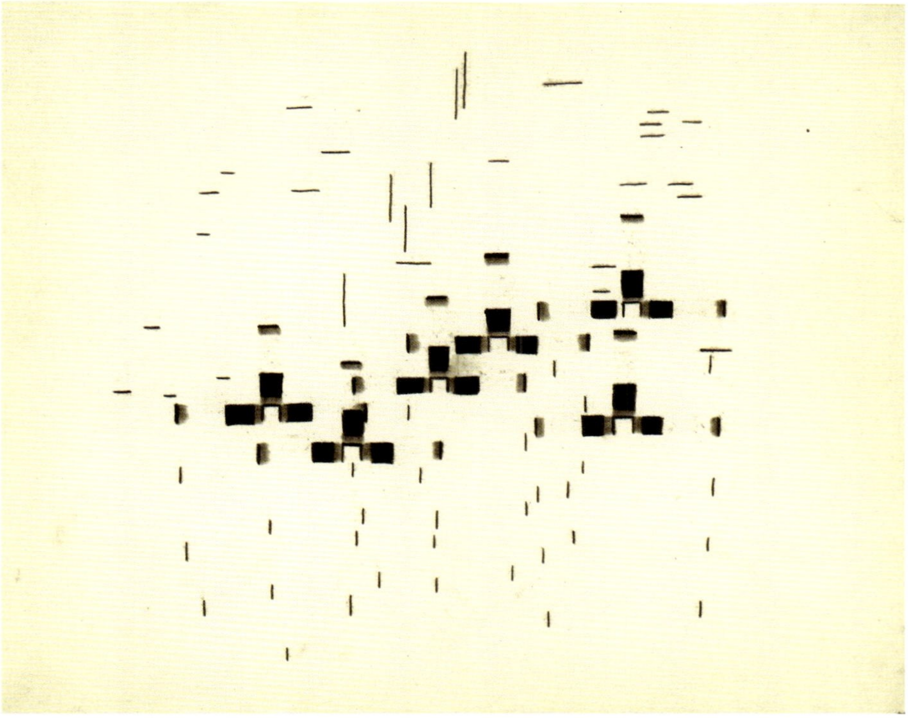

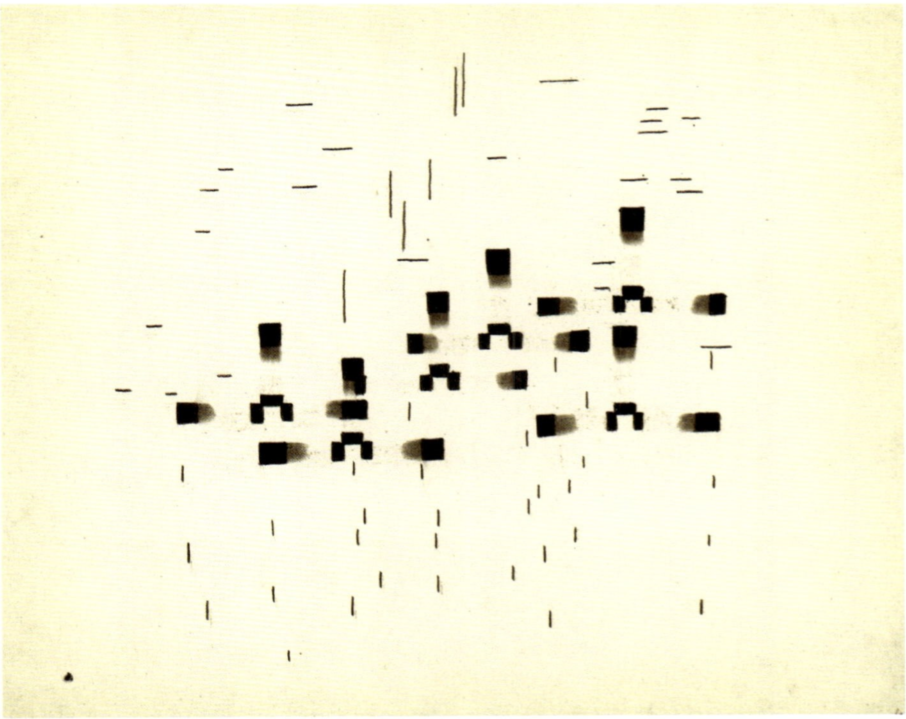

Animation drawings for *Studie Nr. 8* (*Study No. 8*), 1931
Charcoal on paper, 8.8 x 11.1 in. / 22.5 x 28 cm
Collection Center for Visual Music

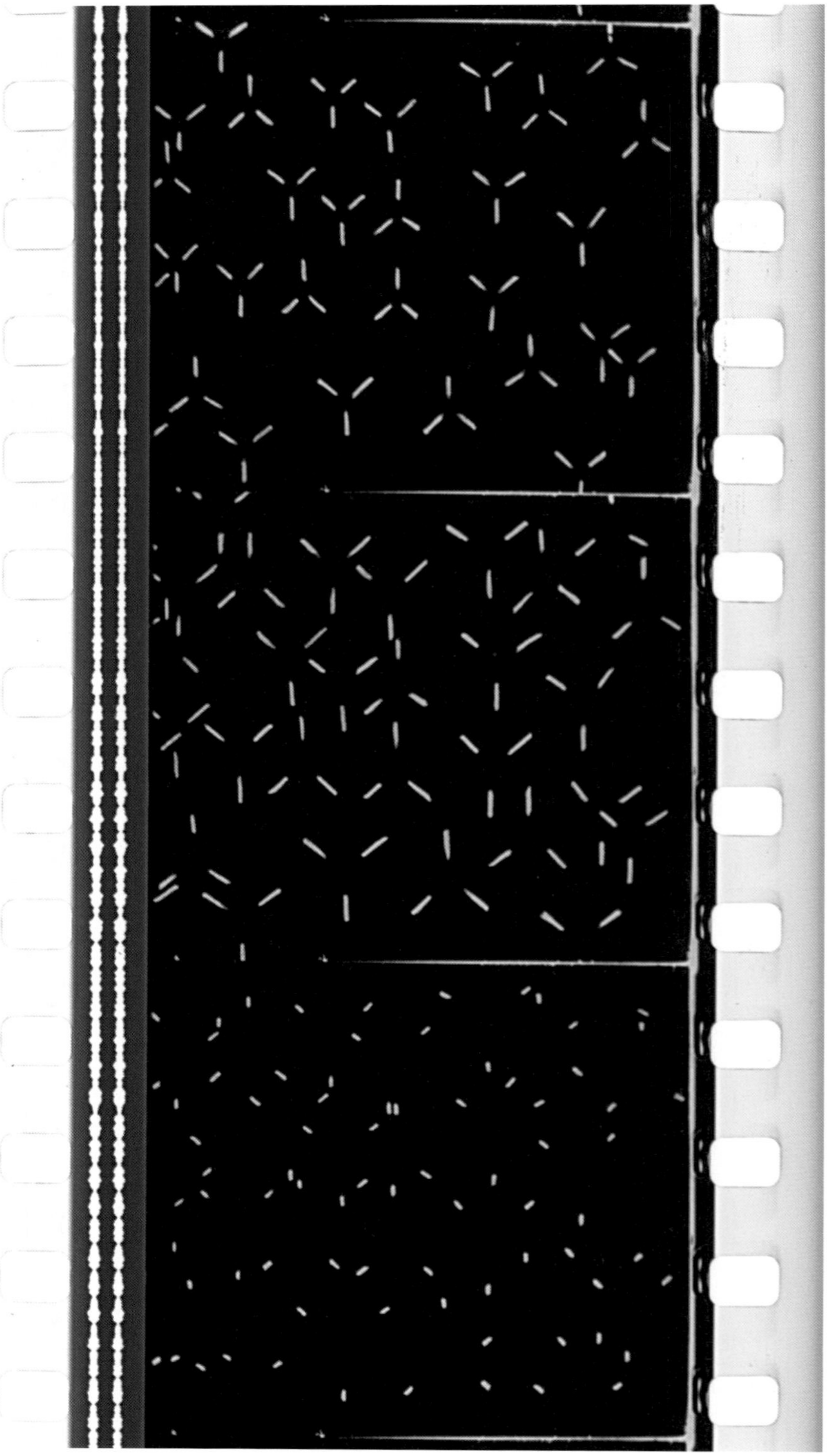

↑
Stills from *Studie Nr. 6* (*Study No. 6*), 1930
35mm, b/w, sound
→
Stills from *Studie Nr. 8* (*Study No. 8*), 1931
35mm, b/w, sound

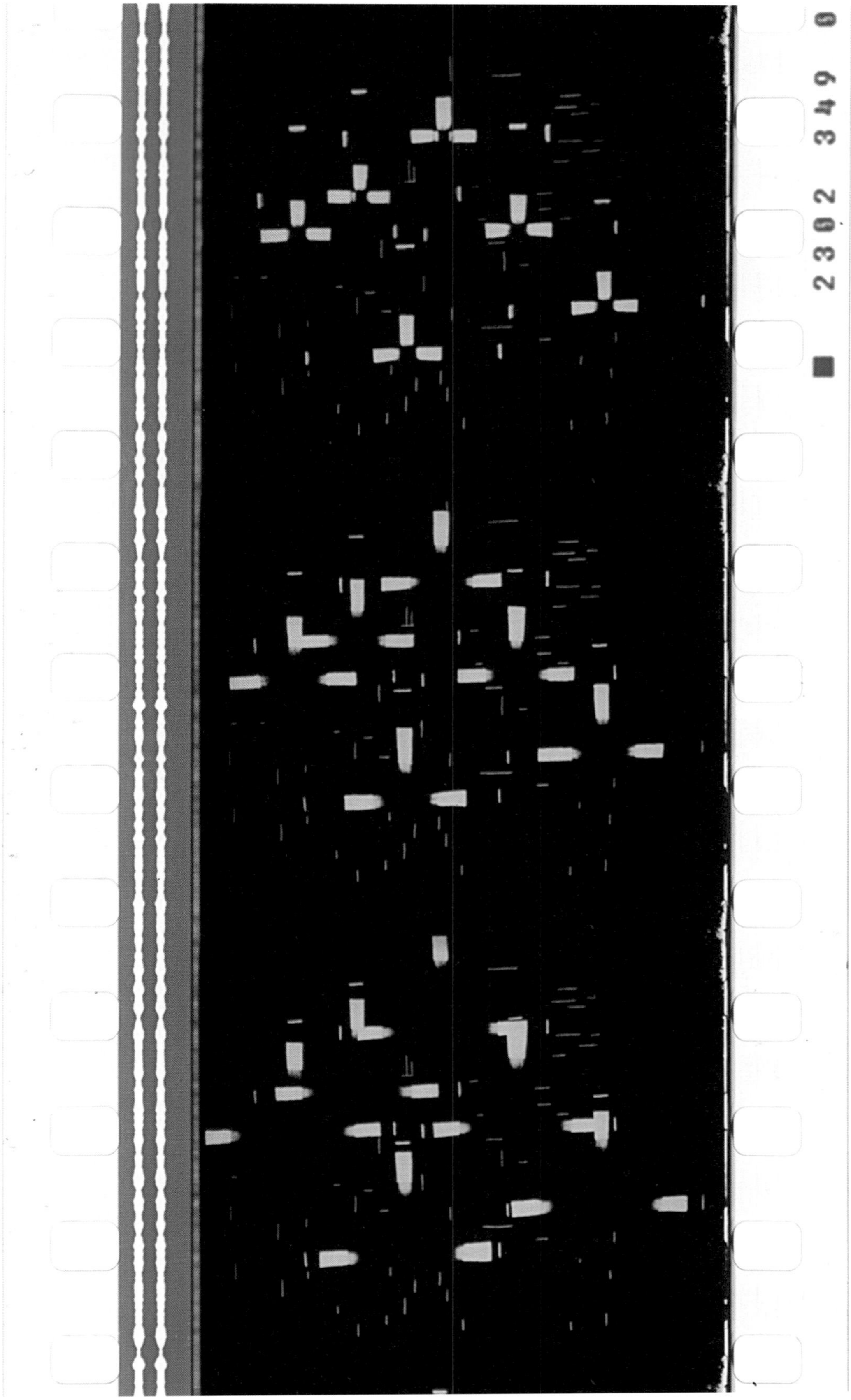

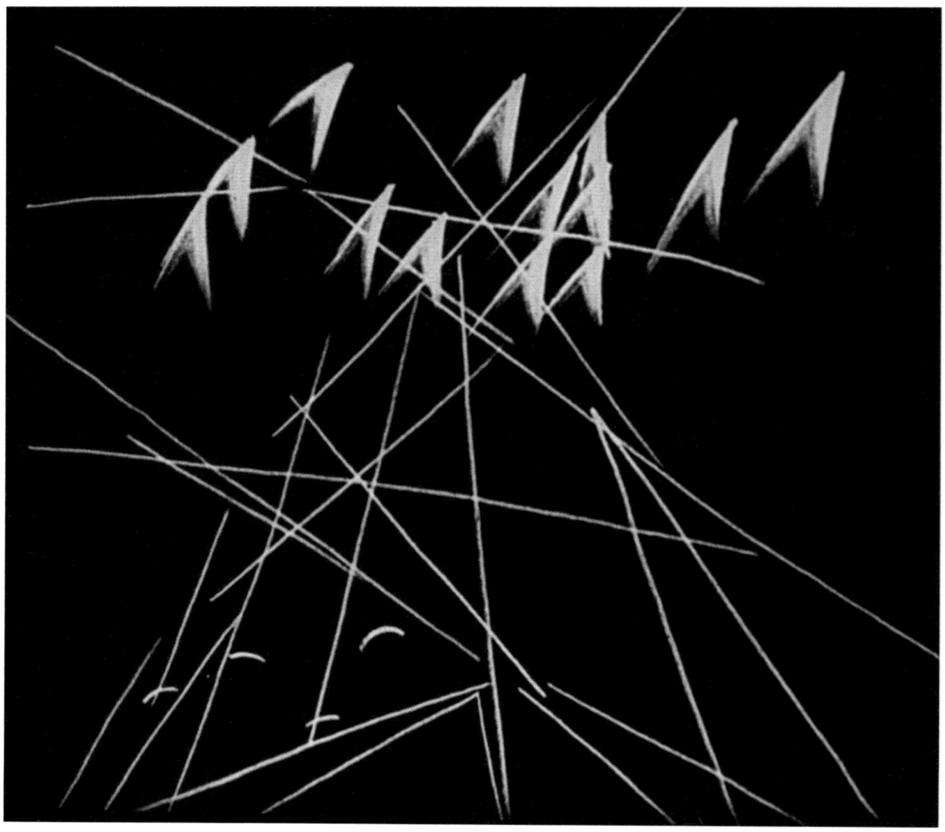

↑
Still from *Koloraturen* (*Coloratura*), 1932
35mm, b/w, sound
←
Stills from *Studie Nr. 8* (*Study No. 8*), 1931
35mm, b/w, sound

Still from *Swiss Trip (Rivers and Landscapes)*, 1934
35mm, b/w, sound

Oskar Fischinger and Hollywood

Oskar Fischinger / Wassily Kandinsky

Where Abstraction and Comics Collide

Esther Leslie

Imagine a series of white and pale green lozenges, irregularly distributed across a larger rhomboid shape composed of rectangles divided into red and deep green, at each of whose tip hovers a scattering of white diamonds. All this sits atop a purple square placed askew on a black rectangle. Blue circles emanate from the center of the image. Imagine, then, how a fraction of a second later these lozenges, rectangles and circles spin away, shape-shifting into triangles and spirals, curves and lines, mutating their colors and forming new combinations. This geometrical drama happens again and again, lyrically pegged to the booms and trills of music. This is animated Kandinsky, or rather a scene from Oskar Fischinger's animated film *Allegretto* (1936–43).

The comparison is not flippant, and Kandinsky had the opportunity to make it himself, for it is reported that he enjoyed a screening in Paris of Fischinger's *Komposition In Blau* (*Composition in Blue*). Fischinger was known to the Bauhaus milieu: his acquaintance László Moholy-Nagy screened his abstract animations and synesthetic optoacoustic experiments at the institute. In turn, Fischinger, who began his career as an animator in the Weimar Germany of the early 1920s, was, according to the film scholar William Moritz, influenced by Kandinsky's theories of the spiritual nature of art, whereby it is a means to a higher truth created by the mystical figure of the artist. At various times in his 40 years of film-making Fischinger found himself confronted with Kandinsky. He may well have spent some time studying Kandinsky's theoretical writings. Certainly he had seen the artworks at close range. He visited, for example, Rudolf Bauer's private gallery-villa. Here in this salon for abstract art, supported by the Solomon R. Guggenheim Foundation, were several Kandinsky canvases alongside other non-objective paintings. Fischinger could refer to the artist's work at will, for he kept in his possession a Bauhaus catalogue with color lithographs by Kandinsky, Hirschfeld-Mack, Albers and others, given to him in 1936 by the gallerist Karl Nierendorf. A later encounter with Kandinsky is revealing. In 1948 Fischinger made seven collages. He clipped reproductions of paintings by Kandinsky and Bauer from old Guggenheim catalogues and stuck on to them cut-outs of Mickey Mouse and Minnie Mouse snipped from Walt Disney comics.
In one collage Mickey stares in horror at the black scribbles at the center of Kandinsky's *Black Lines* (1913), while Minnie points disapprovingly at the knotty mess behind her (fig. 1, p. 90). The worlds of abstraction and comics collide.

This collision between high art abstraction and mass commercial culture is emblematic of Fischinger's career.

Parallel to his experiments in abstract animation (or what he called "absolute creation"), he contributed to commercial culture in the 1930s. In 1933 and 1934 he made a film called *Kreise* (*Circles*). Pulsing rings alter their color and texture as they spin through vortices and are affected by the shapes that bombard them. Only at the close was it apparent that this play of form and color was hitched to commerce. The line "Tolirag reaches all circles of society" turned the film into an advertisement for an advertising agency. This was expedient. As an advertisement, the film evaded the usual censorship restrictions against "degenerate" art, promulgated by the new Nazi government. Fischinger continued to place his animating skills and geometric fascination in the service of commerce in further innovative advertisements in the mid-1930s. *Pink Guards on Parade*, for example, converted the delirious play of spirals into twirls of pink toothpaste squeezed from tubes. Geometrical abstraction found real-world analogues. Sympathetic critics tried to shield Fischinger from the ban on abstraction imposed by Goebbels in 1935 by labeling his films "ornamental" or "decorative." When he was under pressure from the Nazi regime, one critic interceded on his behalf, arguing that the Nazis should rethink their edicts since ornament art was part of an old German tradition that included decorative motives on clothes, books, architecture and landscape. It was to no avail. And anyway an animated advertisement for Muratti with waltzing and parading cigarettes had made Fischinger a name in Hollywood (fig. 2). Paramount organized for him and his films to emigrate, along with a pile of Karl Nierendorf's non-objective canvases, a year before the exhibition *Entartete Kunst* (*Degenerate Art*) opened in Munich in 1937. This "chamber of horrors" represented the demise of Modernism in Germany. The final assault, which

Figure 1 / *Kandinsky/Mickey Mouse Collage*, c. 1940
Collage on paper, 8.5 x 11 in. / 22.5 x 28 cm
Collection The Fischinger Trust, Long Beach, CA

began with the closure of the Bauhaus in 1933, ended with the vilifying parade of 650 artifacts by 112 artists. Works were condemned for their "barbarous methods of representation" as much as their immoral sullying of religion and preaching of political anarchy. With their references to "Negro" and Pacific art, Expressionist works "eradicated every trace of racial consciousness." Reviled too was "art in which the human figure is deformed or idiotic." Worst of all, though, was "the art of total madness." (abstraction and constructivism). Fourteen Kandinsky canvases, deemed "crazy at any price," provided proof of this, even if two were hung sideways.

Kandinsky escaped to France. Fischinger found work in the USA, where commercial film production thrust itself on him in its most unadulterated form. Walt Disney was planning an animated feature illustrating several pieces of classical music and engaged the conductor Leopold Stokowski, who knew that Fischinger had been making animations pegged to music for some time. *Studie Nr. 8* (*Study No. 8*), for example, devised images for Paul Dukas's *The Sorcerer's Apprentice*, a scherzo Disney would later use in *Fantasia*. Unlike Disney, Fischinger did not illustrate Goethe's story, but rather translated the textures and movements of the sounds into spurting and tumbling black and white shapes. In 1938 and1939 Fischinger was hired by the Disney studio as a "motion picture cartoon effects animator" earning $60 a week (fig. 3). Having animated the sparkle of the blue fairy's wand in *Pinocchio*, and thereby converted his abstract powers directly into Disney magic, he produced sketches and try-outs for Bach's "Toccata and Fugue" section in *Fantasia*. In one major sequence, turquoise and green-grey waves were superimposed by a flow of geometric figures in browns, orangey-red and yellow oranges. His twenty seconds' worth of film was worked over by Disney staff and the shapes made simpler, for the assumption was that only then would audiences accept them. Just one figure moved at any one time, and in the background floated clouds in a sky. The non-figurative forms were concretized, conjuring up real-world objects. While Fischinger thought he was utilizing the insights of the color theory he had studied, Disney objected to too extreme a palate and altered the colors. Fischinger's deformed contribution was set among kitschy images derived from jabbing violin bows, ethereal cathedrals and doomy shafts, with the anchoring spectacle of the black-suited conductor who marshals all this energy. Fischinger quit the film in disgust. Clearly still smarting from his experience a decade later, he reflected on the state of cinema, attacking the usual "photographed surface realism-in-motion" that destroys "the deep and absolute creative force":

> Even the cartoon film today is on a very low artistic level. It is a mass product of factory proportions, and this, of course, cuts down the creative purity of the work of art. No sensible creative artist could create a sensible work of art if a staff of co-workers of all kinds each had his or her say in the final creation – producer, story director, story writer, music director, conductor, composer, sound men, gag men, effect men, layout men, background directors, animators, inbetweeners, inkers, cameramen, technicians, publicity directors, managers, box office managers and many others. They change the ideas, kill the ideas before they are born… and substitute for the absolute creative motives only cheap ideas to fit the lowest common denominator.[1]

Fischinger's remarks signaled the end of an era of exchange between avant-garde art and mass culture. In 1932 the situation had been more hopeful. At a premiere of Fischinger's *Studie Nr. 12* (*Study No. 12*) in Berlin, the critic Bernhard Diebold gave a speech entitled "The Future of Mickey Mouse." If cinema was to be an art form, he argued, it needed animation, because that made possible a cinema that had broken free of a naturalistic template and conventional storylines. Animated film defied the inherited artistic genres, forging something new: "living paintings," "musography," "eyemusic," "optical poetry," and "the dance of ornaments." For Diebold, Disney figures, with their elastic and rhythmic universe, had just as much pointed the way as had the "absolute films" of Fischinger, Hans Richter, Walter Ruttmann, Viking Eggeling, and others. Animation provided the exemplar of anti-naturalism in film. All sorts of experimenting artists found that cartoons touched on many things that they too wished to explore: abstraction; forceful outlines; geometric forms and flatness; and the questioning of space, time and logic, that is to say, a consciousness of space that is not geographical but graphic and time as non-linear and convoluted. Animation was proposed as the medium to translate into movement Kandinsky's restful points and dynamic lines in tension. When Rodchenko wrote in 1919 of the line that stands firm against pictorial expressivity, lines that reveal a new conception of the world in construction and not representation, he could have been describing cartoons' flexible and cavalier attitude to representation. This inaugurated an extraordinary episode when Eisenstein could speak of his indebtedness to Disney, Adorno raved about Betty Boop, Vertov and Shklovsky imagined the future of film in cartoons, Oskar Fischinger could go to Hollywood, and

1
From Oskar Fischinger, "My Statements are in My Work," in *Art in Cinema*, ed. Frank Stauffacher (San Francisco: Art in Cinema Society, San Francisco Museum of Art, 1947), 38–40. Reprinted in this volume, pp. 112–13.

Siegfried Kracauer could be disappointed enough in 1941 to condemn *Dumbo* as a setback for the revolutionary movement. And Walter Benjamin could enthuse about Mickey Mouse, writing a defense of Disney's utopian unmasking of social negativity and the rejection of the civilized bourgeois subject by this mouse-shaped figure of the collective dream.

In the 1920s Ruttmann, Richter, and others threw away their canvases in favor of pictures that moved: multiple Mondrians a second. Once on this path they were drawn away from the art world and pulled further into the film world, away from abstraction into montage and staged actuality. Fischinger, despite or because of his encounter with the culture industry at its most intense, was perhaps more than the others committed to preserving film as art, that is to say, in Kandinskyesque terms, as pure form and color, as a spiritual and emotional experience with the artist as prophet. In any case, he did not abandon painting and, in 1947, his animation *Motion Painting No. 1* provided a document of the painting process. He laid Plexiglas sheets on top of each other to enable the generation of mutating shapes and styles. It is a seamless flow of action over eleven minutes, filmed by stop-motion. The artist is absent. The painting seems to paint itself. It echoed Fischinger's first experiments in animation in the 1920s, when he built a device that cut slivers from swirled colored waxes while a camera shutter, synchronized with the movement of the blade, recorded the patterns formed of the whorls and striations of wax. In projection the wax came to life in extraordinary ways, its frame-by-frame record flowing into continuous animation.

Motion Painting No. 1 had been commissioned by Baroness Hilla Rebay, who wanted a film synchronized to Bach's "Brandenburg Concerto No. 3." She hated the result and Fischinger's Guggenheim connections were severed. Not long before, another of his supporters, the art dealer Galka Scheyer, had died. A specialist in what she called "The Blue Four" (Kandinsky, Klee, Jawlensky and Feininger) she had helped him since his first months in the USA. Fischinger never made another major film before his death in 1967. Perhaps the Kandinsky images mutilated by Mickey and Minnie Mouse were a symbol of his final stranding between two worlds.

Originally published in *Tate Etc.*, 7, Summer 2006

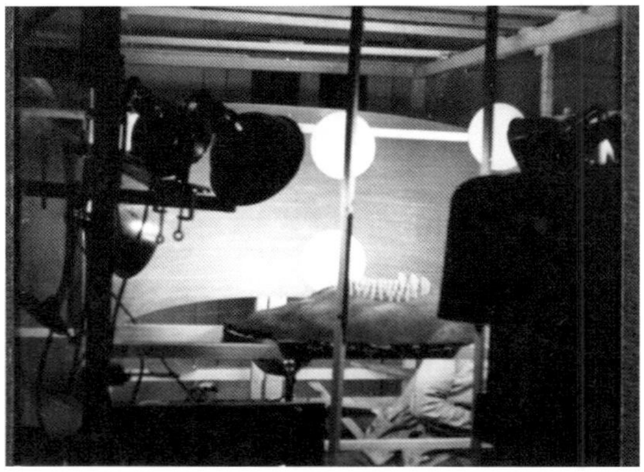

Figure 2 / Animation setup for Muratti cigarette commercial, in Fischinger's Berlin studio, 1934
Collection Center for Visual Music

Figure 3 / Oskar Fischinger working at Disney Studio on *Fantasia*, 1939
Collection Center for Visual Music

Texts, Letters and Documents by Oskar Fischinger

Elfriede and Oskar Fischinger, stills from *Berlin Home Movies* footage, shot in studio of Oskar Fischinger, early 1930s
35mm, b/w, silent

The Composer of the Future and the Absolute Sound Film

Oskar Fischinger

Eye and ear supplement each other in orthogonal function. The eye seizes the exterior, surface, form, and color. The ear seizes through sound, which is particular to each body, the internal structure which the eye spies outwardly. This mutual and supplementary orthogonal composite function [*Gesamtfunktion*] of eye and ear is comparable to the front view of a house (the picture for the eye) and a technical cross-section through the house, (which reveals the internal structure, and which the key of the sound determines for physical bodies).

Soundtrack drawings (ornaments) are at the same time sound images, cross sections of picture-bodies. I have been able to determine, through repeated experiments, the ways in which ornaments produce complex tones as soon as they are scanned with the light aperture of a photoelectric cell. Today in film, sound will be recorded onto the margin of the filmstrip through a transformation of sound waves into light fluctuations. These curves, thus recorded, resemble complex ornamental images. They consist of a constant fluctuation between variously high and variously long impressions [*Zacken*] or fine lines which correspond to those fine fluctuations, just like the grooves of a gramophone record.

This soundtrack drawing on the filmstrip contains the music belonging to the picture. Today both are taken either at the same time or separately such that the film apparatus photographs the exterior image, [for example] the actor, in a word, the visible, while the soundtrack, with its photography of that inner image that is resonant sound—photographs music, language, noise.

For a non-photographic creative process—which is for the independent artist (in creative command) the most necessary presupposition—a vast sphere of activity opens up that seems to have temporarily been buried by the successive development of the sound film, because with the later film only the collective process and the photographing of picture and sound actually mattered. The filmmaker today is a many-headed collective creature [*Kollektivwesen*], consisting of producer, production manager, director, assistant director, architect, cameramen, grips, as well as countless specialized technicians along with actors, authors, manuscript editors, and screenwriters. Each one of these collaborators has an influence on the final result, the finished film. A so-called "collective product" is developed. The director, however talented he may be, is not a sovereign artist in this work process but rather an arranger, and the film itself, even in the most favorable conditions and with great luck, is but the planning and producing of a trashy photo-novel [*Fotokolportage*] devouring approx. 20000 RM per studio day—the author plays an unimportant role.

But there is another, higher-level kind of creative work that is much too sensitive for such an apparatus, and this style of creative work forecloses automatically on any collaboration by additional auxiliary workers in the work process. This truly purest and highest form of creating art proceeds exclusively and directly from a single personality, and art production undertaken in this way, as in works of Rembrandt, Bach, or Michelangelo, are unmediated creations of the highest power which gain immediately [*Gewinnen gerade*] by virtue of the hand-drawn, irrational, and individual. No photo lens could succeed in photographing a landscape as a painter like van Gogh has rendered it, and the function of each photo lens is indifferently mechanical in the end. The most prized photography [is] in the best case a fixed, arranged setting of yet more naturalistically arranged coincidences. And for all the exaggerated claims of feature film production to be the peak of that great development, the handmade film offers the possibility for a pure artistic process. The handmade film consists of many thousands of successive drawings. The drawn, still extremely representational animated films of the "Mickey-Mouse-film" type are undoubtedly the forerunners in this area of the handmade film. Here lie great possibilities for the independently creating artist, for he creates only with what he draws, what he creates himself. The contemporary Mickey Mouse film, which is already reaching the end of its development, brought representational drawing into motion. Until now it has worked primarily in the service of caricature. Figure and plot were still the main point in these films. Movement [was] only a coincidental, inevitable side effect. The absolute film, by contrast, and which is also handcrafted, has already wholly renounced such representational, expressive bridges and for it, light and movement become the main interest.

In dark space are lines of light, figures of light, and movement formed. Figures of light cut through the dark space.

Fantasy will open the last, unlimited spaces of all artistic development. The emerging, abstract film creator—working only from himself, is assured of his technique and handcraft.

He forms image after image in a sovereign manner, his figures of light in space and their movement. Falls of flooding light in movement as he sees it himself bind the eye. He depends only on his signature powers and needs no production manager, cameramen, grips or architect, nor does he need any actors and above all needs nothing but his drawing pencil and his talent. He will also necessarily compose the music for his optical light concert himself, and thus will be able to compose the acoustic stream together with the optical image and in so doing will be able to work in a new and uniform artistic medium.

Innumerable visual artists are today ineffective. The art dealers sit on mountains of images, squandered against the value of the frames. Now a new canvas is offered to these countless artists. Lightplay theatres with their projections and speaker systems await them, and image-and-sound radio will provide them with the highest validation.

Translated by James Tobias

This essay is a new translation of a type-written manuscript similar to a text published by the *Dortmunder Zeitung* on January 1, 1933, under the title and attribution, "'Der Absolute Tonfilm' von Ingenieur Oskar Fischinger" ("The Absolute Sound Film" by Engineer Oskar Fischinger). Though the typescript is undated, it was likely prepared in 1932; Fischinger prepared numerous typescript versions of this essay. The translator would like to thank Sabine Doran for several suggestions that improved the clarity of this translation.

Images from Ornament Sound Experiments

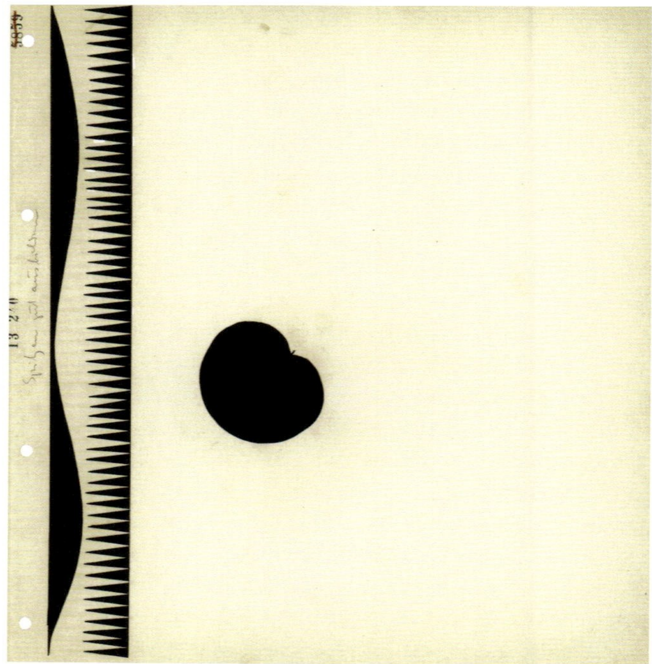

Unshot animation related to the ornament sound experiments, c. 1932–33. If Fischinger had filmed these, the strip on the left side would have been used as the soundtrack.
Paint on paper, 11.6 x 12 in. / 28 x 30.5 cm
Collection Center for Visual Music, gift of The Fischinger Trust

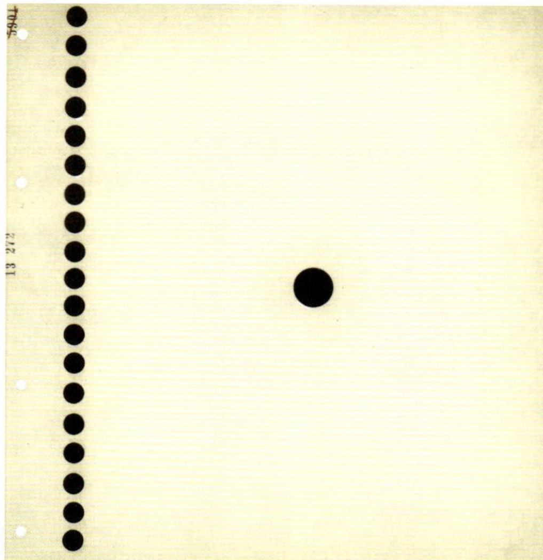

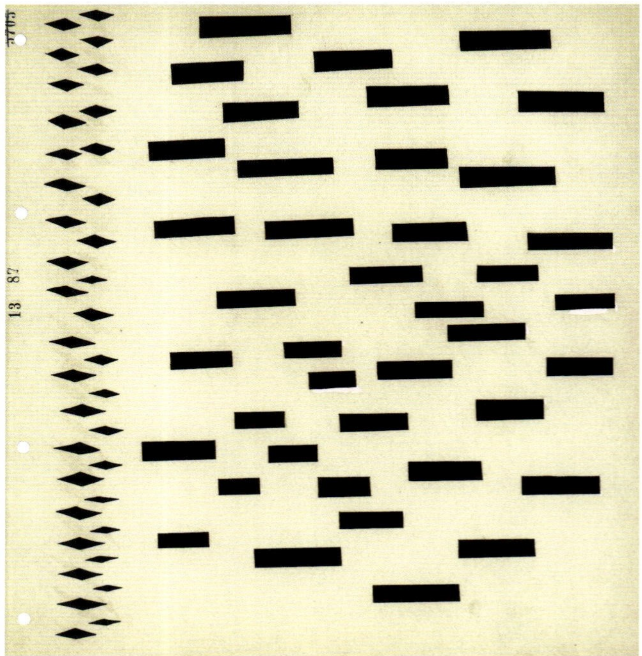

Unshot animation related to the ornament sound experiments, c. 1932–33
Paint on paper, 11.6 x 12 in. / 28 x 30.5 cm
Collection Center for Visual Music, gift of The Fischinger Trust

↑
Display card with examples of Fischinger's ornament sound, no date
Collection Center for Visual Music, gift of The Fischinger Trust
→
Stills from *Ornament Sound*, 1932
b/w, sound (re-creation by William Moritz)

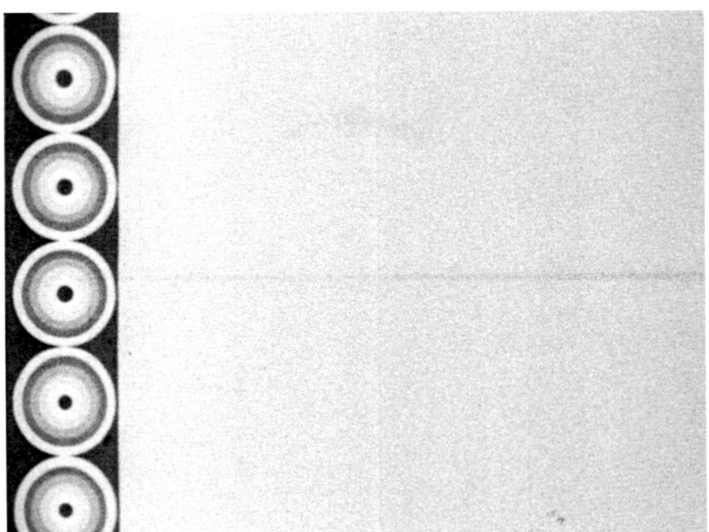

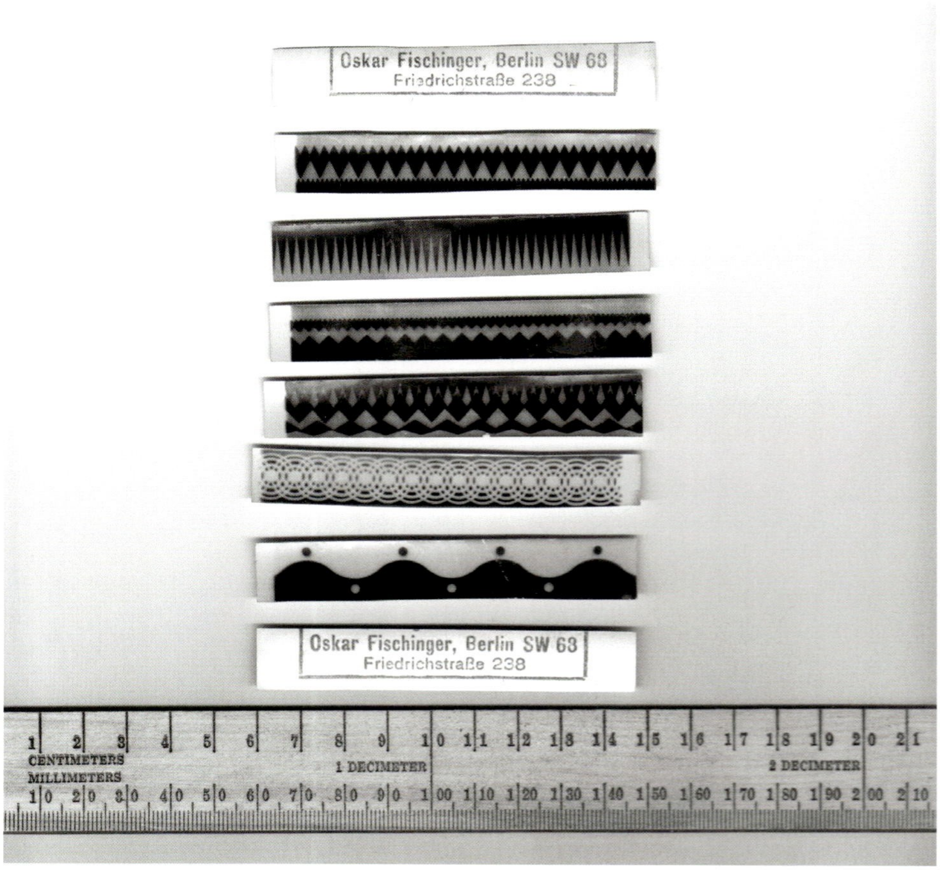

Examples of strips of ornaments used in Oskar Fischinger's c. 1932 experiments. These ornaments were photographed onto the optical track to create sound
Collection Center for Visual Music

Oskar Fischinger with fake rolls of *Ornament Sound* experiments, in his Berlin studio, c. 1932
Staged for publicity, so that his competitors couldn't determine his techniques
Collection Center for Visual Music

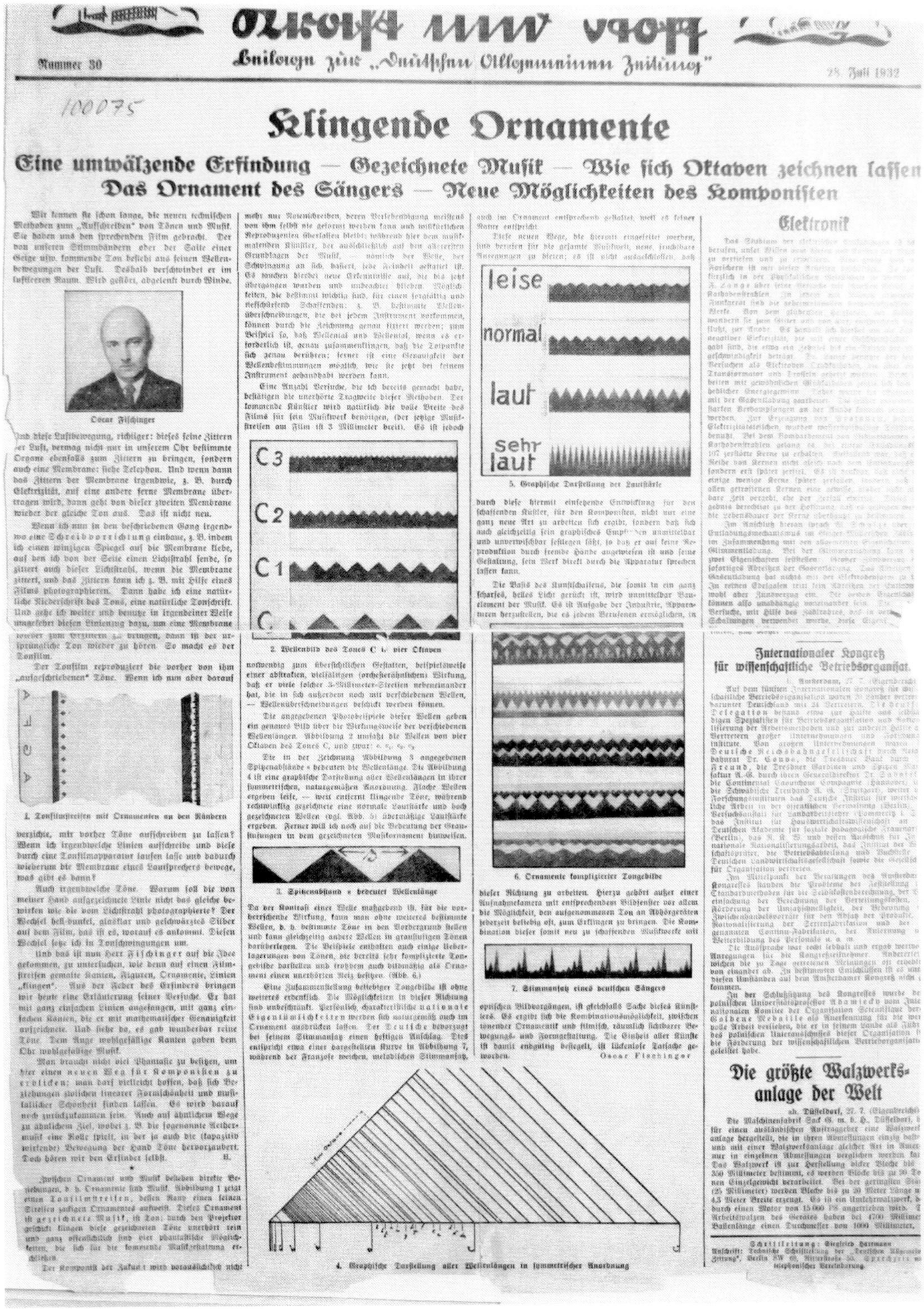

Kraft und Stoff

Beilage zur „Deutschen Allgemeinen Zeitung"

Nummer 30 — 28. Juli 1932

100075

Klingende Ornamente

Eine umwälzende Erfindung — Gezeichnete Musik — Wie sich Oktaven zeichnen lassen
Das Ornament des Sängers — Neue Möglichkeiten des Komponisten

Oscar Fischinger

1. Tonfilmstreifen mit Ornamenten an den Rändern

2. Wellenbild des Tones C in vier Oktaven

3. Spitzenabstand s bedeutet Wellenlänge

4. Graphische Darstellung aller Wellenlängen in symmetrischer Anordnung

5. Graphische Darstellung der Lautstärke

6. Ornamente komplizierter Tongebilde

7. Stimmansatz eines deutschen Sängers

Oscar Fischinger

Elektronik

Internationaler Kongreß für wissenschaftliche Betriebsorganisation

Die größte Walzwerksanlage der Welt

"Klingende Ornamente," *Deutsche Allgemeine Zeitung, Kraft Und Stoff* no. 30, 28 July 1932
Syndicated worldwide. Original newspaper
Collection Center for Visual Music

A Timetable and Music: A Visit to Oskar Fischinger's Color-Sound Animated Film Studio

Date believed to be c. 1934.
Interviewer/author unknown
Collection Center for Visual Music

It's all happening here ...

Oskar Fischinger's studio is right in the middle of Berlin's film district, in southern Friedrichstadt. A man opens the door and greets me with the words, "For heaven's sake, be careful, everything's covered in black here—lamp black." And then I'm standing facing Oskar Fischinger, the man whose uniquely artistic animated films have long been of such interest to me. "Yes, you'll have to forgive us the thick black dust; but we needed it for a black and white animation. We needed rather a lot of lamp black for the black; the usual carbon black wasn't black enough, but we've finished that stage now and the studio is being thoroughly cleaned. Now we're starting on our first big color-film series, colored short films—pure color plays."

Fischinger shows me one of his color-sound films. The narrow, color film strip passes across white paper that is lit from behind by an electric bulb and we soon see those strange, intertwining forms—emerging of their own accord and disappearing again—that we know from Fischinger's black-and-white films, only now they are glowing and flashing in bright colors.

"Color is a wonderful thing," says Oskar Fischinger, "it's much more exciting than black and white, and everyone working here is thrilled that now we're working with hundreds of different colors."

Six to seven thousand different colors

"Presumably you shoot these animations in the same way as usual?" "Yes, each phase is designed and executed sheet by sheet, and then the drawings are shot one after the other—that's how the film is made. For the color shots I use the Gasparcolor system, which easily meets all the demands you could make of a good color film process, and which has more than proved itself in practice. The Gasparcolor system can generate between six and seven thousand different hues and in its own way it's perfect. The shots are taken using three precisely coordinated color filters, which create three separate color exposures; these are then later copied [together] again to create a colored image that exactly replicates the original."

A new world

"And how do you develop the ideas for your films? Do you have screenplays?" "No, you see, this is a completely different kind of film work. Feature films or art films are more or less important, depending on their meaning; but my film work operates on a completely different level. It's all about the purely optical manipulation of light, color, shapes, and movement, which derives not from the subject matter, but from the thing itself wwand the materials. A new, not-real world of color and movement first has to be discovered through an intense, creative effort. In today's feature films and art films, time and again there are shots of real things in the surroundings; in good films, elements in-between and within things also come into play, but always involving real things that exist around us that are filmed for this purpose.

"However, there is another way of making films and filmic works of art, and it takes us in the same direction as music. Music is something that resides and resonates within things. Musical creativity relies on this resonation and creates its forms from within it. Whole universes of connections arise that are not tangible in real terms, but that nevertheless have a legitimate development. Something similar happens with pure black and white or color sequences that arise from lines, light spots, and colors, that describe movements and contain within them a unique potential for development, that are justified in the same way as developments in music. So, since we are talking here of the development of a new optical art, the idea of a "screenplay" no longer applies. The work itself constitutes its own development. It grows and forms during the work process and spectators will subconsciously register and respond to this development—as long as they have eyes to see with and ears to hear with—as long as their souls are open."

Color-music film in 1923

"We know that what you have discovered is a completely new way of filming. How did come up with it?" "Very early on I was already interested in creating a graphic visualization of the main elements that would unfold during the course of a poem. At the age of nineteen I attended a reading one day and suddenly started to draw the emotions that the subject matter unleashed within me. It was as though I was drawing emotional force diagrams: lines that replicated all the main points of the poem—for anyone with the right imagination. But in order to make these linear, drawn representations more widely comprehensible, the lines had to be made to move—and film was the perfect medium for this. Various devices that I had to invent in order to solve the existing technical difficulty of creating a moving representation of this drawn poem ultimately led me to the work I am doing now. It was at the Stadttheater in Munich, in 1923,[1] that Alexander László presented my first films, from years before, in conjunction with his own color-light piano; they met with a very warm reception. These were black and white films with just a few colored effects projected into them. Even the stagehands behind the twelve meter screen (the projection was done from behind) were overwhelmed by the effect. From that point, things moved slowly but steadily forward, until sound came to the movies in 1930, which allowed me to make my first black and white sound-film studies.

"And now these black and white film studies have proved their worth, because they laid the absolutely essential groundwork for the color films that are now on the horizon, and the short color films that are already being made are paving the way for the big, feature-length color films that will soon be here."

Behind the scenes in an animated film studio

We enter a studio where a black-and-white camera is still set up in front of a fantastic scene. The animation has already been shot. Taut black velvet criss-crosses the room. A large silver cross, with some letters below it, can be seen against the

1
This was probably in 1926, according to extant documents; however Fischinger has also variously dated these activities to 1924 or 1925 in other notes. No documentation has been found to support his earlier dates.

invisible black background. The animation was shot upside down; it was the only way to do it, because the letters had to appear to be floating in space.

"Here, at the left, you can see the exact timetable for this animation. On the timetable all the acoustic events are marked, one by one, exactly matching the visual moments." The camera is prepared for a new shot. But while Fischinger explains the strange set-up, the muddle of forms and planes slowly starts to take on a filmic form and coalesces into a film image. One has a sense of the will that has devised this artistic set up. And, on leaving, one is only too well aware that here, little by little, a completely new art form, a very different kind of film, is being fashioned.

Fischinger's Early Color Experimentation

By Cindy Keefer

Fischinger was instrumental in the development of Gasparcolor, a single-strip, three-color film process developed by the Hungarian chemist Dr. Bela Gaspar. Fischinger created many tests in 1933 of this successive exposure color process, and these three stills are from those early tests, scanned directly from the nitrate. He used some of his tinted *Staffs* footage for these tests. Fischinger screened Gasparcolor publicly at the Hamburg Kongress für Farbe-Ton-Forschung (Congress for Color-Sound Research) in late 1933, probably using these tests. He continued to work with the process, making *Kreise* (*Circles*), one of the very first films to use Gasparcolor. Dr. Gaspar was forced to flee Nazi Germany. After a brief time in London (the head credits of Fischinger's *Euthymol Commercial* are "Gasparcolor London") he settled in Hollywood, where he eventually sold his Gasparcolor patents to Technicolor. These early nitrate Gasparcolor tests are currently being restored by Center for Visual Music.

Example of Gasparcolor tests, c. 1933
35mm, color, silent
Collection of Center for Visual Music

Two examples of Fischinger's tinting tests, using some of his black and white Studies footage, on Agfa nitrate stock, early 1930s. He also tested pink, blue, and amber tints in this reel. Collection Center for Visual Music

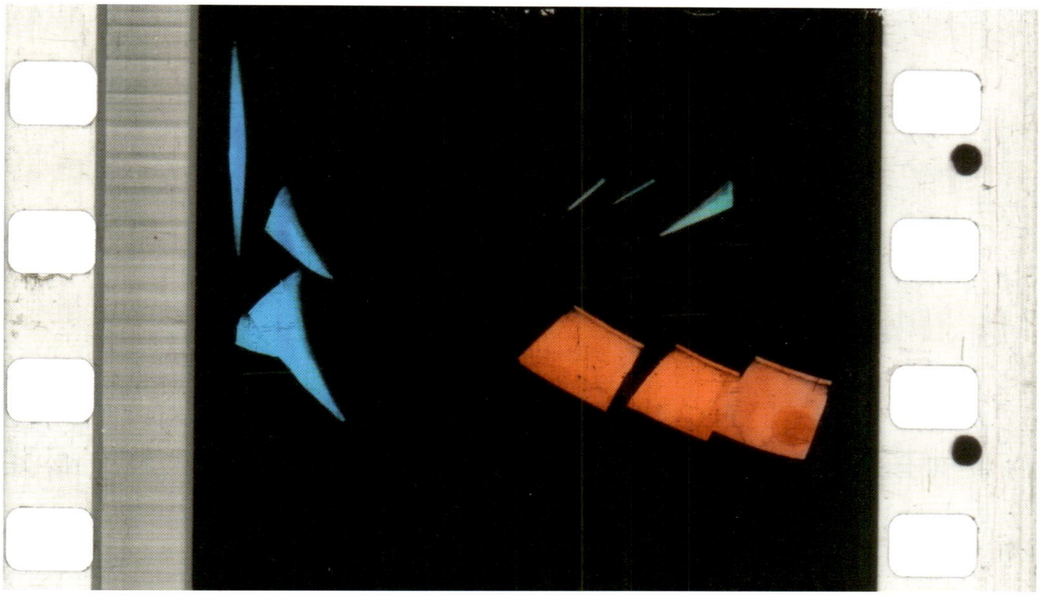

Two examples of Fischinger's hand-painted tests using some of his black and white Studies footage, early 1930s. Collection Center for Visual Music

My Statements are in My Work

Oskar Fischinger

To write about my work in absolute film is rather difficult. The only thing to do is to write why I made these films.

When I was 19 years old I had to talk about a certain work by William Shakespeare at our literary club. In preparing for this speech I began to analyze the work in a graphic way. On large sheets of drawing paper, along a horizontal line, I put down all the feelings and happenings, scene after scene, in graphic lines and curves. The lines and curves showed the dramatic development of the whole work and the emotional moods very clearly.

It was quite an interesting beginning, but not many people could understand this graphic, absolute expression.

To make it more convincing, more easily understood, the drawings needed movement, the same speed and tempo as the feeling originally possessed. The *cinematic* element had to be added.

To do this, the motion picture film was a welcome medium. And so it happened that I made my first absolute film.

Then sound was added to the film. On the wings of music faster progress was possible.

The *flood of feeling* created through music intensified the feeling and effectiveness of this graphic cinematic expression, and helped to make understandable the absolute film. Under the guidance of music, which was already highly developed there came the speedy discovery of new laws–the application of acoustical laws to optical expression was possible. As in the dance, new motions and rhythms sprang out of the music–and the rhythms became more and more important.

I named these absolute films *Studies*; and I numbered them *Study No. 1*, *Study No. 2*, and so forth. These early black and white studies drew enthusiastic response at the time from the most famous art critics of England and Europe.

Then came the color film. Of course, the temptation was great to work in color, and I made thereafter a number of absolute color films. But I soon found out that the simplicity of my own black and white films could never be surpassed.

The color film proved itself to be an entirely new art form with its own artistic problems as far removed from black and white film as music itself—as an art medium—is removed from painting.

Searching, for the last thirteen years, to find the ideal solution to this problem, I truly believe I have found it now, and my new, forthcoming work will show it.

Now a few words about the usual motion picture film which is shown to the masses everywhere in countless moving picture theatres all over the world. It is photographed realism—photographed surface realism-in-motion. ... There is nothing of an absolute artistic creative sense in it. It copies only nature with realistic conceptions, destroying the deep and absolute creative force with substitutes and surface realisms. Even the cartoon film is today on a very low artistic level. It is a mass product of factory proportions, and this, of course, cuts down the creative purity of a work of art. No sensible creative artist could create a sensible work of art if a staff of co-workers of all kinds had his or her say in the final creation—producer, story director, story writer, music director, conductor, composers, sound men, gag men, effect men, layout men, background directors, animators, inbetweeners, inkers, cameramen, technicians, publicity directors, managers, box office managers, and many others. They change the ideas, kill the ideas, before they are born, prevent the ideas from being born, and substitute for the absolute creative motives only the cheap ideas to fit the lowest among them.

The creative artist of the highest level always works at his best *alone*, moving far ahead of his time. And this shall be our basis: That the Creative Spirit shall be unobstructed through realities or anything that spoils his absolute *pure* creation.

And so we cut out the tremendous mountains of valueless motion picture productions of the past and the future—the mountain ranges of soap bubbles—and we must concentrate on the tiny golden thread underneath which is hardly visible beneath the glamorous, sensational excitement, securely buried for a long time, especially in our own time when the big producing and distributing monopolies control every motion picture screen in an airtight grip.

Consequently, there is only one way for the creative artist: To produce only for the *highest* ideals—not thinking in terms of money or sensations or to please the masses.

The real artist should *not care* if he is understood, or misunderstood by the masses. He should listen only to his Creative Spirit and satisfy his highest ideals, and trust that this will be the best service that he can render humanity.

It is the only hope for the creative artist that the art lovers, the art collectors, the art institutes, and the art museums develop increasingly greater interest in this direction, and make it possible for the artist to produce works of art through the medium of the film.

In this connection I wish to express my deep gratitude to one great American institution which has in the past helped so many artists in an idealistic, unselfish way, and which has made it possible for me to do a great amount of research work in the direction of the absolute, non-objective film. I am speaking of the Solomon R. Guggenheim Foundation in New York under the direction of Curator Hilla Rebay.

Originally published in *Art in Cinema*, edited by Frank Stauffacher (San Francisco: Art in Cinema Society-San Francisco Museum of Art, 1947).

300293

About "Motion Painting Nr.1."

A ll my earlier Experimental Films made between 1919 til 1927 and my Film-Studies produced between 1928 till 1933 and all the Color-films which I made from 1933 on till 1946,-consequently lead up to the technique developed in "Motion Painting Nr.1, - the Film which was awarded the Grand Prix at the Belgien Film Festival Brussels 1949. In this Film all my previous works found their conclusion,and "Motion Painting Nr.1..presents in itself a new Art-form of great significants, and enters the Realm Of true creativeness in motion in the field of visual expression, changeing transmuteing Paintings from a static unmoveable almost frozen formation into painted-created-moving-unfolding developing-music like visual presentation in time-step after step, in such a way, that the time element adds a most important Quality or Dimension to it. And this is a entirely new kind of music.Music not created by sounds which follow each other in time unfolding the creative Idea feeling or production of a composer,but a music of a essential visual Motion-Painting natur,- x resulting from a true creative unfoldment development step by step of a painted visual production of a motion-Painter..

The Motion Picture Camera as a Ideal/visual/recording instrument made it possible in oure time, to discover the hidden element of the music-like quality which goes with or is produced by paintings in motion - if they are of a creative nature. The factor of unfoldment of logical growth seems to cary -to produce this music/like/sensation /almost pleasurable/ in the observers.

It may be the result of the extreme clarity and easiness to follow and observe the unfoldment and growth of this creations which results and produces a deeper better grasping understanding in the observer first subconsciously later consciously - of the processes of visual creations through the Painter of the Motion Paintings,who himself is Observer too. The clarity -logical growth -truthfull unfoldment resulting in easier understanding of factors of sincerity and deeper necessities in creations in rhytm time and motion,- release it seems that wonderful feeling of oneness-of harmony with the creative spirit which works and expresses himself/in and/through the works of oure good Artists.-Musicans, Composers,Painters and Motion Painters.

All the hidden factors which make a static unmovable finished painting often only understandable to the trained observer,become clear to the layman to any observer by observing a motion Painting. Every phase of development,every creative thought,every new idea is shown clearly and reveals itself truthfully. Motion Painting Nr.1 is one continuous development. The film has no cut and is fascinating for everyone who can see,since it brings out things,which he himself, has never seen nor dreamed of and which he could never discover otherwise. Itx fulfills and satisfies his deepest desire to be in complete harmony and understanding with the force which creates ,and the ways and means of the creator becomes plainly revealed.
Like good works of Art,such films as Motion Paintingsx Nr.1, have no limitations on when they can be shown and are not fictim of boundaries of time or fashion. In fact the interest in this films grows and multiplys and will be of even greater interest for future generations..

Oskar Fischinger
1010 Hammond Str.
West Hollywood 46 Cal.U.S.A.

III

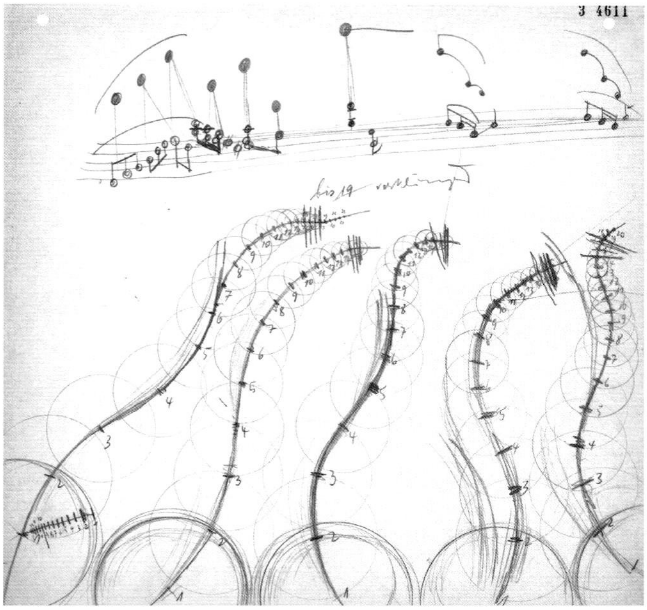

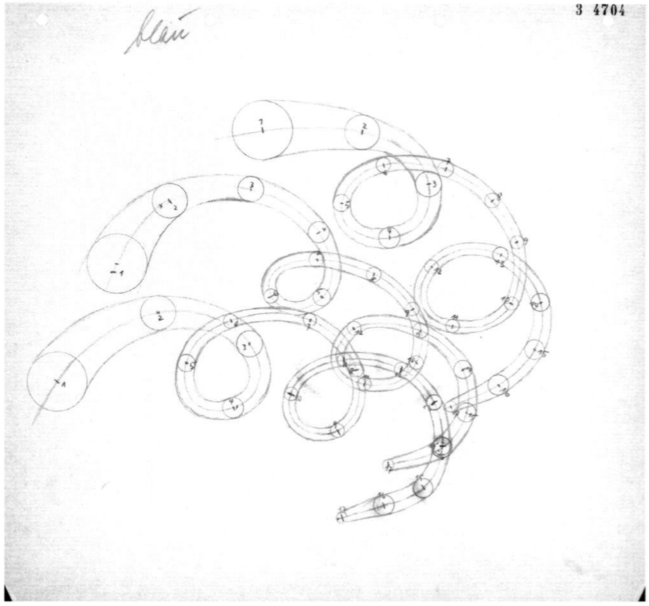

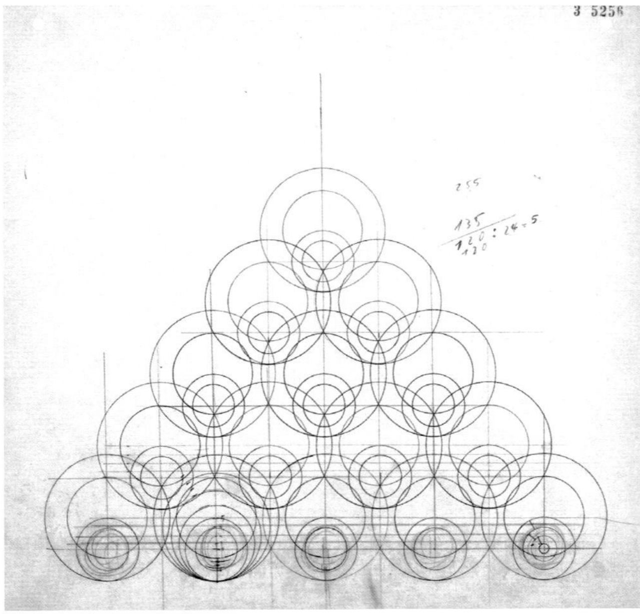

Animation plans for *Kreise* (*Circles*), 1933–34
Pencil on paper, 11.5 x 12 in. / 29.5 x 30.5 cm
Collection Center for Visual Music

Stills from *Kreise* (*Circles*, Tolirag commercial version), 1933–34
35mm, color, sound

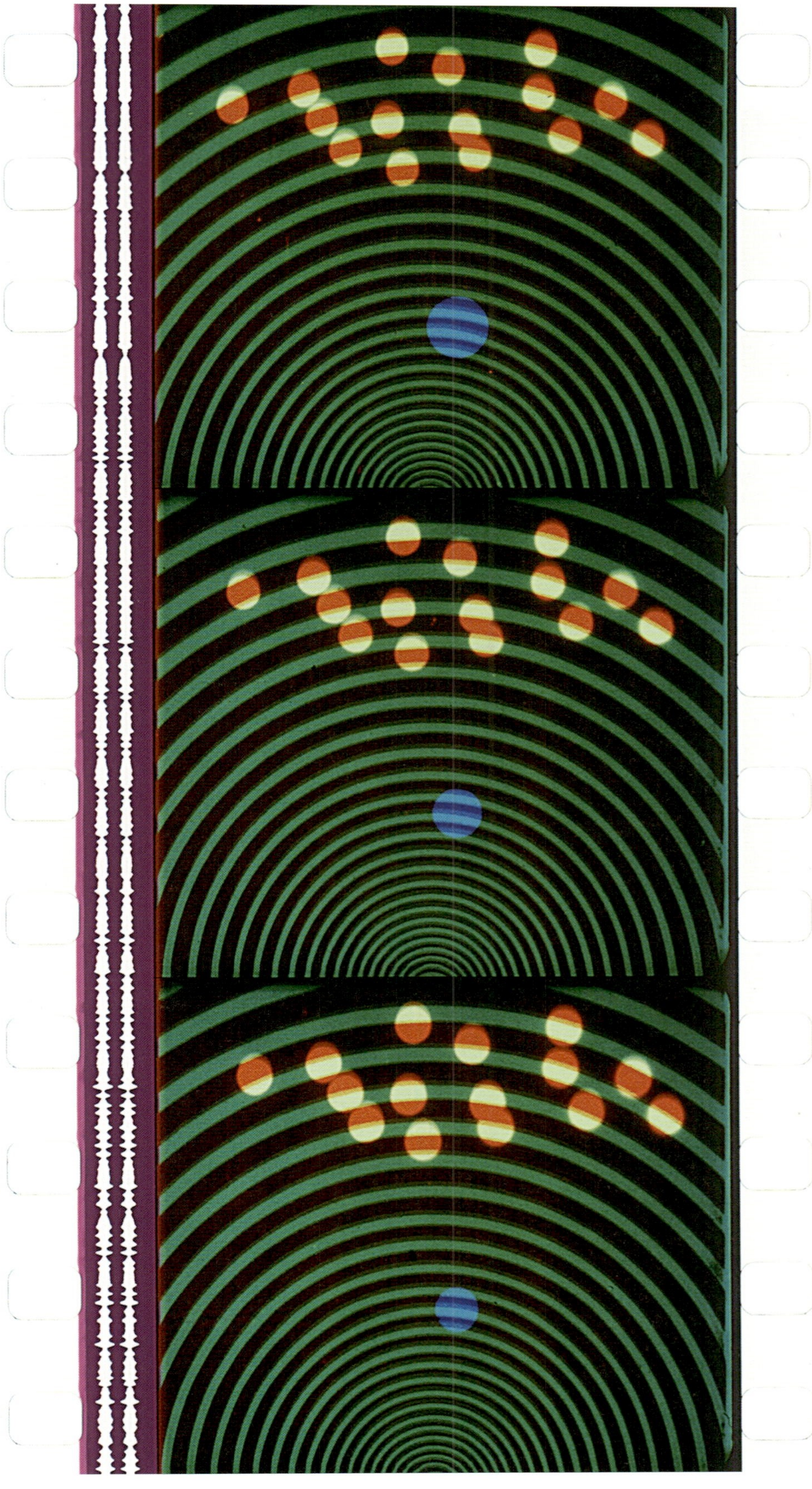

Stills from *Kreise* (*Circles*), 1933–34
35mm, color, sound
Collection Center for Visual Music

KREISE
KREISE
KREISE
ALLE
KREISE
KREISE

3454

Animation designs for *Kreise* (*Circles*), 1933–34
Gouache on paper, 11.5 x 12 in. / 29.5 x 30.5 cm
Collection Oskar Fischinger / Deutsches Filminstitut - DIF, Frankfurt am Main (Germany)

1 2666

1 2663

↑
Animation gouaches for *Quadrate* (*Squares*), 1934
Gouache on paper, 11.5 x 12 in. / 28 x 30.5 cm
Collection The Fischinger Trust, Long Beach, CA
←
Animation gouaches for *Quadrate* (*Squares*), 1934
Gouache on paper, 11.5 x 12 in. / 29.5 x 30.5 cm
Collection Oskar Fischinger / Deutsches Filminstitut - DIF, Frankfurt am Main (Germany)

MURATTI
greift ein!

Jetzt 6 Pf
RATTI
STON
GOLD
CIGARE

Stills from *Muratti Greift Ein* (*Muratti Gets in the Act*)
Commercial, 1934
35mm, color, sound

Stills from *Komposition In Blau* (*Composition in Blue*), 1935
35mm, color, sound

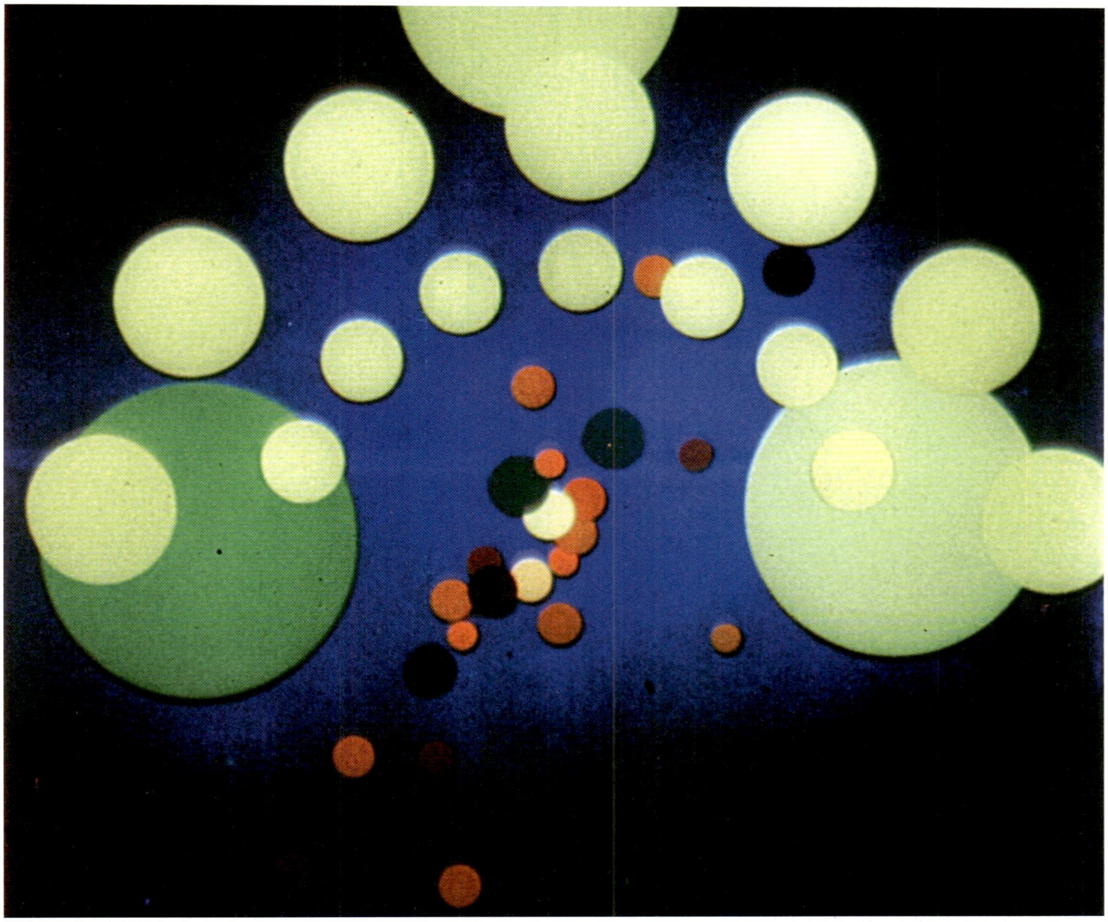

Stills from *Komposition In Blau* (*Composition in Blue*), 1935
35mm, color, sound

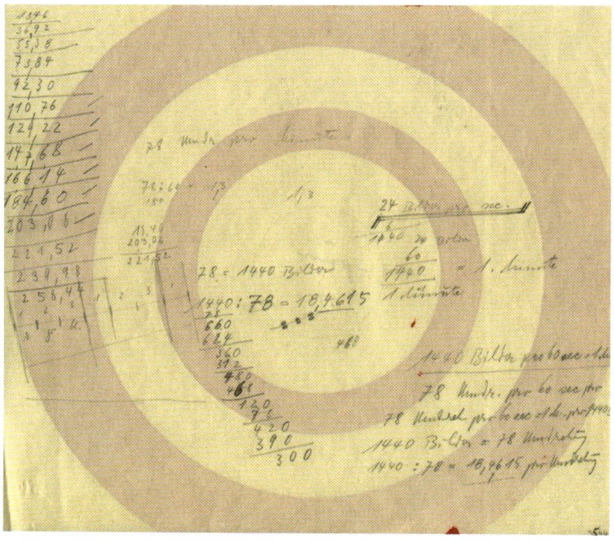

↑
Four painted circles from animation sequence; likely unfilmed, no date, likely 1930s.
Tempera and pencil on paper, 7.9 x 9 in. / 20 x 22.9 cm
Collection Center for Visual Music
←
Reverse of painted animation, showing plans for the sequence

Oskar Fischinger and Music

The Visions of Oskar Fischinger and Alexander László in 1935/36 about a New Way of Visualizing Music

Jörg Jewanski

Filmmaker Oskar Fischinger and the color-light music artist Alexander László collaborated in Germany in 1926. In 1935 and 1936, when László lived in Hungary, they tried to begin a new project for visualizing music: "something that is not music at all but a tapestry of sound." Fischinger emigrated to the United States in 1936, and László followed two years later, but they did not collaborate again. In their unpublished letters, which are evaluated in this article for the first time, they discussed visions for visualizing music that were new for their time. Unfortunately they were never realized.

Germany, 1920s

In Kiel, Germany, in June 1925, a new kind of art was presented in public for the first time: the *Farblichtmusik* (color-light music) of the Hungarian-born German resident pianist and composer Alexander László. He mixed music with colors and forms, in a new type of artistic synthesis he called *Farblicht-musik*, in which he composed the music and presented his own colored associations with it through slide projections onto a screen. With this new work of art, László gave performances until 1927. Thereafter, he devoted himself to film music.[1]

As early as 1921, four years before László's first presentation of his color-light music, the German filmmaker Oskar Fischinger had started making experimental films, mainly showing abstract forms in motion. The first were silent, such as *Wachsexperimente* (*Wax Experiments*) from 1921 to 1926. From *Studie Nr. 2* (*Study No. 2*, c. 1930) onwards he synchronized most of his films to music. Fischinger used popular classical music from the eighteenth and nineteenth centuries, as well as light music—sometimes a little jazzy—that had rhythm and "drive." But he never used contemporary classical music. He probably did this to ensure an easier reception of his films: abstract films combined with music were easy to digest, a combination of the new and the familiar that was accessible for the audience.[2]

Both artists were in contact in the mid-1920s in Munich. The first project they realized together was a performance of László's *Farblichtmusik* (*Color-Light Music*) in Munich, 7 March 1926, where a "film technical innovation" by Fischinger was "co-performed."[3] Probably more performances followed, because Fischinger wrote of "many other places, Cinemas, ectr. [sic]"[4] Afterwards they split up and went separate ways.

1
Jörg Jewanski and Natalia Sidler, eds., *Farbe - Licht - Musik. Synaesthesie und Farblichtmusik* (Bern: Peter Lang, 2006).

2
William Moritz, *Optical Poetry. The Life and Work of Oskar Fischinger* (London, UK: John Libbey Publishing, 2004); and Jörg Jewanski, "Oskar Fischinger," in *Lexikon der Filmmusik*, eds. Manuel Gervink and Matthias Bückle (Laaber: Laaber Verlag, 2012), 173–74.

3
Letter from Alexander László to Oskar Fischinger, March 20, 1926.

4
Oskar Fischinger, unpublished type-script, n.d. (c. 1946?), Collection Center for Visual Music, Los Angeles, cited after: Cindy Keefer, "'*Space Light Art' – Early Abstract Cinema*

Germany and Hungary, 1935–36

In 1933 László (fig. 1) had to flee the Nazis and went back to his hometown of Budapest. Two years later, in July 1935, he was working in the film industry. He again wrote to Fischinger and made a proposal for a new collaboration. He complimented Fischinger's film inventions, but remarked that in his films, the music was the weakest part.[5] This was a criticism of Fischinger's use of popular classical music, which led to an aesthetic conflict: seeing avant-garde films while listening to middle-class music. Fischinger answered that he would welcome a new collaboration, "especially since I know without any doubt that you are the only one who has the right instinct for these things. What I need most for my films is music that is rhythmically and dynamically exciting."[6]

In December 1935 Fischinger picked up the proposed collaboration: "I gradually recognized that the best music for my films is something that is not music at all but a tapestry of sound [*Geräuscheteppich*], woven of rhythm and dynamics—i.e., a sort of Negro music that has no melody, that delivers rhythmic and dynamic intensifications and that can induce dance ecstasy. The orchestra playing this music would have to include the strangest sorts of percussion instruments and, in fact, consist primarily of drums and noise-making instruments (like Talhoff's orchestra, which he put together just the way he wanted it)."[7] In January 1936, László answered positively: "I would love to compose a series of such color-light musical pieces for you, and I am sure that we will be quite a sensation in the international marketplace."[8] This was a remarkable idea, especially if we compare it with other films by Fischinger that were synchronized to music, or with films by other artists of the time.

Fischinger wrote about a tapestry of sound with rhythm and dynamics—but without melody—that had the goal of ecstasy in dance. And he was thinking about an orchestra mainly made up of percussion and noise instruments, similar to Albert Talhoff's orchestra. Talhoff (1888–1956) was a Swiss poet who also composed a little. His most popular work was his unpublished *Totenmal. Dramatisch-chorische Vision für Wort, Tanz und Licht* (*The Call of the Dead: Dramatic Chorale for Text, Dance and Light*, 1930). It was performed many times in 1930 and 1931, but has since been forgotten. For these performances he used a *Klangrhythmisches Orchester* (sound-rhythm orchestra) of only percussion instruments, including gongs, bells, xylophones, vibraphones and various kinds of drums. Because the main instruments used were gongs, the orchestra was also called the *Gongorchester* (gong orchestra).

Figure 1 / Alexander László, c. 1925
Collection Jörg Jewanski

Figure 2 / Postcard *Ein Farblichtkonzert* (A color-light music concert) by Alexander László, c. 1925
Collection Jörg Jewanski

The music in the *Totenmal* consisted of small simple rhythm motifs, which were steadily repeated and which accentuated the stress of the text.[9] Perhaps Fischinger attended one of the performances in 1930 in Munich. He had probably met Talhoff, because both gave lectures at the second Kongress für Farbe-Ton-Forschung (Congress for Color-Sound Research) in 1930 in Hamburg. What kind of music did Fischinger use up to the end of 1935? In 1934 and 1935, he had finished some films, mostly synchronized to nineteenth-century popular classical music, such as his *Muratti Greift Ein* (*Muratti Gets in the Act*), set to music from Josef Bayer's ballet *Die Puppenfee* (*The Fairy Doll*, 1888), or *Komposition In Blau* (*Composition in Blue*) to the overture of *The Merry Wives of Windsor* (1846), a German comic opera by Otto Nicolai. In December 1935, in the same period that he wrote to László proposing his remarkable idea, Fischinger was working on *Lichtkonzert Nr. 2* (*Light Concert No. 2*), which may have been planned to be synchronized to the famous *Rákóczi* march from Hector Berlioz' The Damnation of Faust (1846).

This was the situation in December 1935, when Fischinger wrote to László about his idea of an orchestra of percussion and noise instruments. László was willing to write a composition for him, although he never had composed for such an orchestra. But the piano music for his own color-light music was quite suitable to what Fischinger had meant with "music that is rhythmically and dynamically exciting." László was not content with the music Fischinger chose for his films and as late as August 1935 he wrote to him concerning his film *Komposition In Blau* (*Composition in Blue*): "The artistic side is only partly to my taste, and your use of Nicolai's overture 'The Merry Wives of Windsor' must have resulted from a belief that that would give you an easier field for your work."[10] But this critical attitude could have been a good starting point for a new and different composition.

US West Coast, Switzerland, New Zealand, US East Coast, 1934–40

Looking to other artists who synchronized their abstract films to music at this time, we see that no one in 1935 had realized an idea similar to a "tapestry of sound, woven of rhythm and dynamics."[11] On the East Coast of the US, Mary Ellen Bute had realized her film *Rhythm in Light* in 1934, synchronized to *Anitra's Dance* from Edward Grieg's popular *Peer Gynt Suite No. 1* (1888), followed by *Synchromy No. 2* (1935) to an aria from Richard Wagner's opera *Tannhäuser* (1845). So she used popular classical music for her films, as Fischinger did. Charles Blanc-Gatti did the same in 1938 with his film *Chromophonie*, synchronized to Julius Fučik's march *Entrance of the Gladiators* (1899). Len Lye, born in New Zealand and living in London from 1926, did not use popular classical music for his films, instead using Latin American dance music with elements of jazz, and with a very fast pulse, in *A Colour Box* (1935) and *Kaleidoscope* (1935). This would fit well to Fischinger's idea of a music "that can induce dance ecstasy," although Lye did not use an orchestra of "drums and noise-making instruments." The only film at that time which was synchronized to an orchestra of instruments sounding like drums was done several years later. It is the section of Walt Disney's film *Fantasia* (1940) set to Igor Stravinsky's *The Rite of Spring* (1913). Stravinsky had his orchestra produce sounds similar to "drums and noise-making instruments" by using violins in an intentionally anti-melodic way, with rhythm becoming the most important musical parameter.[12] But the story of the rise and descent of dinosaurs was too trivial and too kitschy to be an aesthetic counterpart to the sophisticated music.

US, 1936–43

So, what happened with Fischinger's and László's project after January 1936? Some weeks later Fischinger left Germany, because the film director Ernst Lubitsch, a German emigrant, had seen *Muratti Greift Ein* (*Muratti Gets in the Act*) and *Komposition In Blau* (*Composition in Blue*) and offered him a job in Hollywood. At that time Fischinger had problems in

---

and Multimedia, 1900–1959," in *White Noise*, exh. cat., ed. Ernest Edmonds (Melbourne: Australian Centre for the Moving Image, 2005), 21–33, here p. 24; also in: www.centerforvisual music.org/CKSLAexc.htm (accessed August 6, 2012). Also Cindy Keefer, "'Raumlichtmusik' – Early 20th Century Abstract Cinema Immersive Environments," in *Leonardo Electronic Alamanac*, 16: 6–7 (2009), 5 pages. Online at www.leonardo.info/LEA/CreativeData/CD_Keefer.pdf (accessed August 6, 2012).

5
Letter from László to Fischinger, July 14, 1935.

6
Letter from Fischinger to László, July 16, 1935.

7
Letter from Fischinger to László, December 5, 1935.

8
Letter from László to Fischinger, January 25, 1936.

9
Fritz Böhme, *Über: Albert Talhoff. 'Totenmal'. Dramatisch-chorische Vision für Wort Tanz Licht* (Munich: Chorische Bühne, 1930); Joseph Bättig, *Einführung in das Werk und die Persönlichkeit Albert Talhoffs*, Diss. (Freiburg: Littau-Luzern, 1963), 19–71; Martin Stern, "Albert Talhoff, 'Totenmal'. *Ästhetische* und politische Kritik eines multimedialen Spiels zwischen Weimarer Republik und Drittem Reich," in *Stimmen – Klänge – Töne. Synergien im szenischen Spiel*, ed. Hans-Peter Bayerdörfer (Tübingen: Gunter Narr, 2002), 573–80.

10
Letter from László to Fischinger, August 19, 1935.

11
Jörg Jewanski and Hajo Düchting, *Musik und Bildende Kunst im 20. Jahrhundert*, chapter: "Musikvisualisierungen: Mary Ellen Bute, Oskar Fischinger, Len Lye" (Kassel: Kassel University Press, 2009), 342–45.

12
For Stravinsky's music see Volker Scherliess, *Igor Strawinsky – Le Sacre du Printemps* (Munich: Fink, 1982). For the relation between music and film, see Irene Kletschke, *Klangbilder. Walt Disney's,"Fantasia" (1940)* (Stuttgart: F. Steiner, 2011), 156–66. (Supplement to Archiv für Musikwissenschaft 67).

Germany with the political system, so he agreed to Lubitsch's offer and arrived in Hollywood in February 1936. László himself left Hungary two years later, in October 1938, because of the Nazis. First he settled in New York, where he continued to work on his own color-light music.[13] There is some correspondence between Fischinger and László between March 1939 and January 1940, but only about their own business affairs. Both were engaged in establishing themselves: Fischinger with his films, László with his color-light music. The only sentence which picked up on their earlier collaboration was written by László in January 1940: "Most of all, it is a great pity that we cannot work together, since we could do something very solid together—of that I am convinced."[14] New York to Los Angeles is a distance of nearly 3000 miles.

Fischinger's first film in the US was *Allegretto* (1936–43), synchronized to *Radio Dynamics* by Ralph Rainger (1901–42), an American who composed popular music, mostly for films. The film *An Optical Poem*, synchronized to Franz Liszt's *Hungarian Rhapsody No. 2* (1851), was delivered to MGM Studios in April 1937. Sometime before March 1937 Fischinger was in contact with the 24-year-old composer John Cage, and may have attended one of his concerts with music for percussion in March 1937.[15] Cage visited Fischinger in his studio and for a few days helped with the execution of the animation for *An Optical Poem*. Some of Cage's percussion music was "rhythmically and dynamically exciting," as Fischinger needed. But there was no further collaboration between them in 1937. Six years later, in 1943, after reading a review of a concert of Cage's percussion music, Fischinger wrote a letter to Cage asking for recordings: "You know which composition would be the best for me and would give me the most possibilities to express something on the screen."[16] There is no answer from Cage, and it is unclear if he actually got the letter. During this time, Fischinger was working on a synchronization of Johann Sebastian Bach's *Brandenburg Concerto No. 3*. It became the music to *Motion Painting No. 1* (1947), his long and final completed music film—set again to popular classical music.

In 1940 László stopped his activities concerning his color-light music to work as a piano teacher and composer.[17] In 1943, the same year that Fischinger tried to contact Cage, László moved to Hollywood, having received an offer to write film music for United Artists and Paramount Studios. In the following decades, until his death in 1970, László wrote the music for around forty movies and also for many popular television series.[18] His life and Fischinger's took a very different course. Fischinger had problems acculturating, finished his last film in 1947 and, because it was difficult to find money for his work, devoted himself to painting. He never did come back to his idea of an orchestra which "consists primarily of drums and noise-making instruments," and he died in 1967. Although they lived in the same city, Los Angeles, for more than twenty years, Fischinger and László had little or no contact.[19]

Their idea in 1935 and 1936 of creating an abstract film based on a "tapestry of sound" would have been a milestone in the history of abstract film, or, in László's words, "quite a sensation in the international marketplace," but the political situation at that time did not provide a fertile ground for such a project. Later, in the US, first the distance between their cities was too big for collaboration, and later, when they lived in the same city, their lifestyles had become too different.

Thanks to The Fischinger Trust and Center for Visual Music for copyright permission for citations from unpublished letters between Fischinger and László. Thanks also to Eric Allen, Bochum, Germany, for translations of the German letter citations.

This article is a slightly revised reprint of "I gradually recognised that the best music for my films is something that is not music at all but a tapestry of sound." "The visions of Oskar Fischinger and Alexander László," in Irina Vanechkina (ed.), *Galeyaev Readings. Materials of the Scientific-Practical Conference ("Prometheus" – 2010), Kazan, October, 2–6, 2010* (Kazan 2010), 95–103.[20]

13
Jörg Jewanski, "Ich brauche mich mit 'Geschäften' nicht mehr zu befassen, nur mit Kunst. Alexander László und die Weiterentwicklung seiner Farblichtmusik im amerikanischen Exil," in *Exilforschung. Ein internationales Jahrbuch*, vol. 16: *Exil und Avantgarden*, eds. Claus-Dieter Krohn, et al. (Munich, 1998), 194–228.

14
Letter from László to Fischinger, January 21, 1940.

15
Richard H. Brown, "The Spirit inside Each Object: John Cage, Oskar Fischinger and The Future of Music," *Journal of the Society for American Music*, 6/1 (2012), 83–113.

16
Letter from Fischinger to John Cage, May 20, 1943.

17
Jewanski 1998 (see note 13).

18
Jörg Jewanski, "Alexander László," in *Lexikon der Filmmusik*, eds. Manuel Gervink and Matthias Bückle (Laaber: Laaber Verlag, 2012), 296–97.

19
Interview by Jörg Jewanski with Oskar Fischinger's widow Elfriede, July 1995, in her home in Long Beach, California.

20
Original publication information:
Ванечкина, Ирина Леонидовна (Ред.), Галеевские чтения: Материалы Международной научно-практической конференции („Прометей"– 2010), Казанъ, 2-6 октября 2010 года.

Oskar Fischinger in his Los Angeles studio working with strips for one of his later experiments with synthetic sound, c. 1948
Collection Center for Visual Music
→
Three strips from the synthetic sound experiments, c. 1948
Paper, each 1.5 x 19 in. / 2.5 x 48.3 cm
Collection Center for Visual Music

The Spirit inside Each Object
John Cage & Oskar Fischinger

Richard H. Brown

Late in his life, John Cage often recalled his brief apprenticeship with Oskar Fischinger in the 1930s as a turning point in his approach to traditional musical composition:

> When I was introduced to him, he began to talk with me about the spirit which is inside each of the objects of this world. So, he told me, all we need to do to liberate that spirit is to brush past the object, and to draw forth its sound. That's the idea which led me to percussion.[1]

This small anecdote quickly became part of the larger body of work known today as "Cagean lore," a series of memories and recollections retold in countless interviews and disseminated via artists, scholars, and journalists. This anecdote in particular has sparked numerous theories, homages, and a long string of citations within the literature surrounding both Cage and the history of visual music, yet little documentation survives from Cage's formative years that outline the details of this interaction.

While Cage's encounter with Fischinger was, in a certain sense, an inspirational moment of spiritual clarity, Fischinger's own working methods for sound synchronization would have had a direct bearing on Cage's interest in contemporary sound synthesis technologies emerging from the Hollywood film industry, in particular those that synchronized sound to visual image via the optical soundtrack. Cage's understanding of this process came about primarily through library research he conducted for his father, John Cage Sr., an inventor and electrical engineer who filed several patents for cathode ray television tubes throughout the 1930s and 1940s, including an "Invisible-Ray-Vision Machine" in 1935 that utilized infrared technology to see objects in the dark.[2] Equally, Fischinger's notion of the "spirit inside each object" was inspired by his research on sound phonography in film. On the audio portion of a sound film, a clear visual representation of sound wave structure appears; the visual nature of this phenomenon inspired numerous theories similar to Fischinger's on the indexical relationship between sound and image and its implications for a composite visual music.[3] Such technological innovations empowered composers such as Cage to explore new methods of temporal organization of sound in a tactile visual interface. With this in mind, one can get a better sense of the encounter between the two artists in an appropriate historical context.

After two years studying at Pomona College, Cage travelled to Europe in 1930 and 1931, and he may have encountered some of Fischinger's ideas and films during this time, although little documentation survives from this early period.[4] However, upon returning to Los Angeles to pursue a career in music, Cage encountered a large population of emigrants fleeing from a war-torn Europe, including Fischinger, who left for Los Angeles in 1936. Cage soon befriended the art dealer Galka Scheyer, who introduced him to the growing legions of artists flocking to the city. Cage spent the first years of his musical training experimenting with complex serial procedures, and he eventually enrolled in courses on music theory and composition with another European émigré artist, Arnold Schoenberg, starting in 1935. As many sources note, it was around the time that Cage first met Fischinger that he first turned away from his formal classical studies and began to incorporate percussion and noise into his musical compositions.

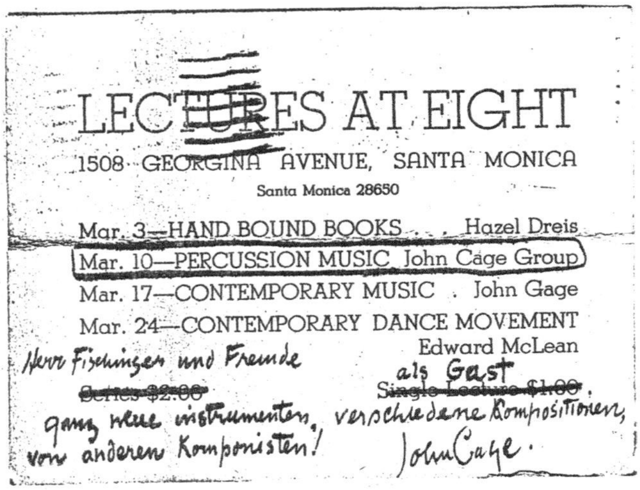
LECTURES AT EIGHT
1508 GEORGINA AVENUE, SANTA MONICA
Santa Monica 28650
Mar. 3—HAND BOUND BOOKS . . . Hazel Dreis
Mar. 10—PERCUSSION MUSIC John Cage Group
Mar. 17—CONTEMPORARY MUSIC . John Gage
Mar. 24—CONTEMPORARY DANCE MOVEMENT Edward McLean
Herr Fischinger und Freunde
als Gast
~~Series $2.00~~ ~~Single Lecture $1.00~~.
ganz neue instrumenten, verschiedene Kompositionen, von anderen Komponisten!
John Cage.

Figure 1 / John Cage, postcard invitation to Oskar Fischinger, 1937
"Herr Fischinger und Freunde; als Gast; ganz neue [I]nstrumenten, verschiedene Kompositionen, von anderen Komponisten" ("Mr. Fischinger and Friends; as a Guest; brand new instruments, various compositions by other composers!")
Collection Center for Visual Music

1
John Cage, *For the Birds: John Cage in Conversation with Daniel Charles*, trans. Richard Gardner, ed. Tom Gora and John Cage (Boston: Marion Boyars, 1981), 68. Cage mentioned his encounter with Fischinger in several other prominent essays and lectures. See, for example, John Cage, "A Composer's Confessions," [1948] repr. in *John Cage: Writer*, ed. Richard Kostelanetz (New York: Limelight, 1993), 31; and Calvin Tompkins, *The Bride and the Bachelors: The Heretical Courtship in Modern Art* (New York: Viking Press, 1965), 86. Notably, it did not arise in the "anecdote" sections of his two major publications of the period, *Silence* (1961) or *A Year from Monday* (1967). After Fischinger biographer William Moritz interviewed Cage and reprinted this anecdote in "The Films of Oskar Fischinger," *Film Culture* 58–60 [1974–75], 37–188. It was repeatedly cited in interviews, including one conducted by Moritz for his biography of Fischinger: *Optical Poetry: The Life and Work of Oskar Fischinger* (Bloomington: Indiana University Press, 2004), 77–78, 165–66.

2
For more on the relationship between Cage and his father's research, see my "The Spirit inside Each Object: John Cage, Oskar Fischinger and 'The Future of Music,'" *Journal of the Society for American Music*, 6/1 (2012), 90–94.

3
The optical sound recording process operates on the principle of inscribing a beam of light onto a strip of photo-electric material. In optical recording apparatuses that utilized the fixed density, variable area, the electric current is transmitted to a mirror that vibrates according to the intensity of sound. A fixed beam of light is projected on the mirror and is reflected onto the soundtrack. With this method, a clear "shape" is inscribed, as the light source is consistent, while the variations in sound pressure cause the electric current to fluctuate, creating an oscillographic curve. When the film is projected, this process is reversed, and the inscribed light patterns are converted to electric current and projected via loudspeakers in the theater. For two detailed explanations of this process, see Jan Thoben, "Technical Sound-Image Transformations," in *See this Sound: Audiovisiology Compendium: An Interdisciplinary Survey of Audiovisual Culture*, eds. Dieter Daniels and Sandra Naumann with Jan Thoben (Cologne: Verlag der Buchhandlung Walter König, 2010), 425–26; and Richard James, "Avant-Garde Sound-on-Film Techniques and Their Relationship to Electro-Acoustic Music," *Musical Quarterly*, 72/1 (1986), 75–78.

4
While it is doubtful Cage came across Fischinger while in Europe, he would have had an opportunity to witness Fischinger's close friend, composer Paul Hindemith, display some of the earliest experiments in overdubbing techniques with phonograph records at the *Neue Musik Berlin* festival in 1931. This festival is discussed in Mark Katz, *Capturing Sound: How Technology Has Changed Music*, rev. ed. (Berkeley: University of California Press, 2010), 110–13. Cage recalled the event years later to composer Ernst Toch's grandson Lawrence Weschler, "My Grandfather's Last Tale," *Atlantic Monthly*, 278/6 (December 1996), 96.

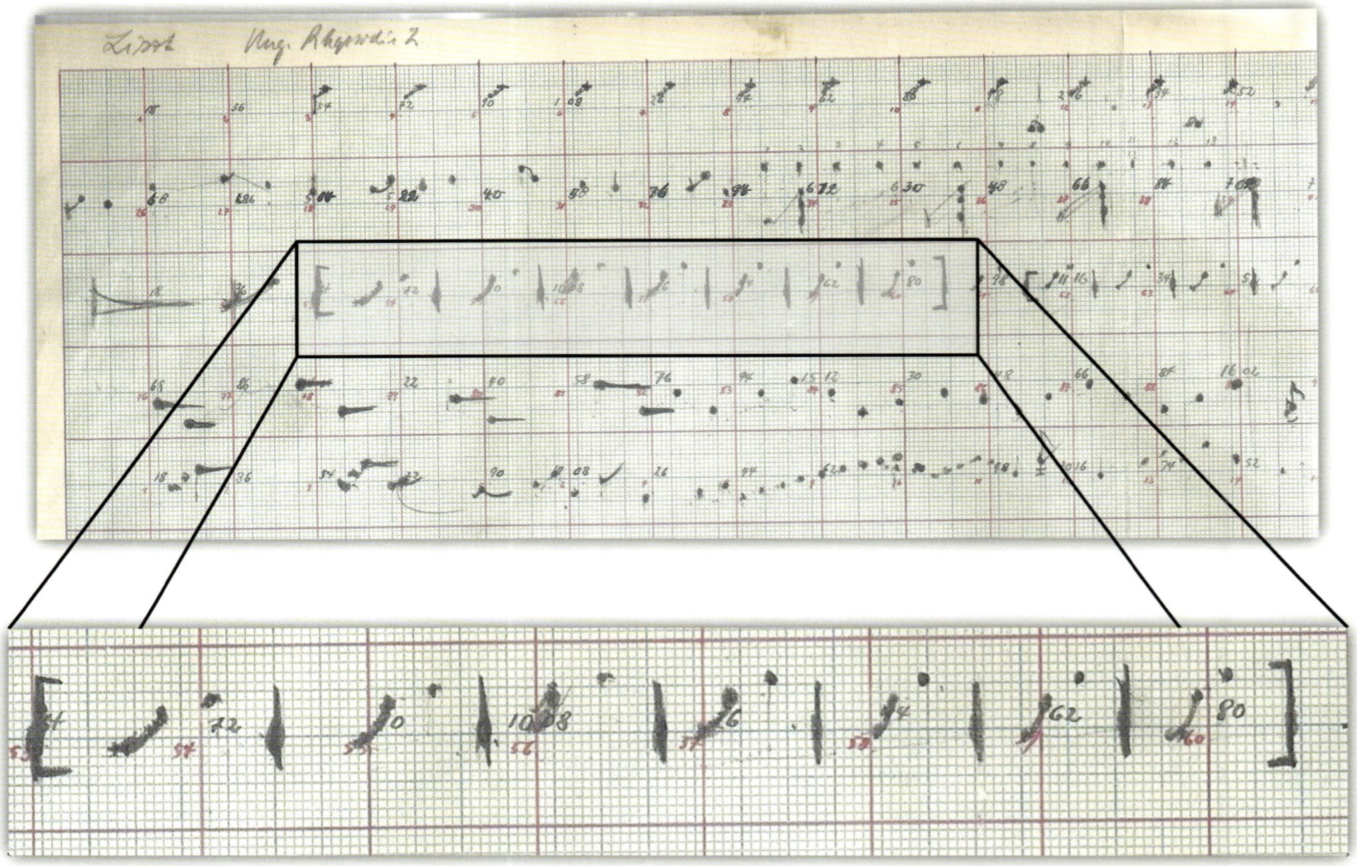

Figure 2 / Graphic notation for *An Optical Poem*, c. 1937
Collection Center for Visual Music

In December 1936 Fischinger received a small contract from MGM Studios for an animated film, *An Optical Poem* (1937), and he rented a studio space for the animation scaffolding. Galka Scheyer introduced Cage to Fischinger sometime before March of the following year. Despite Cage's insistence that Fischinger "led him to percussion," Cage had likely already begun to compose works incorporating percussion instruments before their first encounter. However, a conversation similar to Cage's anecdote could have occurred, because he sent Fischinger a complimentary ticket to a lecture on percussion music at the home of bookbinder and musician Hazel Dreis in March 1937 (fig. 1). Cage's note on the ticket promised a performance of several compositions on new percussion instruments by the "John Cage Group."

An Optical Poem was shot using stop motion animation; dozens of individual paper cutouts of geometric shapes were arranged on the shooting stage and then repositioned after each frame of film was exposed. To outline the animation, Fischinger sketched a graphic-temporal notation of the movement of individual figures across the screen. He used a large scroll of graph paper, where the horizontal plane represented the individual frames. The graph paper was subdivided into individual lines where Fischinger sketched the general movement of the figures over time. The curved lines and straight lines in the example specify a few of the many movements across the screen of the paper cutouts (fig. 2). With these details one can get a sense of the animation process Cage witnessed. Fischinger knew the specific attack points in which each image would appear. In later sections a myriad of figures move across the screen, each corresponding with different attack points, and the coordination of each of the figures within the set was a complex endeavor. As Cage recalled later in life, during his apprenticeship Fischinger looked on, cigar in hand, in the corner of the studio while Cage carefully moved the large paper cutouts of colored geometric shapes a few fractions of a millimeter for each successive frame shot, with a large feather attached to a stick (fig. 3). At one point Fischinger fell asleep, dropping ashes from his cigar into a pile of papers and rags and starting a small fire. Frightened, Cage rushed to splash water on the flames, dousing Fischinger and the equipment in the process.[5]

According to all surviving documentation, Cage's work lasted no more than a few days, and likely ended after the fire incident. Despite the brevity of Cage's apprenticeship, the influence of Fischinger's animation method can be seen in the manuscript for one of Cage's first percussion works, *Quartet*, which displays many similarities to Fischinger's graphic sketches. Although Cage dated the work to 1935—before his first encounter with Fischinger—there is reason to think the date incorrect.[6] Cage's only other percussion piece from his Los Angeles years, *Trio* (1936), used conventional notation and was written for specific instruments, whereas his *Quartet* does not specify instrumentation and is written in a unique graphic notation. Cage's blocking of individual instruments bears a distinct similarity to the animation "staging" in Fischinger's graphs, and it is here that the notion of a "spirit inside each object" has clear scientific and practical artistic implications. Cage had discovered the specific scientific nature of sound-wave structure through film phonography and scientific research for his father, giving him a sense of the indexical relationship between sound and object. In Fischinger's studio he witnessed a miraculous blending of scientific precision with brilliant artistry in the synchronization of sound and image over time. Thus, in just one short encounter, Cage for the first time noticed the connection between sound, object, and duration.

There is no documentation indicating that Cage had further contact with Fischinger until the fall of 1940. While touring Los Angeles with several records of his percussion works, Cage visited Fischinger and played some examples, discussing once again the possibility of a film commission. A number of graphs similar to the one used in *An Optical Poem* in the Fischinger Collection at the Center for Visual Music indicate percussion sounds, although it is unclear from the surviving fragments the specific piece of music in mind. In the coming years, after Cage moved away from Los Angeles permanently, Fischinger did not lose sight of his potential Cage film. After reading the impressive *Life* magazine review of Cage's February 1943 percussion concert at the Museum of Modern Art, Fischinger wrote to Cage, in care of the museum, requesting his newest recordings of percussion music in order to include the commission as part of a new application for Guggenheim support later that summer.[7] In the letter, Fischinger noted, "I have a clear feeling how fertile, expressive, how rich in color your percussion music is,

5
This anecdote was provided to William Moritz in an interview with Cage in the 1980s, and transcribed in his biography of Fischinger (Moritz, *Optical Poetry*, 165–66). Portions of the anecdote are questioned by the Fischinger Trust, and it is possible that Cage or Moritz dramatized certain details, such as smoking near nitrate film.

6
As has been noted by Leta E. Miller, the dating on this manuscript seems to have been added later and is written in red ink on a corner of the first page. It is likely that Cage recalled this date later when he secured his publishing contract with Henmar Press and, like many dates from his early career, was misstated; see: Leta E. Miller, "John Cage and Henry Cowell: Intersections and Influences, 1933–1941," *Journal of the American Musicological Society*, 59/1 (Spring 2006), 59.

7
This contract explicitly indicates that Fischinger was "to use your best efforts to produce a film with percussion music by John Cage." Oskar Fischinger, contract with Solomon R. Guggenheim Foundation, June 18, 1943, The Hilla Rebay Non-Objective Film Collection, Guggenheim Museum Archives, Acc.no. 786445, folder 10.

especially on the screen. Please help me to get your music on the screen, and please do everything possible because it is so important."[8] However, Fischinger's struggles with a severely limited budget and his constant personal and artistic battles with Hilla Rebay cut this proposed project short, and it is doubtful that Cage ever received the letter.

Cage's anecdote about Oskar Fischinger and the "spirit inside each object" provides an insight into several aspects of Cage's emerging ideas on the scientific nature of music. As Cage repeatedly stated in his writings, percussion music was an important transition to the electric music of the future, where recording and synthesis technology required a new approach to the compositional process. The ability to visually interpret sound-wave structure in film phonography provided a tactile medium for creating a time-based structure of sound organization and required new notational approaches in order to coordinate sound and image, ideas Cage would continue to explore during his most influential period in the 1950s and 1960s, all the while recalling this brief encounter as one of the many sparks that ignited his creative fire.

This essay stems from my article examining John Cage's early career in Los Angeles: "The Spirit inside Each Object: John Cage, Oskar Fischinger, and 'The Future of Music,'" *Journal of the Society for American Music* Volume 6/1 (2012), 83–113, ©The Society for American Music. A special thanks to Cambridge University Press for permission to draw upon material from this article.

Figure 3 / Oskar Fischinger working at MGM studios on *An Optical Poem*, 1937
Collection Center for Visual Music

8
Oskar Fischinger to John Cage, May 20, 1943, Fischinger Collection, Center for Visual Music.

Oskar Fischinger's Synthetic Sound Machine

Joseph Hyde

There is a fascinating hidden history that connects early sound cinema from the 1920s and 30s with the electronic music and sound of the 1950s and 60s. This is the evolution of what is variously known as "synthetic sound," "direct sound," or "drawn sound." It involves the direct manipulation of the optical soundtrack technology which became widespread in the late 1920s, to produce new synthetic sounds.

Filmmakers, musicians and inventors around the world began to experiment with this technology virtually as soon as it appeared. If a sound could be captured and represented visually as a waveform, then the reverse process could also be applied, and something drawn by hand, or scratched into exposed film, or produced by photographing directly onto the soundtrack, could then be played through a film projector and heard. This is the foundation of Fischinger's theory that every object contains a sound, famously influential on a young John Cage.

Names associated with this approach include Rudolf Pfenninger, Arseny Avraamov, Evgeny Sholpo, Norman McLaren, and John and James Whitney. Fischinger was also an early pioneer of this practice with his *Ornament Sound* experiments (1932)—these experiments attracted a great deal of press at the time and are well documented. He returned to the technique—in a different form—between 1948 and 1955. Although these later Synthetic Sound experiments are less known, they are at least as groundbreaking as the earlier work, and offer some impressive innovations which Fischinger seems to have only begun to exploit in terms of their full potential.

The archive of the Center for Visual Music contains various parts of the apparatus used to produce these experiments, the Synthetic Sound "machine" (built c. 1948): celluloid strips printed with Fischinger's versions of audio waveforms, glass plates to which these were affixed, a wooden frame to hold these plates (fig. 1, p. 146), and a calibration scale. The archive also contains correspondence, diagrams, and a patent application (apparently never filed) which describe the full apparatus, including placement of camera, lighting, etc (fig. 3, p. 147). In addition, it contains several recordings of the sounds and music produced by the apparatus,[1] including the *Northern Tissue* soundtrack (used in a 1955 commercial), Sibelius' *Valse Triste* (used as a soundtrack for Lumigraph performances), and a number of specially produced "scores" (more closely resembling a modern software sequencer than a traditional music score) based on a template Fischinger produced in 1948 (fig. 2, p. 146).

By cross-referencing these various materials it is

1
William Moritz notes that some of this material was intended to assist the composer Alexander László in a court case in 1948, though the later material was not connected with this case. William Moritz, *Optical Poetry: The Live and Work of Oskar Fischinger* (London, UK: John Libbey Publishing, 2004), 236.

possible to understand the functionality of the apparatus, how Fischinger used it to make sound and music, and indeed how its use might have been developed further. Firstly, the scores can easily be linked to the recordings, and indeed the apparatus, since they depict many of the pieces of music heard in these recordings.[2]

However, it is what the scores reveal about the apparatus itself which is particularly interesting. Some of the key frequencies (pitches) identified by Fischinger on the score template are prominently marked by Fischinger on the machine itself—the yellowish strips at the bottom of the photograph, three-quarters of the way up and right at the top. At each of these points is attached a reference strip of the printed celluloid Fischinger used on the glass slides. These strips and their annotations contain the key to how the machine works, which is simultaneously incredibly simple and extraordinarily ingenious.[3]

It is clear from the patent drawings that the glass plates, with celluloid waveform strips attached, were placed in the slots that can be seen down both sides of the machine, and filmed by a camera placed at the far end of the machine against a light source at the near end. However, while Moritz assumed the function of the slots was to control the volume of the sound,[4] the figures in fact reveal them to control the pitch. What this means is that one could use the *same* slide to produce any pitch (the other slots for the slides corresponding to a chromatic scale), simply by virtue of its placement relative to the camera, with higher pitches simply being further away.[5] This opens up many exciting possibilities: Firstly, potentially infinite polyphony—since there is no reason why multiple slides cannot be used to build up harmony. Secondly, since multiple slides are not needed for each waveform type, it would be easy to make slides with various waveforms. Nothing other than the "triangle strips" has yet been found in connection with the synthetic sound machine, but one can only imagine what this technique might have produced when combined with the earlier *Ornament Sound* figures. Finally, this technique opens up the possibility of harmonics: real-world instrumental tones are made up not of single frequencies, but of multiple (related) frequencies, or harmonics. This would be very easy to simulate using this system by simply arranging multiple strips (with different sized waveforms) on a single slide. One such slide can in fact be found in the collection.

There are several scores in the collection that notate more abstract shapes, rather than recognizable pieces of music. One is rather charmingly annotated "Plank, Plunk, Boing, Blumb, Buzz, Plunk, Plink." It has been previously

Figure 1/ Photograph of main part of Synthetic Sound Machine
Collection Center for Visual Music, gift of The Fischinger Trust

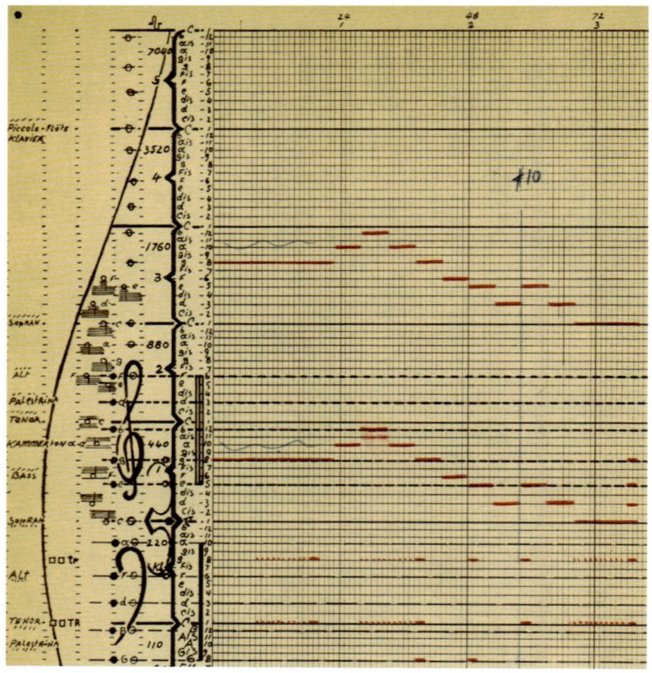

Figure 2 / Template score, page 3 of 5, titled "Bolero" (segment)
Collection Center for Visual Music

speculated that this score may be connected to the *Northern Tissue* soundtrack mentioned above, but the specific contours notated here do not correspond to any of the glissandos and other sounds in the commercial. At the same time, I note that the number of abstract synthetic sound scores found is quite large—far larger than would be merited by such a short sequence (which would require only three pages of Fischinger's template). Some are similar to the "Plank Plunk" score, actually seeming to show different forms of the same motif. Others are constructed differently—there are a large number of "step" shapes cut out of graph paper, and these were used as templates for inscribing complex glissandi onto the template scores. As the abstract sounds used in the *Northern Tissue* advertisement seem like a strange aesthetic mismatch with their context, I question whether this is actually what they were originally intended for. This material leads me to wonder if Fischinger was working on an abstract composition using these materials in the later 1950s. While this can only be speculation at this stage, it is a tantalizing possibility that surely warrants further investigation.

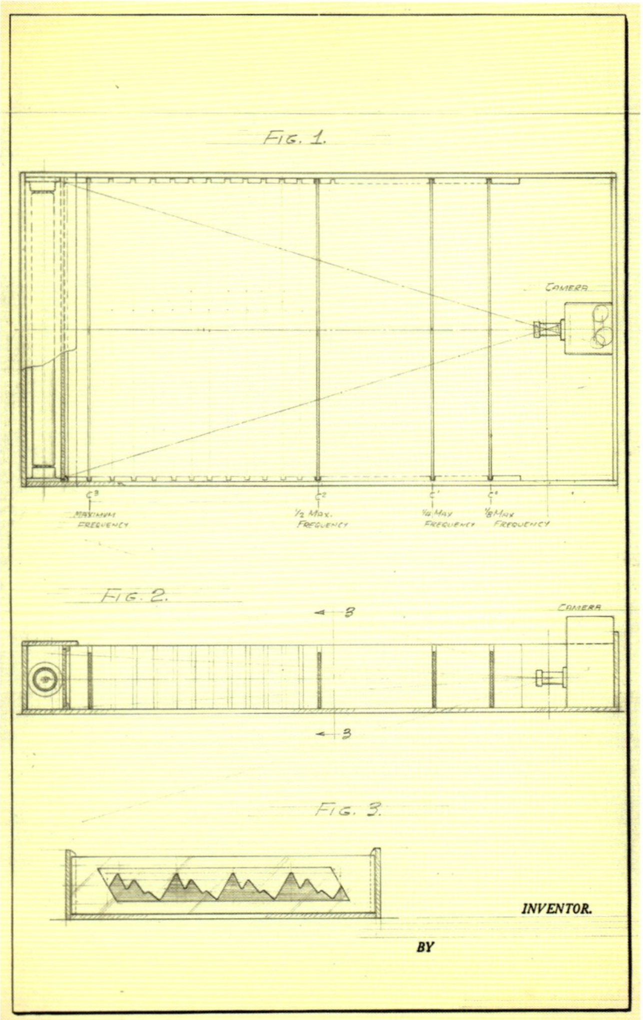

Figure 3 / Diagram for Synthetic Sound patent application (never filed), page 1 of 2, c. 1948
Collection Center for Visual Music

2
Chopin's "Waltz in D flat major, Op. 64, No.1", popularly known as the "Minute Waltz," the "Sabre Dance" from Aram Khachaturian's ballet *Gayane*, and Laszlo's *Faster Than Any Instrument*.

3
The bottom strip is labeled "440 = 18.33." The celluloid strip here is incomplete, but it is easy to extrapolate and observe that there would be just over eighteen triangle formations between the two outer diagonal lines. The next line up is labeled "220 = 9.16." Here, just over nine triangles can be observed between the outer lines. Finally, the top strip is labeled "110 = 4.56," with a strip of 4.5 triangles attached. If we assume that the diagonal lines represent the field of view of the camera (as shown in the patent drawings), then if a glass slide (with "triangle strip" attached) is placed at the position marked "110 = 4.56," then 4.56 triangles would be photographed for every frame. There would therefore be 4.56 triangles, or waveform oscillations, per 1/24th of a second. This would equate to 4.56 x 24 = 109.44 triangle oscillations per second, i.e., the "A" two octaves above concert A. If the same slide is placed at the position indicated by "220 = 9.16," then 9.16 triangles will appear in the field of view of the camera, equating to a frequency of 219.84 (the "A" an octave above). If it is placed at "440 = 18.33," the 18.33 triangles seen by the camera will equate to a frequency of 439.92Hz, or (very close to) concert A.

4
Ibid.

5
To appreciate the ingenuity of this system, it is worth comparing it with what Norman McLaren was doing at around the same time. By the early 1950s, McLaren had evolved a technique rather akin to what Fischinger was doing with the synthetic sound machine, filming pre-produced striped cards frame by frame in much the same way as Fischinger filmed his celluloid/glass slides. However, where McLaren needed a separate card for every required frequency, Fischinger needed only one, with the placement yielding the correct frequency.

Fischinger's Scores
New Perspectives on His Approach to Music

Joseph Hyde

The Center for Visual Music has in its archives a collection of musical scores and score-like material used or produced by Fischinger as part of the creative process in making his films. These scores remind us of the depth of Fischinger's musical interest and knowledge (music being his first choice of career, after all)[1] and allow us to study the musical aspects of Fischinger's work in detail. Musical analysis of any depth is generally considered difficult in the absence of a score—these scores therefore represent a great opportunity to study Fischinger's films from a musical perspective and discover new information about his creative process.

The score collection contains several different types of scores, including published scores, annotated by Fischinger with information pertaining to the animation he was producing. Some of these have been cut up and collaged (fig. 1), usually with graphical additions. Musical scores are generally—and perhaps surprisingly—not proportionally accurate in terms of timing in the way that, say, a computer-based sequencer might be. Cutting up scores in this way allowed Fischinger to represent time accurately—in this sense these scores are in themselves ahead of their time.

More interestingly, there are a number of graphic scores made by Fischinger which represent the music in an abstracted form, i.e. not using traditional music notation (although again, time-accurate). This type of graphic notation became fashionable in contemporary music in the 1940s, and here it can be argued that Fischinger had a direct influence on developments in musical composition: one of the earlier proponents of graphic notation was John Cage, whose earliest graphic scores coincide with his work with Fischinger in the late 1930s. There is in fact a striking visual similarity between the Cage scores of this period and Fischinger's.[2]

The scores from 1948 onwards extend accurate proportional representation to both pitch and time—actually very close to the representation used in contemporary music software as mentioned above. This is no coincidence, because it has become clear that these later scores are not actually related to Fischinger's films, but are rather intended for the production of sophisticated synthesized music, again years ahead of its time. I believe they are intended for Fischinger's synthetic sound machine, which I discuss in a separate essay in this volume.

For the purposes of this short essay, small sections of two of the graphic scores will be examined.

1
William Moritz, *Optical Poetry: The Life and Work of Oskar Fischinger* (London, UK: John Libbey Publishing, 2004), 3.

2
Richard H. Brown, "The Spirit inside Each Object: John Cage, Oskar Fischinger and 'The Future of Music,'" *Journal of the Society for American Music*, 6/1 (2012), 83–113, 97.

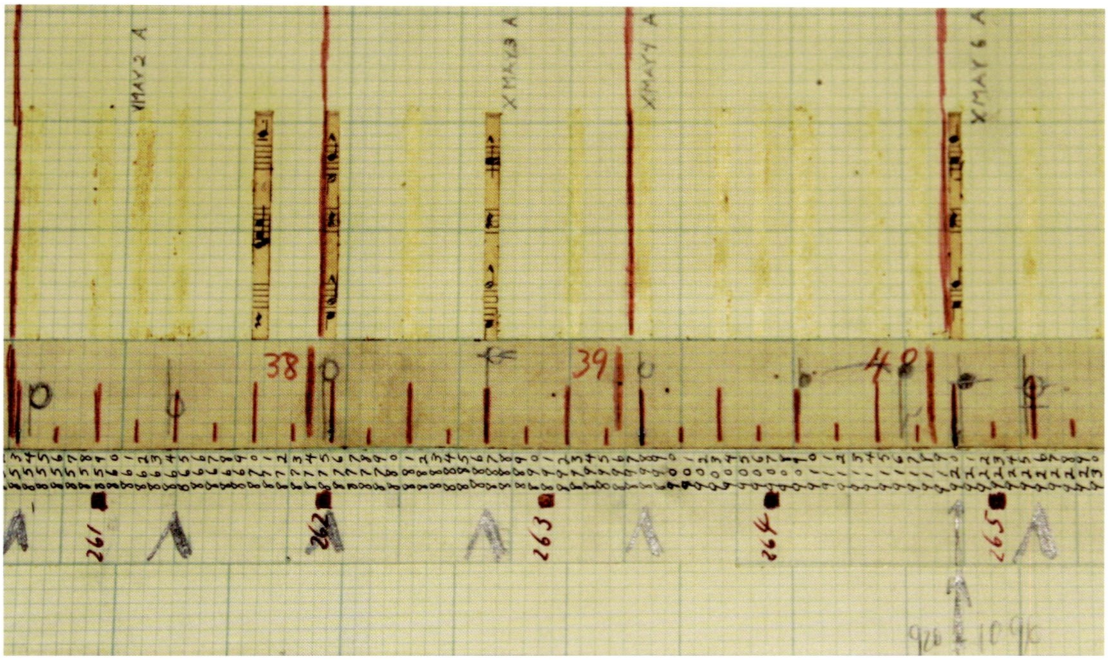

Figure 1 / Cut up score, fragments taken from piano reduction to Souza's "Stars and Stripes" march (excerpt), no date
Collection Center for Visual Music, gift of Fischinger Trust

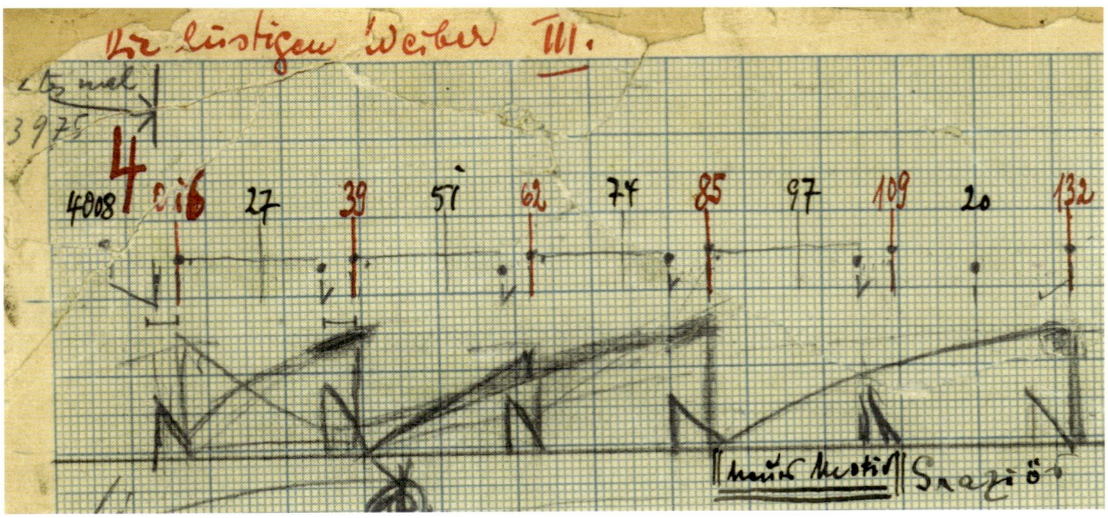

Figure 2 / Graph paper score, page 3 of 3, titled "Die Lustigen Weiber," believed connected to *Komposition In Blau* (*Composition in Blue*, excerpt)
Collection Center for Visual Music

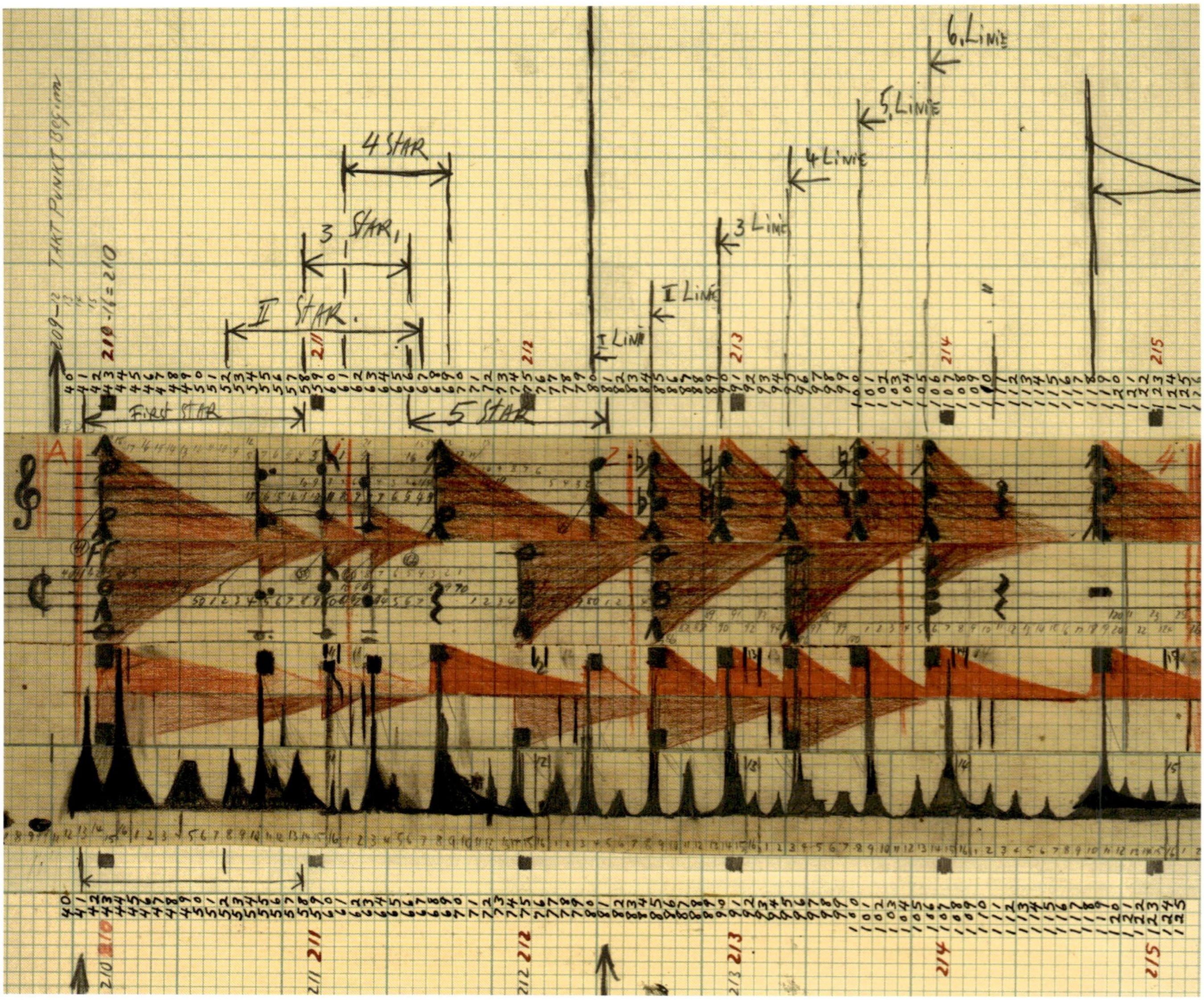

Figure 3 / Graph paper fragment, untitled, believed connected to *An American March*
Collection Center for Visual Music, gift of Fischinger Trust, Long Beach, CA

Example 1: Komposition In Blau

This segment of a graphic score (fig. 2) of the overture to *The Merry Wives of Windsor* by Otto Nicolai (the soundtrack for this film) features two lines of notation, the upper representing a musical outline, and the lower, aspects of the animation. Like many of the graphic scores this is drawn on graph paper, with one square representing one frame of animation.

The start of this segment corresponds with the 4008th frame of the animation.[3] This section of the film features five cubic formations, which rapidly rise and fall from the "floor." Behind these is placed an arrangement of two-dimensional circles, which appear to grow or move towards the viewer. The score represents an accurate representation of the timing of this animation—small peaks representing the rising and falling of the cube formations (rising quickly and falling slightly slower over the "upbeat" into each bar), with curved formations representing the "growth" of the circles, which either take one bar or two bars to complete their animated sequence, as shown by Fischinger's notation.

There are several points throughout the score where the movement of the stop-frame animation is notated in similar detail. Elsewhere, the animation timeline is blocked off with horizontal numbered lines, believed to represent sub-sequences notated in detail elsewhere. These sequences are repeated, and cross-referencing repetitions proves this supposition at least in principle. As an example, sequence 7 at frame 4305 is clearly the same as sequence 7 at frame 4831 (Fischinger's frame numbers), a distinctive sequence where five rounded staffs (somewhat akin to the shapes used in *Staffs* and *Raumlichtkunst*) bounce up and down in time with the downbeat, followed by the appearance of five circles behind them.

Example 2: An American March

This fragment (fig. 3) depicts the first two bars of Sousa's *Stars and Stripes* march, used by Fischinger for this film. The central black and red section represents the music in four distinct representations. The top one shows the main melody, with next line down showing the accompaniment/bassline. The third shows a rhythmic breakdown of the music omitting all pitch information, but still showing the main "events" for both the top and bottom levels of the music. Every note shown in the top three lines has a red "tail" which appears to give an impression of the volume or energy of the notes as they decay. The last offers the most intriguing representation—a series of "spikes" drawn in thick black graphite pencil, some of which align with the events of the first three strips, but many of which do not.

Above this is an area detailing the animation. Although here there is no graphical representation, considerable timing information is given—this gives us a great deal of insight both into the animation for this sequence, and into Fischinger's "interpretation" of the music here.

It is clear that Fischinger has chosen to use these four bars as an exposition to reveal the flag; the first two-bar melodic phrase representing the stars and the second the stripes. This interpretation has logic and charm—the first phrase being rhythmically angular and jaunty, like the graphical form of a star; and the second being entirely regular, both in terms of pitch (an ascending semitone scale) and rhythm (every note being the same length), evoking the uniformity of a series of stripes. Fischinger does indeed illustrate the first phrase with five stars, which would seem to reflect the fact that there are five notes in the melody of this phrase. However, note that while there are five notes and five stars, none are precisely aligned. Since both the music and the animation are meticulously notated to frame accuracy this cannot be a mistake—rather Fischinger seems to have carefully constructed his own syncopated rhythm which reflects but does not mimic Sousa's music.

The second phrase is accompanied by annotations referring to six stripes.[4] It is not immediately obvious how the six lines, or stripes, appear in the animation for this section, which seems on first viewing to consist of a bottom-top wipe revealing the American flag. However, closer examination reveals that each annotation is exactly aligned with the first appearance of one of the six lines of the flag, and that the bottom-top "wipe" is actually something more sophisticated: Fischinger subtly places visual rhythmic emphasis on the white stripes by making them appear more slowly—each white stripe takes four frames to appear, whilst the red stripes (equal in width) take only one. The appearance of each white line is also accompanied by the appearance of one of the six lines of stars, making this "reveal" considerably more complex than it might first appear.

The collection also contains interesting scores connected with *Studie Nr. 8* (*Study No. 8*), *An Optical Poem*, *Muratti Greift Ein* (*Muratti Gets in the Act*), and others, and is further explored in my essay "From Score to Screen: Towards a Musicological Approach to the Visual Music Works of Oskar Fischinger."

3
Note that Fischinger's frame numbers may not correspond exactly to digitized copies of the films, which are likely to be at 30 fps rather than the original 24. In this instance, the frame number can be corroborated with the printed score, annotated by Fischinger and also found in the CVM score collection.

4
Fischinger actually uses the word *Linie* (line).

Essay without Words
Motion Painting No. 1, Insight, and the Ornament

James Tobias

"My Statements are in My Work."
Oskar Fischinger[1]

For a 1956 exhibition of his work at the Pasadena Art Museum, Oskar Fischinger provided a summary description of artistic methods on evident display in *Motion Painting No. 1* (1947, figs. 1–4). Fischinger wrote:

> But painting in motion, combined with music, or painting *without* motion: that is the problem. … "Motion paintings" give to the painter a new potentiality. He must develop and become something like a "visual-motionist," creating not only in space but in time. Within sixty seconds or sixty minutes he must present not only one static, frame-able two- or three-dimensional creations of a virtual nature, but he must also create sentence after sentence of moving, developing visual images changing and changing, in continuously different ways. At times, these may be composed of successive ideas, bringing new life into images. Forms are basic, but changes develop from the orchestration of forms and lines and colors. This is a tremendous new world—a tremendous new tool—a challenge to creativeness comparable only to music.[2]

Fischinger's comments clarify his goals and achievements in arguably his finest film, *Motion Painting No. 1*, in ways we recognize today as both "intermedial" and "transmedial." The intermediality rests in the film's elaboration of musical affect as painting in motion in a carefully modulated synchronization of sound and image. His use of optical sound film confirms the independent art cinema's by then long, varied use of optical sound film to test and breach sound cinema conventions: a resistant mode of transmedia production.[3] A key figure in intermedial and transmedial modernisms, Fischinger's career-long development of musical film, paintings, and media devices consistently resisted limits on artistic expression arising within the standardization and rationalization of industrial film. Yet his comments also present a challenge when placing both *Motion Painting No. 1* and his own body of work in historical retrospect. If his works contain "statements," what, precisely, do they say—and how do they say it?

The "forms, lines, and colors" of *Motion Painting No. 1* recapitulate and develop insights into audiovisual temporality to the extent that musicality in this work extends *beyond* the patterns of temporal relations its formal elements mark off, and to the varying relations of synchronization *between* auditory and visual streams. Granting *Motion Painting No. 1* the status of a film essay highlights the needs to account for the complex temporalities of Fischinger's film work as historical in their own right, and to observe his films' exhibition of continuity and transformation in relation to larger processes of cinema production and of history.

Fischinger highlighted the continuity and metamorphosis cohering in his work as a matter of non-propositional truth value. Describing *Motion Painting No. 1*, he rejected montage orientations and emphasized higher-order continuity, poetic insight, and aesthetic observation: "The film isn't 'cut,' it is a continuity, the absolute truth, the creative truth. Any observer can verify that, and I consider myself an observer."[4] Yet what continues across the interval of the film frame, or over the gaps of political displacement (the flight from the Third Reich) or economic or critical marginalization?[5] What constitutes the "words" communicated in *Motion Painting No. 1's* "sentences" of sound and image?

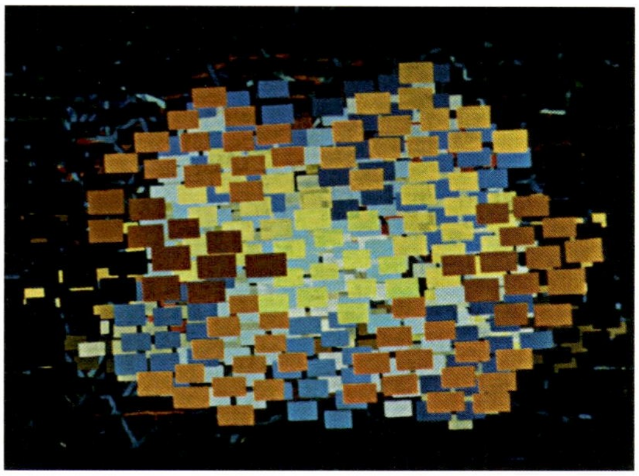
Figure 1 / Still from *Motion Painting No. 1*, 1947
35mm, color, sound

Fischinger painted *Motion Painting No. 1* on successive sheets of Plexiglas, exposing the camera shutter for each stroke of paint (fig. 5, p. 158). The cumulative result projects a constantly transforming sequence of musical paintings in roughly three movements whose non-similar resemblance to one another surprises and satisfies as each develops from the last. Still, the processes of instantiation and return in this film are familiar from his larger body of work. The tessellated patterning seen in *Motion Painting No. 1* appears in earlier canvases such as *Plan* (1938) and later in *Flower* (c. 1950) or *Abstract Landscape* (1959). The stroke-by-stroke patterning (also used by other modernist painters interested in color harmonics) projects a shimmering texture at once whole and fragmented.

Beyond producing historical reference, though, the technique reflexively informs this film's consistency across its non-similar variations. In the opening, a softly glimmering, tessellated field provides the backdrop for a spiral at center frame to bloom upward as it traces its own development. The tessellated background, then, pictures the larger result

1
Oskar Fischinger, "My Statements are in My Work," in *Art in Cinema*, ed. Frank Stauffacher (San Francisco: Art in Cinema Society-San Francisco Museum of Art, 1947). Reprinted in this volume, pp. 112–13).

2
Oskar Fischinger, "A Document Concerning *PAINTING*" (1956), repr. in William Moritz, *Optical Poetry: The Life and Work of Oskar Fischinger* (London, UK: John Libbey Publishing, 2004), 188–89.

3
Today, "transmedia" refers to production across platforms afforded by digital equipment; in Fischinger's time, optical sound film used for sound, image, or synchronized sound and image production arguably afforded an earlier transmedia production.

4
Oskar Fischinger, "True Creation," courtesy of The Fischinger Trust and Archive, available at www.oskarfischinger.org/True%20Creation.html (accessed August 1, 2012); originally published as "Véritable Creation," *Le Cinéma À Knokke-Le-Zoute* (1950), 35–37.

5
Moritz, *Optical Poetry*, passim.

of the additive painting and photographing of color strokes by which the film proceeds. Later in the work a dotted line traces, as if with cinematic needlepoint, what might be abstracted huts against a similarly abstracted landscape across the expanse of the screen-canvas. A tessellating-tracing of part and pattern is disclosed over the course of the work, background glimmer becoming vibrant theme. As this development of part and pattern is introduced, elaborated, and dissolved into yet another field of potential to be developed later, it informs the film's developments and conclusions—and reflexively situates the film in relation to historical motives and contexts.

Figure 2 / Still from *Motion Painting No. 1*, 1947
35mm, color, sound

Graphical ornaments revealing and differentiating processes of instantiation and return in *Motion Painting No. 1* are familiar from the other film work, too. The second movement of *Motion Painting No. 1* presents concentric circles formed as a spiraling line traces its own contours, finally closing off each cycle as the line's leading edge draws back to the center of the now completed spiral. New iterations open up from each closed figure until the field of vision becomes a network of concentric circles drawn as flattened spirals. These spiral and circular forms are readily identifiable across Fischinger's body of work, from the *Spiralen* experiments (*Spirals*, 1926), to the circle-themed *Kreise* (*Circles*, 1933–34) or the pulsing orbs of *Radio Dynamics* (1942) among others. In *Motion Painting No. 1*, though, their development is resolved in terms of unexpected coherence. Instead of spiral or circle becoming dominant, a network mapping the hearts of the spiral-circles to one another emerges and gives rise to the next—third—movement, in which distributed movement across space becomes primary. Circle; spiral; spreading mesh: the complex graphical synthesis of cinematic space and time plays loosely against the vigorous *ritornello* of Bach's "Brandenburg Concerto No. 3." Just as music and image move together more or less closely but always pulse forward, each movement of the film proceeds in terms of topographical transformations, not always predictable, and mediated by the duration of the painterly line traced stroke by stroke. While the developmental revelations the film exhibits proceed in forward-moving, linear temporality, the return and development of complex graphical and audiovisual relations cannot be reduced to a simple linear relation.

Figure 3 / Still from *Motion Painting No. 1*, 1947
35mm, color, sound

Rather, historical duration, cinematic time, and sustained spectatorship are mediated in terms of pulsing gesture, revealing the process of composing poetic insight as aesthetic observation. The film thus prescribes an interpretive process within which insight into audiovisual relation as explication of entangled cinematic and historical time is subjected to aesthetic observation. In its formal recurrence, the rhythmic spiral of part-and-pattern appears as the visual complement of the concerto's *ritornello*. The circling spiral ornament becomes the temporalized emblem of our rhythmic, open-ended observation of the film as attention wanders from image to sound, to sound and image, to image: attention and distraction at play. The result is a superabundant measuring of poetic insight as aesthetic observation according to musical instrumentalities rather than technical ones.

Fischinger described this rhythmic effect as an "optical dance":

> This music, concerto by Bach, is like a smooth river flowing on the side of open fields— And what you see—is not translated music, because music doesn't need to be translated on the screen—to the Eyes music is in itself enough—but the optical part is like we walk on the other side of the river—sometimes we go a little bit farther off (away) but we come back and go along on this river, the concerto by Bach.[6]

Motion Painting No.1 is the virtuoso instance; we see this play of attention and distraction throughout Fischinger's career. The play of part and pattern, continuity and transformation unfurled in *Motion Painting No.1* informs this film's recapitulation of both Fischinger's compositional methods to this point *and* the larger history of aesthetic invention underpinning this film. Ultimately, this history is that of modernisms aiming to reveal the unseen and unheard energies of both a relativistic cosmos and a potentially creative mass culture. *Motion Painting No.1* presents the modernity of graphically composing processual media art, but it also presents an essay on method and on the historical motivations and achievements of method: an essay, without words, on musicality, modernity, and time.

Fischinger's use of part and pattern via motion ornaments such as spirals and circles to project "creative truth" has been criticized as semiotically naïve. Mistakenly describing Fischinger's sound ornaments as continuous, linear curves, Levin argues that Fischinger was unable to produce a semiotically rigorous, acoustically specific, combinatorial (and thus identifiably modern) "techno-logic of writing" sound.[7] The mischaracterization is as common as it is useful to reconsider. Fischinger's sound ornaments or spiral motifs are only particular motion ornaments; for him the temporalized ornament functioned as a contingent, creative heuristic affording aesthetic experimentation wherein technical development followed poetic insight, and wherein poetic insight was to be communicated in terms of "sensory force,"[8] meaning, affectively rather than in semiotic or technological terms.

Less interested in a semiotics of synthetic sound (or of a simulation of synesthesia), Fischinger was more interested in a process in which creative insight might cohere in trans-subjective, aesthetic observation shared by artist and audience alike. Poetic insight observed to cohere aesthetically in its affective communicability was what he referred to as "creative truth." Not propositional, representational, or neuropsychological, this affective communicability mobilized continuity and transformation at times irreducible to one another and irreducible to the logics of technical inscription delivering it. It is precisely the irreducibility of sound and image to one another's spatiotemporal rendering (whether or not closely synchronized), and his resistance to systematizing technics underlying that irreducibility, that makes Fischinger's work consistently modern.

Motion Painting No.1 is the summary document of Fischinger's animation of cinema's potential to musically modulate, to reveal as affective force, the unseen, unheard pulse of modern temporalities and epistemologies. In his words, *Motion Painting No.1*'s "sentences" of temporalized ornament neither systematize visual notation or acoustic transcription, nor translate musical form or psychological experience, but give particular insight into affect's communicability:

> Sometimes it is dark and you see in the darkness nothing but your own feeling your own movements your own pulse and the rapture of your heart your blood this is what you see what goes with the music—the Stars the Heaven the Darkness and the Light of your own love your own heart The Light of your mind The Dancing Light of your blood—and your feeling.[9]

6
Oskar Fischinger, "A Document Related to Motion Painting I," in Moritz, *Optical Poetry*, 185.

7
Thomas Levin, "'Tones from out of Nowhere: Rudolph Pfenninger and the Archaeology of Synthetic Sound," *Grey Room*, 12 (Summer 2003), 32–79, 50–59.

8
Oskar Fischinger, unpublished typescript, Collection Center for Visual Music, Document 300160, c. 1932. Here Fischinger argues that graphical composition methods might remedy loss of fidelity in reproduction and of detail when executed by others, but: "Even a creative artist may not be able to do so [that is, recreate an original work beyond its original instance and format of composition], potentially, since his own development always advances farther, and processes specific to their times may not be able to be recovered in their original purity, requisite form, and sensory force."

9
Oskar Fischinger, "A Document Related to Motion Painting I," in Moritz, *Optical Poetry*, 185–86.

This comment confirms that the affect at stake here is that of the ecstatic: the withdrawing of borders between inner and outer movement. But how does the work, so particular to its own intermedial, transmedial moment, attain to the particularity of feeling? Fischinger's mysterious comments suggest not semiotic ill-rigor, but the temporal ornament as a material, reflexive sign-form instantiated as an aesthetic-perceptual series to be repeated, transformed, disseminated, or dispersed. Contemporary analog to Bloch's "carpet motif,"[10] the temporal ornament provided both container and content for the affective communicability evidenced in the measured sensory experience of the work.

Semioticians note that film's indexicality is always entangled with iconic and symbolic traits.[11] Fischinger's 1930s comments on "sounding ornaments" suggest he understood the same to be true of sound inscription, but also illuminate his concerns with temporalized ornament, affective communicability, and technical process. He describes one ornament as a target shape sounding like an electric bell when projected.[12] In practice, that target shape would repeat as a pattern varying in size (the focal distance of the camera effected differences in volume). The temporal ornament, in Fischinger, has aesthetico-perceptual duration when rendered as an event-series, but *need not be a sign in the semiotic sense*. Fischinger notes that similar vibrating circles used in early cartoons denoted the ringing of a bell: a mnemonic aspect of the ornament-as-event-series, determined in part through familiar mass cultural experience, lends itself to the temporalized ornament's deployment in a highly—not primarily—technical process.[13]

In the temporal ornament, symbolic, iconic, or indexical meanings may mingle as potential values to be determined in a workflow conditioning and conditioned by aesthetic actions producing new artworks and new aesthetic forms, processes, and relations. Once observable in terms of sensation, meaning is left to the observer to determine. If he described one ornament as sounding like a bassoon to demonstrate "an inner relation to this instrument," such relation subsists in vibration corresponding to higher-level, potential motion—affect to be actualized in sensible motion, not in representation. As he makes clear in his typescript "The Composer of the Future," particular visual or auditory perceptions disclose not presence but movement: change.[14] The temporal ornament affords a rendering of poetic insight communicable to observation in sensory force.

As pressing in his time as in ours, the problem of relating insight to action as creative and technical act has less to do

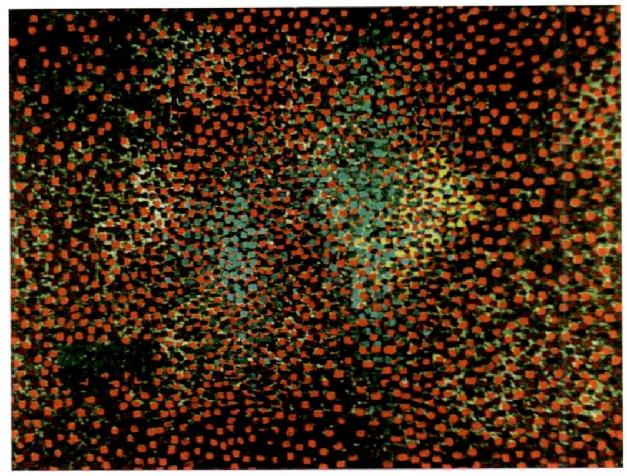

Figure 4 / Still from *Motion Painting No.1*, 1947
35mm, color, sound

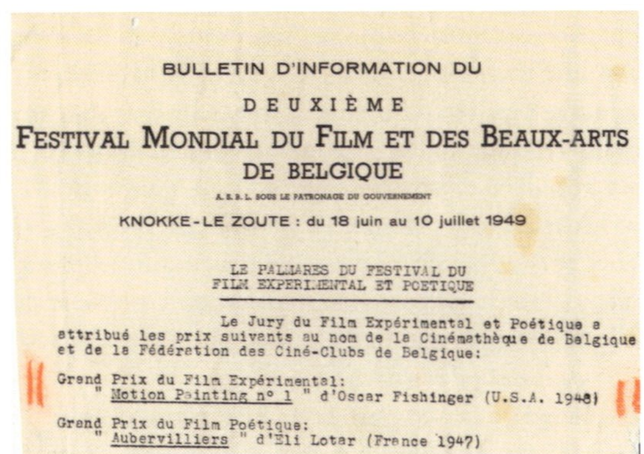

BULLETIN D'INFORMATION DU

DEUXIÈME

FESTIVAL MONDIAL DU FILM ET DES BEAUX-ARTS

DE BELGIQUE

A.S.B.L. SOUS LE PATRONAGE DU GOUVERNEMENT

KNOKKE-LE ZOUTE : du 18 juin au 10 juillet 1949

LE PALMARES DU FESTIVAL DU
FILM EXPERIMENTAL ET POETIQUE

Le Jury du Film Expérimental et Poétique a attribué les prix suivants au nom de la Cinémathèque de Belgique et de la Fédération des Ciné-Clubs de Belgique:

Grand Prix du Film Expérimental:
" Motion Painting n° 1 " d'Oscar Fishinger (U.S.A. 1948)

Grand Prix du Film Poétique:
" Aubervilliers " d'Eli Lotar (France 1947)

Figure 5 / Award from *Festival Mondial du Film et des Beaux-arts de Belgique*, Knokke-Le Zoute, 1949
During this period Fischinger used both the Americanized "Oscar" and the German "Oskar," though he settled on "Oskar," as used on his film head credits
Collection Center for Visual Music

with representational theory than with *phronēsis*, or bringing insight to bear on particular, situated experience.[15] As Brogan explains, for Heidegger, *phronēsis* is a "noetic" holding in view of "the particular being that appears in the fullness of its being at the moment ... without *logos* in one sense, [it] remains a simple saying of being in a higher sense."[16] *Phronēsis* shares with *technē* a capacity for disclosing. *Technē* discloses "produced beings"; *phronēsis* leads to action disclosing the particularity of human being itself (174–75). And as Vorris Nunley recently suggests, as *phronēsis* articulates practical wisdom, intellect or virtue, it brings the theoretical to bear upon use such that the shared fortifies the subjective.[17]

Needing to invent industrial techniques in support of particularly modern, popularly accessible, and critically singular aesthetic projects, Fischinger and others had to re-frame the Heideggerian distinction between *technē* and *phronēsis* in terms like those Nunley emphasizes. They re-framed the particularity of modern human existence differentiable from a technics of produced beings as a problem of the particularity of poetic insight enabling media reception as creative act of observation. Here, musical expressivity exhibits the fullness of the particular artwork in its technical exhibition, substituting for the industrial instrumentalization of sound and vision a *phronēsis* shared, within limits, with the audience. This counter-cinema joined competing efforts to intervene in the subjection of the cinematic apparatus to the financial and artistic constraints of studio production.

For Fischinger, the temporalized ornament correlated poetic insight and aesthetic observation with a sensory force experienced as a particular, creative truth of being-in-mass-mediation. The spiraling parts and patterns of *Motion Painting No. 1* externalize insight as an art in, and of, differential motion, in an ecstatic, affective cinema: "The Light of your mind The Dancing Light of your blood—and your feeling." To render such insight cinematic demanded a poetic act beyond the powers of technoscience:

> There are many things in nature before which our mind remains in wonder, without the mind's eye mastering or a sophisticated cortex penetrating this mysterious, evocative weaving to descend into the darkness of the unexplored and clarify still unseen relationships. Here even the physicist must halt, and here lie, too, the boundaries of his world. Only poets gifted with higher imagination may perhaps intuitively see into deeper darkness, to penetrate it and glimpse relationships that can not be proven immediately.[18]

Motion Painting No. 1 disclosed unprovable insights to audience eyes and ears in radiant fashion in its day. Today it offers a historical essay without words recapitulating the creative forces it disclosed, along with the material histories that the film's exhibition of those forces still communicates.

10
James Tobias, *Sync: Stylistics of Hieroglyphic Time* (Philadelphia: Temple University Press, 2010), 89–98.

11
Peter Wollen, *Signs and Meaning in the Cinema* (Bloomington: Indiana University Press, 1972).

12
Oskar Fischinger, Collection Center for Visual Music, Document 300160.

13
A second ornament produced a "flute-like tone" bearing "a startling resemblance to the figure of a snake," suggesting more the relation of snake charmer to snake than of the snake to itself.

14
Oskar Fischinger, "The Composer of the Future and the Absolute Sound Film," unpublished typescript, Collection Center for Visual Music. Included in this volume (pp. 96–97).

15
Among many examples, see the history of neuroscientific and aesthetic insight in modernisms in Eric Kandel, *The Age of Insight: The Quest to Understand the Unconscious in Art, Mind, and Brain, from Vienna 1900 to the Present* (New York: Random House, 2012).

16
Walter Brogan, *Heidegger and Aristotle: the Twofoldness of Being* (Albany: SUNY University Press, 2005), 175.

17
Vorris Nunley, *Keepin' It Hushed: The Barbershop and African American Hush Harbor Rhetoric* (Detroit: Wayne State University Press, 2011), 47.

18
Oskar Fischinger, untitled, undated typescript, Collection Center for Visual Music, Document 300165, c. 1932. Author's translation.

Figure 6 / Oskar Fischinger in his Hollywood studio with panels from *Motion Painting No. 1*, 1949
Collection Center for Visual Music

Oskar Fischinger and Visual Music

Fischinger Misconstrued Visual Music Does Not Equal Synesthesia

Paul Hertz

Art that links together compositional elements in different sensory modalities is frequently labeled "synesthetic art." The term tends to confuse rather than to clarify. Synesthesia, the involuntary experience of a stimulus in one sensory modality reliably causing a specific perception in another, is a neurological phenomenon. People may be synesthetic. Art works are not.

It is particularly inappropriate to characterize Fischinger's visual music as "synesthetic." It was not a term he advocated. His work reveals a strong formal understanding of music. Works that include a soundtrack do not always display strict correspondence to musical events, but they are always informed by them. Where there is correspondence, of phrasing to spatial motion or of rhythm to shifts in scale, for example, the correspondences vary within a given composition and across the entire oeuvre. It is emphatically not synesthetic.

Why is "synesthetic" such a readily used adjective for visual music? Confusion about poetic language and confusion over the cognitive effects of art that crosses boundaries between media or that addresses multiple senses seem to elicit most misuses. The language that some artists used in writing about cross-modal art has confused matters further.

Long before the current vogue for synesthesia or synesthetic art, in the nineteenth century, "fusion of the senses" served as an engine for innovation in poetry, theater and opera. The sociologist-philosopher Pierre Leroux saw in the accord of the senses a moment when the perception of "harmonic vibrations" inherent in natural phenomena opens the mind to an experience of Nature's inner meaning: "when this accord is expressed, it is a symbol."[1] Charles Baudelaire, perhaps influenced by Leroux, set in motion a new poetics: "Nature is a temple of living pillars…where perfumes, sounds and colors correspond."[2] A generation later, Arthur Rimbaud prided himself on creating "a poetic language accessible some day to all the senses," to which he reserved exclusive rights of translation.[3] In Symbolist poetics, fusion of the senses operates as an act of imagination mediated through art, not as a re-creation of sensory experience. Language that blends the senses signals, through its halo of associations in the mind of the reader, the possibility of transcendent insight.

Contemporary with Symbolism, a movement towards fusion of the arts took place within theater and opera. The

1
Pierre Leroux, "De la Poésie de notre époque," 1831, citation from *Symbolist Art Theories*, ed. Henri Dorra (University of California Press, Berkeley, 1994). Notably, Leroux understands the accord of the senses to be produced not by a neurological condition but by "harmonic vibrations" inherent in natural phenomena, perhaps in reference to the mathematics of wave functions emerging at the time he wrote.

2
Charles Baudelaire, "Correspondances," in *Fleurs de Mal* (pub. 1857).

3
Arthur Rimbaud, "Alchemy of the Word," in *Rimbaud: Complete Works* (Chicago: University of Chicago Press, 1966), 193–95.

intent was to create a spectacle where different arts and sensory modalities would coincide. The Wagnerian *Gesamtkunstwerk* is arguably its most famous manifestation. The project of a synthesis of the arts gave rise to a metaphoric language similar to that of the Symbolists, though its intent was more practical than poetic. A dramaturgy that aimed to encompass diverse art forms and sensory modalities found it convenient to map their languages onto one another. Again, there is no literal fusing of the senses, rather there is conceptual mapping and blending within a language whose purpose is to join multiple arts upon a single stage.

Similarly, the use in visual art of a formal language derived in part from music is not the same as fusion of the senses: it is the conceptual scaffolding for a new art form. Artists who were interested in creating a new, abstract visual art turned to music as a readymade descriptive and formal language. In his theoretical writing, Wassily Kandinsky uses both music and speech as extended metaphors for visual abstraction. In *On the Spiritual in Art* (1912) in particular, he implies that cross-modal fusion can evoke spiritual insight. In this, he echoes not only Symbolist poetics but the popular mysticism of Theosophism, which turned tropes back into literal, if elusive, experience—those adept in spiritual disciplines may expect to experience a transcendent fusion of the senses.

Of course, the use of the word "synesthetic" to describe visual music, intermedia, or multimodal art in general isn't necessarily intended to suggest that a *neurological* fusion exists. The problem lies not in inaccuracy with respect to its original, scientific meaning, but with the way it elides a whole series of historical developments, assuming that they can all be explained by one tendency, a synesthetic tendency. They cannot. One is tempted to attribute this to laziness, but the real problem may lie in the way we once conceived of art history from Romanticism on: as a succession of avant-gardes driven by aesthetic and social advancement. Though the avant-garde has withered, the idea of progress it fostered persists, with its crises and resolutions. Disciplines as diverse as chaos theory and network theory are providing us with new models of causality in the digital humanities. These models may serve us better to understand the historical development of visual music, intermedia, and cross-modal art—as a diachronic web of influences and ideas, rather than as a unified tendency.

Fischinger's visual music has been mistakenly labeled "synesthetic art" because the meaning of the word "synesthesia" has been stretched, particularly in writing about art from the 1960s on. Gene Youngblood, in his landmark book *Expanded Cinema*, applied it to emergent new media art that allows simultaneous perception of "harmonic opposites." He used the term to distinguish non-linear "evocative" cinema from expository "narrative" cinema. However, he specified that "synesthetic cinema" would be "primarily poetic in structure and effect."[4] The ethnomusicologist Alan P. Merriam may have been combating the loose interpretation of synesthesia popularized during the psychedelic 60s ("I hear colors" was a catchphrase of the times) when he devoted a chapter of his text *The Anthropology of Music* (1964) to distinguishing many different forms of sensory cross-modality, embedded in perception, culture and language, of which synesthesia was but one small manifestation.[5]

We would then advocate that "synesthetic" be reserved for work that actively sought the label, however misapplied, and not stretched to include visual music, intermedia, or all cross-modal art. It is important to keep our terms straight because that will help us to understand the history of their use and consequently the history of new art forms. It will unconfuse us. That is an end devoutly to be desired.

4
Gene Youngblood, *Expanded Cinema* (P. Dutton and Company, New York, 1970), 92.

5
Alan P. Merriam, "Synesthesia and Intersense Modalities," in *The Anthropology of Music* (Evanston: Northwestern University Press, 1964).

Oskar Fischinger, Berlin, early 1930s
Collection Center for Visual Music

Optical Expression: Oskar Fischinger, William Moritz and Visual Music

An Edited Guide to the Key Concerns

Cindy Keefer

Oskar Fischinger is credited as the father of Visual Music, but what does this really mean? What were his thoughts on "visual music," a phrase not found in his writings until the mid-1940s (along with "optick music" and "augenmusik")? Is he labeled the father of the genre due to his far-reaching influence on generations of animators and filmmakers, rather than as its strongest practitioner?

Yet any question as to Fischinger's place in the genre presupposes a more basic one: what exactly is visual music? There is a hundred year history of Visual Music on film, and a bibliography stretching back centuries. Interest in the correspondences of sound to color, and music to image, extend back to Aristotle, Pythagoras, and Issac Newton. Today, definitions of Visual Music rapidly change as the field expands.[1] William Moritz, who devoted thirty-five years to the study of Fischinger and Visual Music, described in 1986 "A music for the eye comparable to the effects of sound for the ear," and asked, "What are the visual equivalents of melody, harmony, rhythm and counterpoint?"[2] Moritz also explained:

> Visual music enjoys a long and complex history - from the philosophical speculations of Aristotle and Leonardo, through the color organs of Father Castel and Rimington, Scriabin's Mysterium, to the abstract animated films of Eggeling, Ruttmann and Fischinger, the Dada/Surrealist "poems" of Man Ray or the Satie-Picabia-Clair *Entr'acte*, or the equally Surrealist films of Len Lye. This tradition ranges from works of a luxuriant organic Romantic dynamism (such as Thomas Wilfred's Lumia) to more spare, strictly geometric and mathematically precise works such as the Bauhaus "Light-Show" performances.[3]

Simplistic ideas of Visual Music presume a direct illustration or translation of music and thus Fischinger's earlier films are sometimes mistakenly written off as "Mickey Mouse synchronization." Yet a more accurate preliminary definition of Visual Music would be "the translation of a specific musical composition (or sound) into a visual language, with the original syntax being emulated in the new visual rendition."[4]

"My films are no illustrations of music," Fischinger declared in a 1947 statement, "Corrections to Richters [sic] Article." He explained that in his early Studies he used music simply as "an architectural ground plan" from which he took the time and rhythm [transcription of original]:

> With the absolute film, music is used to put it over, but the development of optical expression, the invention of new ways of motion in coordination with the Rythmus given in

> the music ... the invention of new Ways of motion is the main ... Idea, the main force, and the time—or Rythmus cordination with music is secondary of less importance. People who say that [these] films are illustrations to music, are...poor in their imagination...or say so intentionaly to lessen the impact of [these] works (for personal reasons...Probably Richters reason). I found out this way of saying (illustrations of music) is mostly used by people who feel themselfes to be my adversarys because maybe subconsciously they would like to have done it themselfes but for some reason were unabble to do it.[5]

Fischinger also noted in this 1947 statement that not all of his films are sound films; according to his dates, he made silent films for ten years before making any of the synchronized Studies. In a letter to Hans Richter written in the same period (June 16, 1947), he stated, "I never tried to translate sound into visual expressions."

Not surprisingly, Moritz argued against simplistic readings of Fischinger's work with his assertion that, in visual music, music requires sophisticated levels of synchronized imagery:

> Fischinger's tight synchronization to jazz in a film like *Allegretto* demonstrates that music demands more than just a thump-thump-thump rhythmic beat—rather a complex, layered "symphony" of integrated parts, with rhythmic background, harmonic supports, melodic bravura solos—and some overall integrity of color and form to suggest the structural dynamics of key signatures and development/resolution patterns in the music.[6]

Elsewhere Moritz explains:

> Similarly in Fischinger's *Allegretto*, we see a viable visual equivalent for orchestral music, with rhythmic pulsations of circles and matrix hue in the background to suggest rhythm and general key signature, while several layers of shapes in various mutating colors and clusters move in complementary patterns in the foreground to suggest melodies, harmonies and counterpoints. Not surprisingly, *Allegretto* is immensely satisfying, and has an almost infinite re-play value. The same could be said of other Fischinger films (including the silent *Radio Dynamics*).[7]

Asked, "What are the goals of your *Farbenfilmspiele* [color film plays]?" Fischinger himself emphasized affective, even spiritual qualities associated with musical effects and experience:

> Just as audible music is born out of the immaterial from the soul, first from one soul and then again and again can be born through others, and the invisible tones of this music fall into the soul of the listener and move him, so are these optic, unfolding, creative, abstract color-symphonies not to be sought in the material. The material that the colors mediate in the film on the projection wall are only comparable to instruments. The color-movement over the screen leaves hardly any traces behind. The color-light waves fly through the eye into the soul of the observer just like sound waves of music.[8]

Along these lines, Fischinger emphasized film's potential to achieve properly musical effects similar to, but independent of, those of musical sound: "This art emphasizes the effect of music. It is to music what wings are to birds. Figures and forms have a definite effect on the consciousness. When they are in color the effect is emphasized. The staccato movement of rows of geometrical figures on the screen will get the same reaction from a person as the staccato sounds from a musical instrument."[9]

Within the idea of general correspondences between auditory and visual forms lies the notion of a descriptive

1
Jack Ox and Cindy Keefer, "On Curating Recent Digital Abstract Visual Music," Abstract Visual Music Project, New York Digital Salon, School of Visual Arts, 2006.

2
William Moritz, "Towards an Aesthetic of Visual Music," *Asifa Canada Bulletin* (Montreal: ASIFA Canada), 14/3 (December 1986). Online at www.centerforvisualmusic.org/TAVM.htm

3
William Moritz, "James Whitney Retrospective," *Toronto 84 International Animation Festival* (program notes Canadian International Animation Festival, March 1984). Collection Center for Visual Music, Los Angeles. Online at www.centerforvisualmusic.org/library/WMJamesWRetro.htm

4
Ox and Keefer, 2006 (see note 1).

5
Transcription including original spelling of excerpt from 1947 document titled "Corrections to Richters [sic] Article about the History of the Avantgarde." Unpubished typescript. Richter's article was published in the 1946 *Art in Cinema* catalog and contained numerous errors, particularly about Fischinger. Fischinger was so angry about the misrepresentation of his and others' work, and Richter's rewriting of their histories, that he wrote in a June 13, 1947 handwritten draft of a letter to Richter, "You are not worthy to polish Ruttmann's shoes, if he were still alive," and "all that was good in your work you stole from Eggeling." Fischinger wrote numerous drafts of letters to Hans Richter during this period correcting Richter's errors; it is not known which of these drafts was actually sent. All documents, Fischinger Collection, Center for Visual Music, Los Angeles.

6
"Visuelle Musik: Höhlenmalereien für MTV? (Visual Music: Cave Painting to MTV?)," *Sound & Vision*, ed. Walter Schobert (Frankfurt: Deutsches Filmmuseum, 1993), 132–45. Online at www.centerforvisualmusic.org/library/WMCavePtgs.htm

7
Moritz, 1986 (see note 2).

8
Question and answer from unpublished typescript, interview with Fischinger by Bert Reisfeld, likely c. 1950. Collection Center for Visual Music, Fischinger Document 300610. (transl. Amy Hough)

9
Oskar Fischinger, quoted in, Herman G. Weinberg, *Foreword to the Invitation Preview of the Representative Work of Oskar Fischinger*, at the 5th Avenue Playhouse, New York, 1948. Collection of Center for Visual Music.

equivalence of specific instances: visual music as "translation." The direct translation of image to sound is sometimes labeled as a 'pure' type of visual music, as in Fischinger's 1930s *Ornamente Ton* (*Ornament Sound*), and in works by Norman McLaren (*Synchromy*), Barry Spinello (*Six Loop Paintings*), Lis Rhodes (*Dresden Dynamo*), Guy Sherwin (*Soundtrack*), Richard Reeves (*Linear Dreams*), Devin Damonte and other filmmakers. Moritz explains the origin of Fischinger's interest:

> Having studied Pythagoras, alchemy, and Buddhism, he was fascinated by the notion that every element and object contained an essential personality that could be revealed by the visionary artist who found a technical formula through which the material could speak for itself. These ideas survived throughout Fischinger's work and bore fruit in the 1930s, when he filmed representational shapes and abstract ornaments onto the sound-track area of the filmstrip in order to release the innate sounds locked inside silent, or nonmusical, objects—a theory he explained to Edgard Varèse and John Cage with crucial effect on their compositions.[10]

Fischinger's texts on this work are included in this volume, online, and in Moritz's *Optical Poetry*: *The Life and Work of Oskar Fischinger*. It is interesting to discover that Fischinger was on the other hand critical of transformations of sounds to images made mechanically. He felt all had the same result, and lacked the soul of the artist: "just a sound vibration changed into a light vibration—through mechanical means." He emphasized that, "A machine has no spirit."[11]

Fischinger's last major film, *Motion Painting No.1*, is perhaps his most creative use of varied music synchronization. Numerous statements and notes by him exist about this film.

> And what you see—is not translated music, because music doesn't need to be translated on the screen—to the Eyes music is in itself enough—but the optical part is like we walk on the side of the river—sometimes we go a little bit farther off (away) but we come back and go along on this river, the concerto by Bach.
> The optical part is no perfect synchronization of every wave of the river—it is a very free walk, nothing is forced, nothing is synchronized except in great steps.
> The film is in some parts perfectly synchronized with the music, but in other parts it runs free—without caring much about the music—it is like a pleasant walk on the side of a river—If the river springs, we on the side do not necessarily spring to it—but go our own free way—sometimes we even go a little bit away from the river and later come back to it and love it so much more—because we were away from it. Sometimes we go up a little while on the side of the river and the river goes low through a tunnel or under a bridge but we are all the time with the river near the river we hear the sound of the river and we love it and the river is the music of Bach.[12]

If musical form, experience or effect was key for Fischinger's goals, it appears that this was not because of any aesthetic value assigned to music over other art forms, but because music provided key insights for developing this art of movement. For Fischinger, "In *Motion Painting Number One*, for the first time, visual music was born, creating that deep, emotional, almost pleasurable feeling (as we know it) that we get from good music."[13] A few years later, Fischinger spoke of his intent, his work, and his expectations:

> What always interested me about film was the possibility to draw and paint movement, configure movement, develop graphic lines, dots and shapes in movement, exhibit them, change them, give them expression, let them voice feelings, give them their own life, let them entertain, so to speak. I managed with the help of Trickfilm Technik [sic] to give my thoughts expression and give life to lines. On thousands of white papers I drew lines, which changed from paper to paper and then in film on the screen resulted in a fluid overall movement. … I expected through incessant work and study … to bring graphic concerts to the screen. In other words: I wanted to create visual music. … I believe I've been successful in considerably contributing to the creation of a new art form, of which developmental possibilities today are still completely overlooked. The meaning will most likely be able to be for the first time fully and entirely captured by later generations, although today there are people who are ready for it and who contribute a great understanding and a real enthusiasm.[14]

10
William Moritz, "Abstract Film and Color Music," in *The Spiritual in Art: Abstract Painting 1890–1985*, exh. cat., Maurice Tuchman, Judi Freeman, et al. (New York: Los Angeles County Museum of Art/Abbeville Press, 1986), 301. In this quote Moritz also cites, re Varese and Cage: Calvin Tomkins, *The Bride and the Bachelors* (New York: Viking, 1968), 86–87; and John Cage, interview with author [Moritz], New York, 1974.

11
Fischinger's draft of his letter responding to one from Ralph K. Potter, 1946. Unpublished. Fischinger Collection, Center for Visual Music, Los Angeles.

12
Fischinger's notes about Motion Painting No.1, published as "A Document Related to Motion Painting I," in William Moritz, Optical Poetry: The Life and Work of Oskar Fischinger (London, UK: John Libbey Publishing, 2004), 185.

13
Fischinger, in Weinberg (note 9).

14
Interview with Bert Reisfeld, unpublished and undated typescript 300615, possibly c. 1950. Fischinger Collection, Center for Visual Music, Los Angeles.

IV

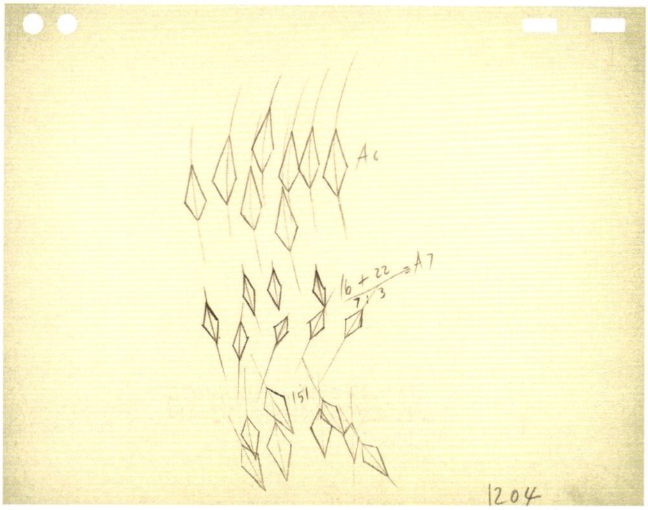

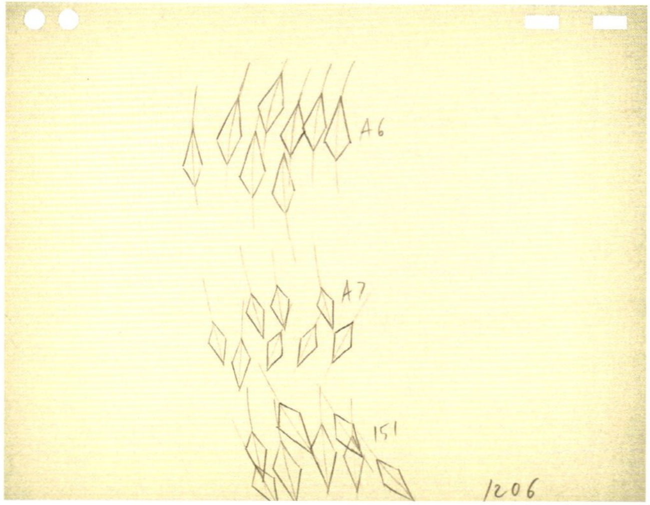

Animation drawings for *Allegretto*, 1936–43
Pencil on paper, 8.8 x 11.1 in. / 22.35 x 28.1 cm
These were used as a guide under transparent animation cels, which were painted according to the pencil drawings and notes
Collection Center for Visual Music, gift of The Fischinger Trust

Stills from *Allegretto*, 1936–43
35mm, color, sound

Molecular Study, 1965
Oil on canvas, 36 x 48 in. / 91.5 x 122 cm
Collection The Fischinger Trust, Long Beach, CA

Space Abstraction No. 3, 1966
Oil on canvas, 48 x 35 in. /122 x 89 cm
Collection The Fischinger Trust, Long Beach, CA

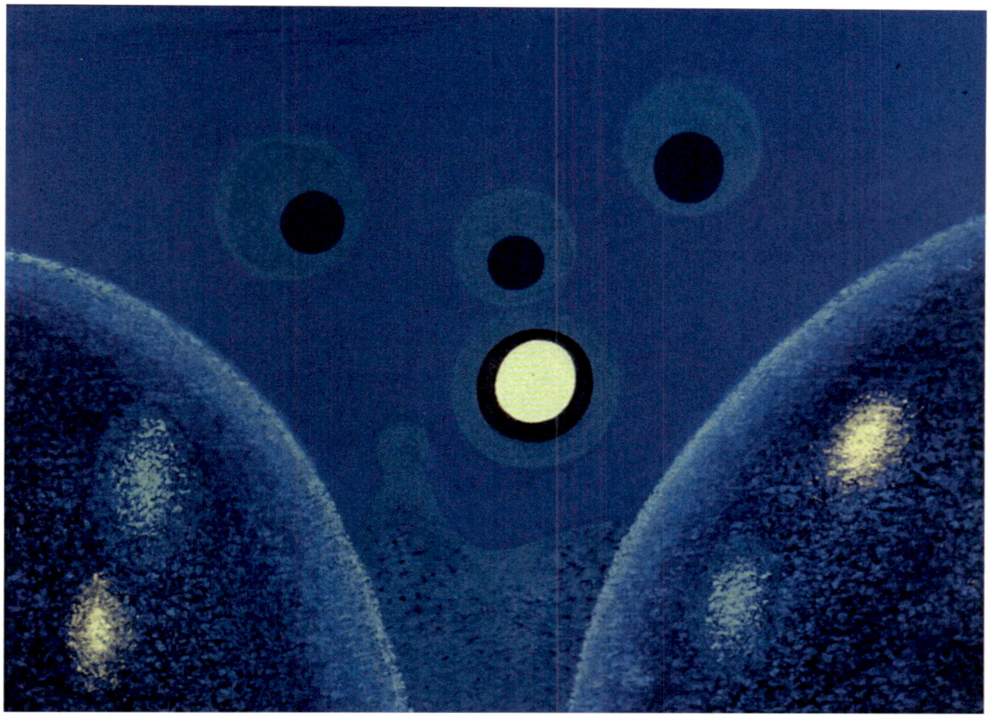

Stills from Fischinger's later experiments with his motion painting techniques, 1957–60
35mm and 16mm fragments, color, silent
Collection Center for Visual Music

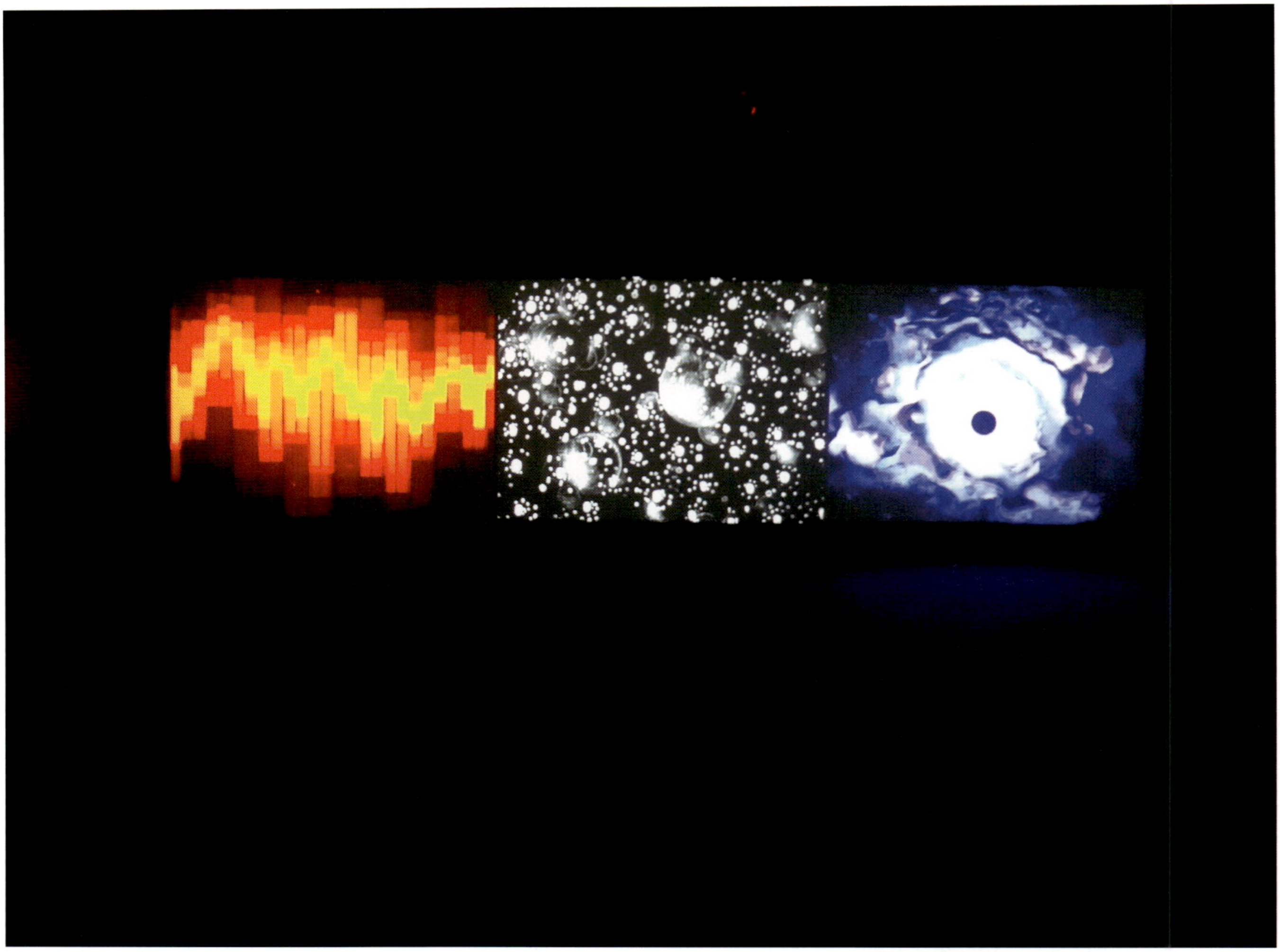

Raumlichtkunst, c. 1926/2012 (restoration/re-creation from Fischinger's 1920s originals)
Three-screen projection: three 35mm films transferred to high-definition video, b/w and color, accompanying sound
Installation views: Whitney Museum of American Art, New York, 2012
Collection Center for Visual Music

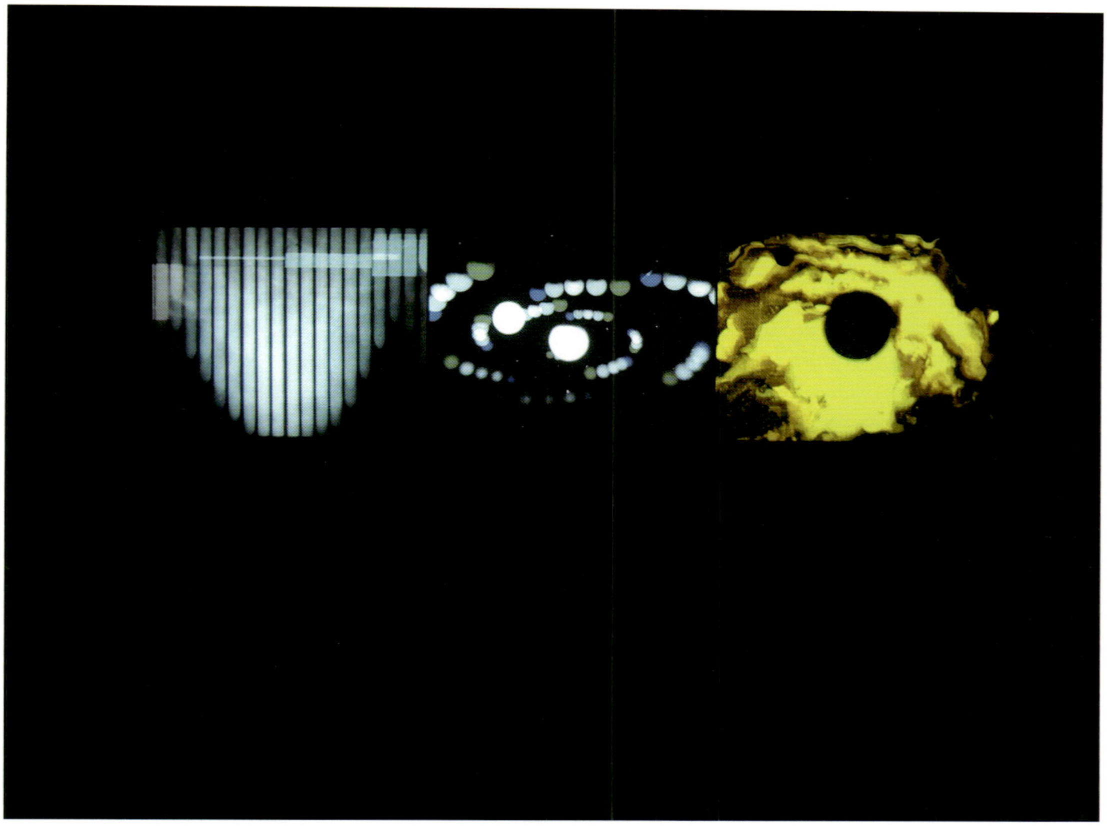

Oskar Fischinger's *Raumlichtkunst*
(c. 1926/2012)
By Cindy Keefer

In 1926, Fischinger and Hungarian composer Alexander László began to perform multimedia shows in Germany with reels of Fischinger's abstract films, projected colored lights from László's color organ instrument, and painted slides. After their brief partnership ended that year, Fischinger began performing his own shows titled *Fieber* (*Fever*), *Vakuum* (*Vacuum*), and *Macht* (*Power*). From texts and press, we now understand these shows as his attempts to create some of the very first cinematic immersive environments. Fischinger performed several different versions of these multiple projector shows in the late 1920s, using up to five 35mm film projectors, color filters to create light effects, slides, and reels of black and white, tinted, and hand-painted abstract film.

Fischinger wrote "Eine neue Kunst: Raumlichtmusik (A New Art: Space-Light-Music). ... Of this Art everything is new and yet ancient in its laws and forms. Plastic-Dance-Painting-Music become one. The Master of the new Art forms poetical work in four dimensions. ... Cinema was its beginning. ... Raumlichtmusik will be its completion." Soon afterwards he changed the name to *Raumlichtkunst*.

Raumlichtkunst has been re-created as a three-screen high-definition installation, in an edition of five. It was recently exhibited at The Whitney Museum, New York, is currently at Tate Modern, London, and is included in the exhibition at EYE Filmmuseum.

Working with reels of Fischinger's original 1920s nitrate film, consisting of Agfa and Goerz Tenax film stock, positive and negative, Center for Visual Music (CVM) restored the 35mm film by photochemical processes. CVM then transferred the new preservation materials to high definition video, digitally restored the color, and produced the three-screen re-creation of his c. 1926–27 performances. The re-creation does not attempt to represent any one specific performance, rather the concept and effect of Fischinger's series of shows. *Raumlichtkunst* is presented as three continual loops, offset, creating constantly varying combinations. No documentation exists of the original music used, other than reports of "various percussive" accompaniment. The current installations use Varese's "Ionisation" and two versions of "Double Music" by John Cage and Lou Harrison.

Raumlichtkunst, c. 1926/2012 (restoration/re-creation from Fischinger's 1920s originals)
Three-screen projection: three 35mm films transferred to high-definition video, b/w and color, accompanying sound
Collection Center for Visual Music

Testimonials

In the early 1970s I wanted to make films that were visual music. It was possible in theory to follow musical structure as a means to composing a film, but I was not seeing such ideas in practice within the films that I was seeing at the time . In my search for such films and filmmakers, I discovered some early avant-garde filmmakers, among them Oskar Fischinger. His films were a revelation to me and I realized that the visual music I was looking for was a different one.

I was amazed by the freedom of designs in motion within the pace of sound in Fischinger's films. It seemed to me that, along with Richter and Lye, Fischinger had opened new fields within the art of films. When I first saw the atoms splitting in *Studie Nr. 8* (*Study No. 8*) and the white flashes in later Studies, what surprised me most was the power and the potential of those white lines creating melodies and rhythms within the specificity of the apparatus. Treating lines as melody was a constant in all his work, whether in paintings or films.

If the motion is frozen or suspended within painting, there are nonetheless moments with potential further development to come, as shown in *Motion Painting No.1*. This film emphasized a dimension of performativity which is been crystallized within the Lumigraph as much as in *Motion Painting No.1*. Here the music of colors and lights is live, whereas the recording of *Motion Painting No.1* induces delays while the Lumigraph performance works in the present.

With the Lumigraph, Oskar Fischinger gave life to a live cinema; light becomes an instrument to play with. In films, Fischinger created three-dimensional effects through inward and outward movements spiraling toward the center of the screen, as he had done earlier in *Spiralen* (*Spirals*); in his paintings, movement is often off-centered and aligned along the diagonal. With *Motion Painting No.1* and *Quadrate* (*Squares*), Fischinger articulated the two possibilities, with one medium dissolving and becoming another. Flip books are an early form of this shift.

Resolution of movement is achieved through a modulation of tensions according to melodic lines or dynamic beat, for which repetition and variation are essential.

The pleasure of discovering the multiple aspects of Oskar Fischinger's work would not have been possible without William Moritz and Elfriede Fischinger. I'll never forget waking up in Elfriede's house after a long trip from New Zealand to LA and facing a stained glass of an Oskar Fischinger logo, hanging on the entrance door.

Illuminating.

yann beauvais, filmmaker and critic
Recife, Brazil

I was just graduating from college in painting when I saw Fischinger's films at the 1946 Art in Cinema festival at the San Francisco Museum of Art, and that inspired me to start making films instead of just painting canvases. He was very supportive of my work, and recommended me for a Guggenheim Fellowship on the basis of my first film.

My most impressive memory of him is the lingering imagery of the Lumigraph show he performed, also at the San Francisco Museum of Art, in 1953. His films had been shown in the auditorium, which was treat enough, and then the curtains were closed for a brief intermission. Then the lights faded out slowly, and the hall was completely black for several minutes, so your eyes began to adjust. Some music—I think Sibelius' "Valse Triste"—arose out of the darkness, and in mysterious synchronization with the sounds appeared soft, glowing images where the movie screen had been. I could tell that this was not a film: the luminous presence of these lithe colors was quite different even from the illusions of the high-contrast black and white films we had just seen. These irregular, always-changing shapes could flicker and pulsate, and when they swirled around, they could leave a vague trail like a comet's tail. The bright, saturated colors had a ghostly three-dimensional presence. The shapes changed so easily—occasionally resembling some hard, complex object, but most often amorphous clusters or discrete points of light—however they seemed so dimensional, so solid. Sometimes the lights would disappear and appear suddenly, but other times they would fade in and out extremely slowly—just as one color might glow exquisitely in saturated duration or suddenly jump to another hue, with brilliant, tasteful timing.

When the music was over, we were plunged into total darkness again. The audience erupted with wild applause. Fischinger wouldn't let anyone backstage to inspect the Lumigraph because it would have destroyed the magic (just as he didn't like to tell about his filmic techniques—and I have followed his wisdom in that). Actually, the mechanism of the Lumigraph was rather primitive, handmade, but the way he performed proved his innate artistry, his natural sensitivity, that could turn even the simplest things into a luxurious, magical illusion of cosmic elegance. That was very inspirational to me: much of my work after that had more of the quality of Lumia, and relied more on simple, handmade devices.

Jordan Belson (1926–2011), filmmaker/artist
San Francisco, US (1971)

Given to William Moritz, and previously published in Moritz's Optical Poetry: The Life and Work of Oskar Fischinger *(London, UK: John Libbey Publishing, 2004). Reprinted with permission of Center for Visual Music.*
See p. 193 for an article about Fischinger's Lumigraph

Oskar Fischinger, First among Equals

We shall attempt to put in order the scattered tesserae of that mosaic that the first cinematic abstractionists created. Who influenced whom, who was greater than somebody else, how did he or she deal with the combination of sound and image? These are the questions that concern us. Was Oskar Fischinger a greater artist than his colleagues? This writer thinks yes.

For the sake of discussion and understanding, let's suppose that *qualitatively* they were all equals: Walther Ruttmann, Len Lye, Oskar Fischinger, Mary Ellen Bute, Norman McLaren.

Richter was busy claiming the falsified or non-existent dreams that money could buy for himself.

Ruttmann was a great, discombobulated mind. He anticipated many of the stylistic solutions of his colleagues, but then he fell into the jaws of Nazi propaganda and died, leaving some confused writings and no successors.

I met Len Lye in 1975. He complained he was old, sick and tired, needed a rest, and didn't want to talk. Then we lost track of him, only to find him waterskiing on the Annecy Lake one hour later. Lye was a jocular genius, a witty man, a merry poet.

Mary Ellen Bute was a pert, strong American woman of Scottish ancestry. She was the typical Grand City intellectual and was always thinking of the public and of a backer for her projects, whether they were abstract animated films or cultivated live-action adaptations of literary greats.

Oskar Fischinger was—from his beginnings—a classic. He had an imposing personality that no one undervalued at any Kongress für Farbe-Ton Forschung (Congress for Color-Sound Research) and remained true to himself even in front of the major forces of Hollywood. He gathered in his house—even when he became poor—many young artists, among whom was another genius, the twenty-six years younger Jordan Belson. Fischinger took care to encourage and to promote these artists, and sometimes to recommend them to the Guggenheim Foundation.

Oskar Fischinger brought the culture of Old Europe to the United States. A great artist, he was also a great example, in every sense—an example that was copied, and fruitfully so.

With Fischinger, American non-representational animation became big, great and grand. After his death, it continued to be so, thanks to his wife Elfriede and his biographer William Moritz, two people whom we will miss always.

I did not mention Norman McLaren. A completely different man, with different style and aims, McLaren was a soloist but definitely not an egocentric. A leftist, he was concerned with the social progress of mankind, to the point that he went to Spain during the Civil War and to China and to India for humanitarian missions, despite his bad health.

McLaren was not a gregarious man and didn't like intellectual panels or cultural disputes. He surrounded himself with very few intimate friends. But he helped everyone who asked him for help, answered every letter that was sent him, and wrote endless pages of explanation about the techniques and the tricks he had invented.

Furthermore, McLaren was backed by his adopted country, Canada. During the 1960s and 1970s, the Canadian embassies worldwide would lend, for free, his pictures to any cultural group and even to individuals. Canada was trying to build its own cultural credibility, and imitators of McLaren rose in Europe, Asia, and South America, in the same way imitators of Fischinger rose in the United States.

McLaren was twenty-seven years younger than Ruttmann, fourteen years younger than Fischinger, thirteen years younger than Lye. With hindsight, I'd portray him as a great experimentalist, but only partially an abstractionist. He was a Knight of the Cause, but his cause was the invention of movement, not necessarily the invention of Visual Music. McLaren's last two films were ballets, and he stated: "If I hadn't been a filmmaker, I'd have been a choreographer."

To close, I'll take the liberty to say my opinion: *qualitatively* Norman McLaren was the only one who could challenge Fischinger in the Olympus of the Masters.

Giannalberto Bendazzi, film critic and historian
Milan, Italy

* A series of four Kongress für Farbe-Ton Forschung (Congress for Color-Sound Research) was held in Germany between 1927 and 1936, organized by Dr. Georg Anschütz.

Oskar Fischinger's animated contribution to the avant-garde moving image is often aligned to so-called "experimental" film, Modernist and Absolute film. While he is rightly located in these historical canons of painting, sculpture, and film, his influence on contemporary art is also unmistakable. It is a tribute to the Center for Visual Music's tireless championing and preservation of this work that Fischinger's *Raumlichtkunst* is now on display in the 2012 *Structure and Clarity* collections exhibition and will be added to the permanent collection at Tate Modern, London. The first film I saw from Fischinger was in a class at the University of Zurich on music video. This then-new genre of music-motivated film and video made use of a plethora of animation techniques, mainly non-digital. Over time it became increasingly obvious how big a debt the mostly young artists working with abstract form owed to Fischinger, to say nothing of the usurpation of his style by advertising and commerce.

Many who experience Fischinger's timeless films today are charmed by their elegance and buoyant vibrancy, and his visual interpretation and spatial choreographies of music, color and abstract forms. What did and does strike me most about his oeuvre is the incredible variety of techniques and experimentation. From object animation in *Komposition In Blau* (*Composition in Blue*) and *Muratti Greift Ein* (*Muratti Gets in the Act*) to additive painting in his masterpiece *Motion Painting No.1*; and the almost vertigo-inducing visual maelstrom of his wax slicing experiments, which stand comfortably alongside the "Stargate" sequence in Stanley Kubrick's *2001: A Space Odyssey*.

There is so much more that could be said about his creative vision, but I leave that to the other contributors to this volume. Instead, I'd like to say a few words about his legacy. Nowadays, a few of Fischinger's films are online, and this is often students' first encounter with the work, not least because overworked lecturers choose the ease of online platforms rather than projecting film or buying high-quality digital copies. But there's nothing quite like seeing a big-screen projection of Fischinger's work (or any celluloid-based film). The difference in experience is like that between seeing a photograph of a Gerhard Richter painting, and standing in a gallery in front of the real thing, with all its minutely monumental detail.

A few years ago I visited the Center for Visual Music to talk with Cindy Keefer about the challenges of running archives and especially the care and knowledge needed to protect and preserve artworks used to make animation. Over those hours, Cindy showed me some remarkable "stuff," including original paintings and drawings that were stand-alone artworks but also revealed the profilmic fine-arts material base of the cinematic medium. Seeing those originals, and understanding their relation to the artist's hand and his creative process, helped me to look at (and teach about) Fischinger's films in a new way, and it became all the more clear why it is important that we show these works as much as possible in their original formats, especially to those not yet familiar with them.

Dr. Suzanne Buchan, Professor of Animation and author of
The Quay Brothers: Into a Metaphysical Playroom (2011)
London, UK

I wanted to make some kind of Visual Music, so I was studying with Mr. Joseph Schillinger, actually struggling along, because he had very complex mathematical ideas about the correspondences of musical and visual structures. One day, worn out by this hard concentration, I decided to just go to the movies and relax. I've forgotten what the feature was, but in those days, the early 1930s, it was probably full of songs and dances—but I don't remember because first came a short subject, a little animation by Fischinger set to a jazz song "I've Never Seen a Smile Like Yours." It was .the simplest thing, drawn lines fluttering about in graceful swirls in perfect time to the music. Suddenly it all made sense for me. That was how to do it, not by mathematical theories, but rather an intuitive choreography.

I was happy to meet Mr. Oskar Fischinger half a dozen years later when he visited New York. He was a very sweet man, modest, with a good sense of humor. I suggested we might work together on something, but it never worked out.

Mary Ellen Bute (1906–83), filmmaker
New York, US (1969)

Given to William Moritz, and previously published in Moritz's Optical Poetry: The Life and Work of Oskar Fischinger *(London, UK: John Libbey Publishing, 2004). Reprinted with permission of Center for Visual Music.*

The color saturation and dynamic motion of *Allegretto*, Oskar Fischinger's two-and-a-half minute abstract masterpiece, stunned me during a chance sighting on a local New York PBS TV channel in the early 1970s. I had never before seen a film so sensually immersive. My curiosity about this film and a filmmaker that I had never heard of was intense. It was richly satisfied at a presentation at the 1976 Ottawa International Animation Festival, where film historian and Fischinger biographer William Moritz and Elfriede Fischinger, the filmmaker's widow, presented a cogent, intriguing lecture aptly titled "The Importance of Being Fischinger."

Subsequently, the close friendship with Elfriede and Bill that I and my spouse Joe Kennedy enjoyed for nearly thirty years was based on the awe and love we all felt for the supreme film legacy of Oskar Fischinger and his life. Like the radiating forms of his spellbinding film *Kreise* (Circles), his influence continues to ripple outward to enthrall audiences around the globe.

John Canemaker, Oscar-winning animator, animation historian, author, and teacher
New York City, US

The work of Oskar Fischinger has had a continuing influence on our filmmaking since we began in 1960. His dedication to the use of the medium of motion picture film to make a significant time-based visual art—often in the face of lack of interest or opposition from the art establishment—has always been a source of inspiration. His pioneering work with color (such as the use of retinal color mixes in *Radio Dynamics*), his multi-screen presentations, and his work with manipulation of the screen surface in real time, as with the Lumigraph, directly influenced our own essays into similar possibilities in our *Expanded Cinema* presentations.

We were fortunate enough to acquire several 16mm prints of key Fischinger works in the 1970s, thanks to our association with William Moritz and, through him, Elfriede Fischinger. The close study of these films, and our use of them in lectures on film art, could only benefit our work and that of the younger filmmakers we encountered. It is wonderful to see that his art is now finding a wider audience.

Arthur and Corinne Cantrill, filmmakers
Castlemaine, Australia

Fischinger's work has been with me for many years and I'm still discovering it today. I was blown away to discover animated abstraction being practiced so many years ago, and immediately felt an affinity. The techniques and stories behind it have made for fascinating reading. This history, like his films, seems to expand upon study. The devotion and vision necessary to make it (and apparent in the work itself) adds a new layer of experience for the modern viewer now accustomed to the use of computers. I am only left wondering how the audience felt all those years ago. What a novel experience it must have been.

My first tastes of Fischinger were from DVDs and blocky compressed online videos. But now—thanks to the Center for Visual Music digitally remastering *Raumlichtkunst* and bringing it to the Whitney Museum—I have experienced a whole new dimension of his work, projected in HD on three large screens. He was working not only with abstraction in space and time, but also with nonlinearity.

I wish he could see the world today. He influenced me, and he also influenced artists working across the spectrum (as he did himself). Just the other day I was watching the video of Roger Waters' *The Wall* on tour again in 2012. I was struck by the images of goose-stepping hammers, and how similar they are to Fischinger's Muratti cigarette commercial *Muratti Greift Ein* (*Muratti Gets in the Act*). When I went online to look it up I discovered my memory was actually of a Lucky Strike commercial which was knocked-off from Fischinger fourteen years after his 1934 original. And so the story grows.

Scott Draves, software artist and founder of The Electric Sheep
New York, US

26 August 2012

Dear Cindy,

Following up on our earlier conversation on the roots of VJing, there is a general misguided history where VJing is erroneously framed as live cinema with a direct link from experimental visual music, later followed by 60's light shows and peppered with liberal doses of synaesthesia. With all these precedents we are only looking at aesthetics and partially at technique while over looking the conceptual and theoretical precedents. There is a shift in medium, intention, environment and narrative between these. We can't draw a straight line and end on VJing.

What I propose are very exact historical references particularly Oskar Fischinger's Raumlichtkunst concept which was a multi-projector performance; and Man Ray and Lee Miller's White Ball created for a I930 party in Paris. All party guests were dressed in white and Ray and Miller projected tinted films by George Méliès on them while they danced.

W

With these specific precedents we see VJs also activate the space of their performance by spatializing their media and creating meta-narratives. Wasn't Oskar's work about meta-narratives of image and sound, a new audio-visual medium, an aesthetic and conceptual narrative separate and different from the two originating media used to create it, just as a VJ mix?

Xárene

Xárene Eskander, media artist
Santa Monica, US

Oskar, Elfriede, Bill, and Me

In August 1998 I was on the west coast to speak at the Society of Animation Studies conference about abstract filmmaker Jim Davis. Elfriede Fischinger (who I had known previously) and Bill Moritz were present too. I wrote in my journal:

> Elfriede Fischinger was there—she *said* she came just to hear me, but I doubt that—but she was engaged by what I said. She interrupted when I talked about the lack of support for Davis in the 1940s. She said that Oskar had the same experience on the West Coast. Afterward she said she liked the Library of Congress-preserved sound film (*Thru the Looking Glass*, 1953) by Davis. When Moritz said he did not like it, she took gleeful exception to his opinion. We all had a late lunch afterward and then they drove back to Long Beach.

Subsequently I spent several days at Elfriede's home and saw at least sixty of the paintings Oskar had made in the 1950s, when he was unable to raise funding needed to make more films. Among the paintings I remember there were at least six that had circular images that resembled night sky objects, like the moon. Oskar's books were also in the house; I found 1920s books on astronomy on the shelves. I do not think they were solely used as research materials for his work on Fritz Lang's *Rocket to the Moon*. Celestial images are something he wrote about in the 1940s, and that I saw in much of his work.

The number and variety of his paintings was just astounding—and their obvious cinematic character led me to rethink my response to *Kreise* (*Circles*) and his other films.

These notes focus on two films, both dominated by circular forms. They are different because of the decades in which they were made; one in black and white, and one in color; one silent and one precisely linked to music. They are united, I believe, by Fischinger's wish to expand the flat, two-dimensional space of the screen into a deep, three-dimensional space. He used optical means in the one case; optical and musical means in the other.

Fischinger used circular forms in many of his films, but they were usually subordinate to the motions of the staffs or the sperm-like forms that dart across the screen in formations like birds. In *Spiralen* (*Spirals*, 1926) and *Kreise* (*Circles*, 1933–34) the circular forms are visually central.

Spiralen (*Spirals*) is composed of brief shots of round forms containing different patterns swirling in towards a central point. Visually it is as if the screen has been punctured. As Moritz noted in his 1974 article on Fischinger in *Film Culture*, these movements have a pronounced Op Art effect.

The 16mm version of this film was assembled by Moritz after Fischinger's death. The title is apparently Fischinger's, but the specific selection of the different spiral footage was made by Moritz in that version. He said there was much of this kind of original footage, some for use in backgrounds, and some, like the initial sequence in *Spiralen* (*Spirals*), stood on its own.*

In *Kreise* (*Circles*) there is no question of Fischinger's intended form. It is a finished film commissioned by an advertising agency (Tolirag) with a synchronized music track (*Venusberg Music* by Wagner, then Grieg's *Huldigung's March*). In this film the circular forms (rings) also race away towards a central vanishing point, but they differ from those in *Spiralen* (*Spirals*). In *Kreise* (*Circles*) whole circular forms speed away from us, not just their contents as in *Spiralen* (*Spirals*). There is an impression of depth, but it is not as acute as in *Spiralen* (*Spirals*). I think this is related to the music, which changes as the circular rings fly away.

Fischinger was aware of how sound could condition the reception of his images. When he made *Radio Dynamics* (1942) he requested that no sound accompany it. He wanted us to *see* his visual music.

Ende

Robert Haller, Director of the Jerome Hill Library, Anthology Film Archives
New York, US

* In his 1974 *Film Culture* essay, "The Films of Oskar Fischinger," Moritz wrote that, "The first two sequences are so much alike that I have little doubt they were once part of the same finished film." (p.90)

A deeply spiritual person and a life-long student of religious mysticism, Oskar Fischinger envisaged a spiritual function for his films. He understood the prolonged and painstaking process of manufacture as itself a devotional practice (as did Jordan Belson and others whom he influenced), and he expected that his films would be apprehended directly and intuitively by the spectator without their passing through a stage of verbal articulation or ratiocination. Given these aspirations, it is perhaps inevitable that the itinerary of his life would read as an allegory of the impossibility of a fully humane public culture in the twentieth century. Glimpsing film's potential to synthesize previous mediums and provide unique expressive capacities, he developed it into an art that was simultaneously popularly pleasurable and yet formally sophisticated; an art that was capable of being put to commercial uses while still sustaining profound imaginative functions. But no sooner had he attained formal mastery of his chosen medium than he was trapped between political interests categorically opposed to such utopian use of it: fascism in Germany and the capitalist entertainment industry in the United States. Fleeing one, he found himself simultaneously imprisoned by and excluded from the other. The career which promised so much in the early 1930s was aborted and though he left a handful of masterpieces, he never realized his magnum opus: the feature length abstract animation, the true visual symphony.

Despite the financial exigencies that prevented him from making films for the last twenty years of his life, Fischinger was a revered figure in Southern California. Especially after the Art in Cinema screenings in San Francisco in 1947, where an entire program (one tenth of the whole series) was devoted to his work, his combination of aesthetic and technological inventiveness and spiritual interests made him the chief inspiration for the Los Angeles avant-garde generally. He was a decisive influence on John Cage and on several generations of California filmmakers, the source of a distinct local tradition that included Jordan Belson, Charles Dockum, John Whitney and his brother James, and Jules Engel. Belson worked primarily in San Francisco, where Harry Smith, who also admired Fischinger immensely, worked briefly, while the Whitneys, who met Fischinger in 1939 on their return from Europe, were integral to the Los Angeles avant-garde cinema for four decades.

David James, film historian
Los Angeles, US

Adapted extract from David E. James, The Most Typical Avant-Garde: History and Geography of Minor Cinemas in Los Angeles *(Berkeley: University of California Press, 2005).*

In May 1991, I invited Elfriede Fischinger and William Moritz to the Impakt festival in Utrecht, and they brought two seemingly endless programs: one was about visual music and the other was a retrospective of films by Oskar Fischinger. It was an amazing day, a group of about sixty people saw both screenings and still years after that event, people would come up to me to tell me that they had been there too and that it was so special. For me, it was a very important experience to finally get to see all these films, and to get a sense of the culture around them through Elfriede and Bill's stories. The Fischinger films appeared to me in a totally different league than those of the other pioneers of the first half of the twentieth century; to me his work appeared that of a modernist giant, comparable to Le Corbusier, Schoenberg or Kandinsky—a giant who did not write books but who defined a completely new artistic language by speaking it so eloquently in color and musical movement. The sensory explosion of that day focused my wandering interests on wanting to make films myself.

Joost Rekveld, artist and educator
Amsterdam, the Netherlands

Oskar Fischinger / Aftershock into Today

I encountered Fischinger's work quite late—around 2001, in the middle of my studies at Bauhaus University, Weimar. At the time, "New Media" found itself in one of the efflorescences of its exhaustion—what had become possible through technical progress stood ineptly in the foreground, always looking blatantly towards the future. During an exchange program in England, the horizon of Fischinger's films completely opened up to me as a collection of works that had remained incredibly effective despite the distance of many decades.

The sheer extent of conceptual and formal ideas overwhelmed me. Fischinger's ceaseless research—laying a bridge between imagination and realization with every step—is still unparalleled today. Whether it was static or motion painting, image-creating machines or silhouette and wax animation, each work clearly followed his vision, despite innumerable technical, financial and personal obstacles.

Some of these problems, such as the costs for film prints or camera equipment, have now been minimized thanks to digitalization and technology's declining prices. The world could in fact be full of unique and personal artistic universes. So what has happened? It seems that many users of technology misread the concept of having a malleable tool, instead following paths laid out by software manufacturers and Hollywood. Digital processes for creating film, usually abstracted from reality, appear as technically precise, slurred representations that narrow the space for imagination or personal expression. In an echo of Disney's attempt to constrain Fischinger in a corset, today's users voluntarily accept a mold in order to become masters of the situation in a seemingly endless sea of possibilities. Yet despite the tremendous, unprecedented possibilities of our time, this virtualization of risk, the industrial pressure of efficiency and the constant noise on all channels lead to a dulling of artistic exploration.

A further point, something that has scarcely improved since Fischinger, is the recognition of the experimental moving image in the museum context.

After a wave of media art in the last few decades that specifically reflected the medium, one would assume that the proliferation of technology which has permeated all aspects of life would finally arrive in the museum. However, when one finds film, or video art as the case may be, presented today in a generally appropriate manner in museums, it is overwhelmingly naturalistic, focusing mainly on the human, and in some instances surreally exaggerated. Beyond this it is mainly exhibited in a rectangular frame, conforming to centuries-old pictorial representation without addressing the freedom that projected images offer.

At present one rarely encounters maturely formulated abstraction, in part because the advertising and event industries have appropriated abstract visual images and projection, misusing them as ornamental filler. These examples are often rendered with a high level of technical skill, but are nevertheless soulless, inconsiderate forms of perfection. In addition, while every curator communicates by smart-phone and email, an undefined fear of technology remains inherent in the art world. Since the process of digital or digital-analog hybrids is extremely complex, it is often mistaken as unartistic or artisanal. That computers are merely a tool to the manifestation of the artist's thoughts remains overlooked, despite, or perhaps precisely because nowadays even technophobes have acquired a seemingly self-evident acquaintance with word processing or image manipulation software.

Thus abstract-digital film fills only a niche. Given the pioneering accomplishment of Oskar Fischinger, and taking this as a postulate for his possible consequence, one has to conclude that abstract film unfortunately does not represent the artistic and technological saturation of our age. Historically observed, the training of our optical senses remains unparalleled, but visionary creation falls so far behind the voracious image-producing industry that the effect of his wonderfully idiosyncratic films still remains unbroken and timeless. When an art form has already achieved such maturity from the relative start of its conception, all living artists should feel challenged to sketch a similarly clear, personal utopia and work tirelessly to realize this.

Robert Seidel, artist, filmmaker and curator
Berlin, Germany

You can tell how much I admire Fischinger: the only film of mine that I ever gave a real title to was *Homage to Oskar Fischinger* (*Film No. 5*, in the current scheme of things). I learned concentration from him—visiting his home and seeing how he could sit serenely in that small house, crawling with what seemed like a dozen children, and still paint those stunning pictures. That great film *Motion Painting* makes the process seem deceptively simple—and it was simple for him: the images really did just flow from his brush, never a ruler or compass, all freehand—but you can't see all the obstacles he had to overcome in order to even work at all. Something so wonderful happened in that film, and in those paintings, something so much better than all the Pollocks and other stuff that the museums fight to get hold of. Did anyone ever fight to save Fischinger's things?

Harry Smith (1923–91), filmmaker, artist, ethnomusicologist
New York, US (1977)

Given to William Moritz, and previously published in Moritz's Optical Poetry: The Life and Work of Oskar Fischinger *(London, UK: John Libbey Publishing, 2004).*

I was introduced to Oskar Fischinger's animation one sleepy, 1980s afternoon in the concrete bunker of the Rhode Island School of Design's Animation Department. As our professor began to play *Studie Nr. 8* (Study No. 8) in 16mm, I immediately became alert, and I believe I did not even blink for the film's full five minutes. I'd never seen movement in such a pure form and with such sophistication—simple lines dancing on screen, not "Mickey Mousing" the music, but rather in counterpoint, as if the images were another instrument, hitherto missing, from Dukas' *Sorcerer's Apprentice*. The images had me laughing, grinning ear-to-ear with joy, and then, finally, in tears. I was stunned, and curious, how images without a face, bodies, or nature, could evoke such powerful, primordial emotion.

Fischinger's work became the fundamental inspiration for what I had been calling, defensively, and for lack of a better term, "useless programs," works of interactive computer graphics that had no more use than, say, a poem, a song, or a work of art. Soon after seeing Fischinger's film, I began writing a program called *Motion Phone* that let people create Fischinger-like abstract films in real-time, collaboratively over a network. That work of art became my entrée into the field of interactive art, and the launch of a career that later spawned million-selling apps in the app store, and visual music collaborations with Björk that resulted in the debut of a new medium: the 'app album.'

Whenever I give a talk, I begin with a brief history of dynamic abstraction, including Joseph Cornell's magical boxes, Marcel Duchamp's Rotoreliefs, Thomas Wilfred's *Clavilux*, and, first and foremost, the masterful films of Oskar Fischinger. Repeatedly, I tell students and practitioners that time-varying abstraction was perfected in the 1920s by this man, and that to fail to study his work might doom one to spend a whole life clumsily re-inventing the wheel.

Fischinger's work not only forms the foundations for the later magic of 1960s light shows, 1980s MTV, and 2010s apps, but also provides a lesson to interaction designers—the people responsible for how our iPhones, computers, and TVs talk to us. Fischinger understood something deep and primitive about the human brain. His films represent a crystallization, a super-stimulus of form, movement, and color that bores down to the fundamentals of how we perceive. His works teach us the roots of emotion and perception, and, I daresay, a spiritual connection to our most fundamental nature, how physicists now understand each of us to be not merely blobs of matter, but, more true to the subtlest reality, as immaterial, moving bodies of light.

Scott Snibbe, interactive artist and entrepreneur
San Francisco, US

Appendices

Oskar Fischinger Filmography

All films originally 35mm unless noted. Lengths refer to extant versions. Brackets denote film titles assigned later by someone other than Fischinger (often Elfriede Fischinger and/or William Moritz). English translations of German titles in parentheses on first mention. See Jeanpaul Goergen's "Timeline" in this publication for original lengths of the films registered in Germany, up to 1936 (p. 42).

Stromlinien (*Currents*), c. 1922. Experiments, tinted, silent, short fragments.

Wachsexperimente (*Wax Experiments*), 1921–26, b/w and tinted, silent, various lengths, various different versions of these experiments. In distribution today: a 35mm b/w version of 4 minutes (at 24 fps), and a 16mm version compiled by William Moritz of 11 minutes (at 18 fps), with a head title added. This 16mm version includes some *Stromlinien* (*Currents*) and tinted *Wax Experiments* material. It is believed that much of the original tinted *Wax Experiments* material has not survived.

[*Orgelstabe*] (*Staffs*), 1923–27. Experiments, b/w and tinted, several versions, varying lengths. *Staffs* material is incorporated in both [*R-1 ein Formspiel*] and *Raumlichtkunst*.

Pierrette I, from *Münchener Bilderbogen* Series 1924–26, b/w, silent, unfinished, length unknown. The 5 minute version in distribution today is a Moritz re-creation. It is unclear on which of the other films of this series Fischinger worked, and his exact role.

[*Spiralen*] (*Spirals*), c. 1926, b/w, silent, experiments, original length unknown. Several versions exist today: a 35mm, 2 minute version, and a 16mm, 2 min. 44 sec. version with a later head title added by Elfriede Fischinger and Moritz.

Raumlichtkunst multiple projector cinema performances, c. 1926–27. A series of performances, some with individual names, e.g. *Fieber* (*Fever*), *Vakuum* (*Vacuum*), *Macht* (*Power*), b/w and tinted, 35mm, accompanied by non-sync sound. Two re-creation attempts exist from surviving nitrate material:
a [*R-1 ein Formspiel*], 1993 re-creation from c. 1926–33 material, b/w, tinted and color, 6 min. Cinemascope 35mm re-creation by William Moritz / Fischinger Archive (single screen). No press or documentation has yet been found to confirm that Fischinger gave any performance by this name.
b *Raumlichtkunst*, 2012 restoration and re-creation from c. 1922–26 material, b/w, tinted and color. Three-screen projection (installation) by Center for Visual Music, comprising three reels of 35mm film transferred to high definition video. Continual loops, with varying offsets, accompanied by non-sync music.

[*Seelische Konstruktionen*] (*Spiritual Constructions*), c. 1927, b/w, silent, 7 min.

Munich Special Effects Work, 1927, b/w, for *Sintflut* (*Noah's Ark*, or *The Flood*), Director: Josef Berger.

[*München–Berlin Wanderung*] (*Walking from Munich to Berlin*), 1927, b/w, silent, 3 min.

Berlin special effects work, 1927–32: animated special effects for *Dein Schicksal* (*Your Fate*), 1928, Director: Erno Metzner; several UFA films including *Welt Krieg, Zweiter Teill* (*World War, Part 2*); *Frau im Mond* (*Woman in the Moon*), director: Fritz Lang, 1929; an AAFA Film in 1928; commercials for Axselrod's and Dr. Spieker's Yogurt; *Die Forster Christl* (*Christy the Forester's Daughter*); *Das Blaue vom Himmel* (*The Blue of Heaven*); *Das Hohelied der Kraft* (*The Hymn of Energy*, 1930). [1]

Miscellaneous early Berlin work: Various b/w tests and experiments. Various b/w fragments of animation tests and effects, including "The Entrepreneur" and "Studie Transmannfilm" fragments. Various unshot b/w and color animation drawings.

Studie Nr. 1, c. 1929, b/w, other details unknown. Likely accompanied by live organ music.

Studie Nr. 2 (*Tanzende Linien*, *Dancing Lines*), c. 1930, b/w, 2 min. Originally synchronized to sound on gramophone record, "Vaya, Veronika."

Studie Nr. 3, 1930, b/w, silent. 4 min. Originally synchronized to sound on gramophone record, "Vinka" by Will Coste.

Studie Nr. 4, 1930, b/w, length unknown (lost). Possibly synchronized to sound on gramophone record, "Auf Wiedersehen" by Mischa Spoliansky.

Studie Nr. 5, 1930, b/w, sound, 3 min. 15 sec. Originally titled *R. 5—Ein Spiel in Linien*. Several versions exist, an early silent version (likely synchronized to sound on gramophone record), and one with sound on optical track, synchronized to "I've Never Seen a Smile Like Yours" from the film *The Perfect Alibi*.

Studie Nr. 6, 1930, b/w, sound, 2 min. Music: "Los Verderones" by Jacinto Guerrero.

Studie Nr. 7, 1931, b/w, sound, 2 min. 30 sec. Music: "Hungarian Dance No. 5" by Johannes Brahms.

Studie Nr. 8, 1931, b/w, sound, 5 min. Music: *The Sorcerer's Apprentice* by Paul Dukas.

1
See for further details William Moritz, *Optical Poetry* (2004), Bibliography, pp. 208–11; and *Optische Poesie*, Deutsches Filmmuseum (1993), p. 105.

Studie Nr. 9, 1931, b/w, sound. 3 min. Credited as "School of Oskar Fischinger, drawn by Hans." Made under Oskar Fischinger's supervision. Music: "Hungarian Dance No. 6" by Johannes Brahms.

Studie Nr. 10, 1932, b/w, sound, 4 min 30 sec. Music: from "Aida" by Giuseppe Verdi. Some of the animation was executed by Hans Fischinger.

Studie Nr. 11, 1932, b/w, sound, 4 min. Music: "Eine Kleine Nachtmusik" by Wolfgang Amadeus Mozart.

Studie Nr. 12, 1932, b/w, sound, 4 min. 30 sec. Credited as "School of Oskar Fischinger, drawn by Hans." Music: "Candle Dance of the Kashmiri Brides" from *Feramors* by Anton Rubinstein.

Koloraturen (*Coloratura*), 1932, b/w, sound, c. 1 min. 30 sec. Music: "What Could be so Lovely as Your Love?" aria from the film *Gitta Entdeckt ihr Herz* (*Gitta Finds Her Heart*).

Fiesta Commercial, 1932, b/w, details and length unknown.

Tönende Ornamente (*Ornament Sound*) c. 1932, b/w, sound (various fragments exist; the 2-minute 35mm version, and a longer 16mm version in distribution today are Moritz compilations, c. 1972). Some of these experiments may date earlier than 1932.

Studie Nr. 13 [*Coriolan Fragment*], 1933, b/w, sound, unfinished. Music: "Overture to Coriolan" by Ludwig van Beethoven.

[*Liebesspiel*] [*Love Games*], c. 1931–34, b/w, silent, 2 min. Several theories exist regarding the possibility that this may be the "missing" *Studie Nr. 4*.

Kreise [Tolirag Ad Version], 1933–34, color, sound, 1 min. 48 sec. Full original title: *Alle Kreise erfasst Tolirag* (*Tolirag Reaches all Circles of Society*). Possibly the first film completed in Gasparcolor. Music: Venusberg ballet music from *Tannhäuser* by Richard Wagner, and the ending of "Triumphal March" from *Sigurd Jorsalfar* by Edvard Grieg. Commissioned by the Tolirag ad agency.

Kreise [Abstract Version], 1934, color, sound, 1min. 48 sec. Gasparcolor. Music, same as above.

Ein Spiel in Farben (*A Play in Colors*) a.k.a. [*Studie Nr. 11A*], 1934, color, sound, 3 min. A color version of *Studie Nr. 11*. Fischinger was not satisfied and did not distribute this version.

Quadrate (*Squares*), 1934. Color, silent, original length unknown. Gasparcolor.

Muratti Greift Ein (Muratti Gets in the Act), 1934, color, sound, 3 min, Gasparcolor. Music: from *The Doll Fairy* by Josef Bayer.

[*Swiss Trip* (*Rivers and Landscapes*)], 1934, b/w, sound, 11 min. Music: "Brandenburg Concerto No. 3" by Johann Sebastian Bach.

Muratti Privat Commercial, c. 1935, b/w, sound, 3 min. Music: excerpts from "Turkish Rondo" and other work by Wolfgang Amadeus Mozart.

Euthymol Commercial (*Pink Guards on Parade*), 1935, color, sound, unfinished (Moritz re-creation on video, 2001, 3 min). Gasparcolor. Music: excerpts from "Poet and Peasant" overture by Franz von Suppé, "Si j'étais Roi" by Adolphe Adam, and fragments of jazz and march music.

Miscellaneous later Berlin work: Series of Gasparcolor tests, 1933. Another b/w Muratti ad. Various commercials for Borg and Meluka cigarettes. "Home movie" footage from Berlin studio (b/w, silent); various b/w cigarette tests. Titles for Merkur company; logos for film companies Europa and Rota (1934). Special effects for *Annette im Paradies* (*Annette in Paradise*), 1934. Various other short animated tests and fragments.

Komposition In Blau (*Composition in Blue*), 1935, color, sound, 4 min. Gasparcolor. Music: Overture to "The Merry Wives of Windsor" by Otto Nicolai. Fischinger's last film made in Germany.

Allegretto [Early Version], 1936, color, sound, 2 min. 30 sec. Begun at Paramount but not completed in color there. Original title was to be *Radio Dynamics*. Music: "Radio Dynamics," by Ralph Rainger.

An Optical Poem, 1937, color, sound, 7 mins. Music: "Hungarian Rhapsody no. 2" by Franz Liszt. Made for MGM.

An American March, 1941, color, sound, 3 min. 45 sec. Made with partial support from The Museum of Non-Objective Painting, New York. Music: "Stars and Stripes Forever," by John Philip Sousa.

Radio Dynamics, 1942, color, silent, 4 min. A head credit proclaims "Please! No Music. Experiment in Color Rhythm."

Allegretto, [Late Version], 1936–43, color, sound, 2 min. 30 sec. Gasparcolor. Made with support from The Museum of Non-Objective Painting, New York; final version of the film begun at Paramount. Music: "Radio Dynamics," by Ralph Rainger.

Motion Painting No.1, 1947, color, sound, 11 min. Technicolor. Made with support from The Museum of Non-Objective Painting, New York. Music: "Brandenburg Concerto No. 3," by Johann Sebastian Bach.

[*Stereo Film Test*], 1952, color, silent, 30 sec. Left and right eye films, meant for projection with silver screen and 3D glasses.

Muntz TV Commercial, 1952, b/w, sound, 1 min.

Oklahoma Gas Commercial, 1952, b/w, sound, 1 min. [*Bon Voyage Party*], 1953, b/w, silent, 4 min. Home movies shot by Fischinger during children's party at his home in Hollywood.

[*Later Motion Painting fragments*], 1957–60, Color, silent, c. 2 min. (originally 16mm for the 1957 fragments and 35mm for the 1960 fragments).

Miscellaneous US work: Designs (not used in film, heavily adapted) for *Fantasia* (1940); various tests and fragments including one titled *Concerto* (1945); title sequence for *Jane Eyre*, 1944 (not used in film). Unfinished drawings and cels for [*Organic Fragment*] project, 1941 (later painted and filmed by Barbara and Elfriede Fischinger and William Moritz). *Pure Oil Commercial* and *Sugar Pops Cereal Commercial* (both unfinished, 1950s). Special effects work for "Space Patrol" television show. Synthetic soundtrack for *Northern Tissue Commercial*, c. 1955. Various short tests and unshot animation drawings. Various 8mm home movie footage.

Selected Chronological Bibliography

Schneider, Rudolph. "Formspiel durch Kino." *Frankfurter Zeitung* (July 12, 1926).

Böhme, Fritz. "Der Tanz der Linien." *Deutsche Allgemeine Zeitung* (Berlin, August 16, 1930).

Lichtfeld, Lou. "Fischingers muzikale Films." *De Groene Amsterdammer*, no. 2800 (January 31, 1931).

Behm, Walther. "Abstrakte Filmstudie Nr. 5 von Oskar Fischinger (Synästhetischer Film)." In *Farbe-Ton-Forschungen*, vol. III, edited by Georg Anschütz, 367–69. Hamburg: Meissner, 1931.

Diebold, Bernhard. "Über Fischingerfilme: das ästhetische Wunder." *Lichtbildbühne* (June 1, 1932).

Eisner, Lotte. "Lichtertanz." *Film-Kurier* (June 1, 1932).

Fischinger, Oskar. "Was ich mal sagan mochte..." *Deutsche Allgemeine Zeitung* (Berlin, July 23, 1932).

Fischinger, Oskar. "Klingende Ornamente." *Deutsche Allgemeine Zeitung, Kraft Und Stoff*, no. 30 (July 28, 1932). Syndicated worldwide; several different versions exist, both published and unpublished. English version: "Sounding Ornaments," in Moritz, *Optical Poetry* (2004) and online at www.centerforvisualmusic.org/Fischinger/SoundOrnaments.htm

Böhme, Fritz. "Tönende Ornamente: Aus Oskar Fischingers neuer Arbeit." *Film-Kurier* (July 30, 1932).

Fischinger, Oskar. "Der Absolute Tonfilm: Neue Möglichkeiten für den bildenden Künstler." *Dortmunder Zeitung* (January 1, 1933). Syndicated. A version of this article is in this volume, pp. 96–97.

Schamoni, Viktor. "Das Lichtspiel. Möglichkeiten des absoluten Films." Dissertation, Munich, 1936.

Parsons, Louella. "Movie-Go-Round." *Examiner* (March 6, 1938).

Johnson, R.V.D. "Animating Music," *Minicam*, vol. II, no. 5 (January 1939).

Fischinger, Oskar. "My Statements are in My Work." In *Art in Cinema*, edited by Frank Stauffacher, 38–40. San Francisco: Art in Cinema Society-San Francisco Museum of Art, 1947. Reprint: New York: Arno Press, 1968, and in Scott MacDonald, ed. *Art in Cinema: Documents Toward a History of the Film Society*. Philadelphia: Temple University Press, 2006. Reprinted in this volume, pp. 112–13.

Fischinger, Oskar. "Véritable Creation." *Le Cinéma À Knokke-Le-Zoute* (1950): 35–37. Available online at www.oskarfischinger.org/True Creation.html

Fischinger, Oskar. *My Paintings/My Films*. Beverly Hills, CA: Frank Perls Gallery, October 1951. Brochure.

Renan, Sheldon. *An Introduction to the American Underground Film*. New York: Dutton, 1967.

Weaver, Mike. "The Concrete Films of Oskar Fischinger." *Art And Artists*, vol. 4, no. 2 (1969): 30–33.

Long Beach Museum of Art. *Bildmusik: Art of Oskar Fischinger*. Exhibition catalog. Long Beach, CA: Long Beach Museum of Art, 1970.

Curtis, David. *Experimental Cinema*. London: Studio Vista, 1971.

Starr, Cecile. *Discovering the Movies: An Illustrated Introduction to the Motion Picture*. New York: Van Nostrand Reinhold Co., 1972.

Moritz, William. "The Films of Oskar Fischinger." *Film Culture*, nos 58–60 (New York: Film Culture, 1974): 37–188. [Contains factual errors.]

Moritz, William. "The Importance of Being Fischinger." *Ottawa '76 International Animated Film Festival Program* (Cinémathèque québecoise, 1976). Online at www.centerforvisualmusic.org/library/ImportBF.htm

Russett, Robert and Cecile Starr. *Experimental Animation*. New York: Van Nostrand Reinhold Co., 1976. Revised edition: New York: Da Capo Press, 1988.

Moritz, William. "Fischinger at Disney - or Oskar in the Mousetrap." *Millimeter*, vol. 5, no. 2 (1977): 25–28, 65–67. Online at www.centerforvisualmusic.org/OFMousetrap.htm

Canemaker, John. "Elfriede! On the Road with Mrs. Oskar Fischinger." *Funnyworld*, no. 18 (Summer 1978): 4–14. Online at www.oskarfischinger.org/OntheRoad2.htm

Hein, Birgit, and Wulf Herzogenrath, eds. *Film Als Film, 1910 bis heute*. Cologne: Kölnischer Kunstverein, 1978: 74–78.

Moritz, William. "Non-Objective Film: The Second Generation." In *Film as Film: Formal Experiment in Film, 1910–1975*. Hayward Gallery/Arts Council of Great Britain, 1979. Online at www.centerforvisualmusic.org/MoritzNO-OFexcerpt.htm

Janiak, Larry and Dave Daruszka. "Oskar Fischinger: An Interview with Elfriede Fischinger." *Zoetrope* (1979). Online at www.oskarfischinger.org/EFZoetrope.htm

Rosenblum, Gordon. *Fischinger: A Retrospective of Paintings and Films by Oskar Fischinger, 1900–1967*. Denver, CO: Gallery 609, 1980.

Fischinger, Elfriede. "Writing Light," in *Fischinger: A Retrospective of Paintings and Films by Oskar Fischinger, 1900–1967*, exhibition catalog, edited by Gordon Rosenblum. Denver, CO: Gallery 609, 1980. Reprinted in *The Relay* 3, no. 2 (May 1984): 4–7. Reprinted in *First Light*, edited by Robert A. Haller. New York: Anthology Film Archives, 1998: 30–34. Online at www.centerforvisualmusic.org/WritingLight.htm

Moritz, William. "You Can't Get Then from Now." (Part I). *Los Angeles Institute of Contemporary Arts Journal* 29 (1981): 26–40, 70–72. Online at www.centerforvisualmusic.org/WMThenFromNow.htm

Canemaker, John. "The Abstract Films of Oskar Fischinger." *Print Magazine* 37, no. 2 (March/April 1983): 66–72.

Moritz, William. "Towards a Visual Music." *Cantrills Filmnotes* 47, 48. (Melbourne: Arthur and Corinne Cantrill, 1985): 35–42.

Maur, Karin, ed. *Vom Klang der Bilder: Die Musik in der Kunst des 20. Jahrhunderts*, 416, 417. Munich: Prestel, 1985.

Ehrlich, Susan E. *Five Los Angeles Pioneer Modernists: A Study of the 1940's Paintings of Peter Krasnow, Knud Merrild, Oskar Fischinger, Lorser Feitelson, and Helen Lundeberg*. PhD dissertation, University of Southern California, 1985.

Moritz, William. "Abstract Film and Color Music." In *The Spiritual In Art: Abstract Painting 1890–1985*, exhibition catalog, edited by Maurice Tuchman, 296–311. New York: Abbeville Press with Los Angeles County Museum of Art, 1986. Dutch version of essay: Moritz, William. *Het Mysterie In De Abstracte Film*. Amsterdam: Stichting Nederlands Filmmuseum, 1987.

Beauvais, Yann and Deke Dusinberre, eds. *Musique Film*, Scratch/Cinémathèque Française, Paris, May 1986.

Moritz, William. "Der Traum von der Farbmusik." In *Clip, Klapp, Bum. Von der Visuellen Musik zum Musikvideo*, edited by Veruschka Body and Peter Weibel, 17–51. Cologne: DuMont, 1987.

Bendazzi, Giannalberto. *Cartoons: Il cinema d'animazione, 1888–1988*. Venice: Marsilio Editori, 1988. English edition: *Cartoons: One Hundred Years of Cinema Animation*. Translated by Anna Taraboletti-Segre. London: John Libbey & Co. Ltd., 1994.

Peacock, Kenneth. "Instruments to Perform Color-music: Two Centuries of Technological Experimentation." *Leonardo* 21, no. 4 (1988): 397–406.

Ehrlich, Susan. "Oskar Fischinger." In *Turning The Tide: Early Los Angeles Modernists, 1920–1956*, edited by Paul J.Karlstrom and Susan Ehrlich, 63–67. Santa Barbara: Santa Barbara Museum of Art, 1990.

Ehrlich, Susan. "Southern California's Modernist Dawn." *Artspace: A Magazine of Contemporary Art*, vol. 16, no. 6 (Fall 1991): 80–81.

Moritz, William. "Film Censorship during the Nazi Era." In *Degenerate Art: The Fate of The Avant-Garde in Nazi Germany*, edited by Stephanie Barron, 184–91. New York and Los Angeles: Harry N. Abrams, with Los Angeles County Museum of Art, 1991. German edition: *Entartete Kunst: das Schicksal der Avantgarde im Nazi-Deutschland*, 184–91. Munich: Hirmer, 1992.

Lorenz, Marianne. "Kandinsky and Regional America." In *Theme & Improvisation: Kandinsky & The American Avant-Garde*, 159–62. Exhibition catalog. Dayton and Boston: Dayton Art Institute with Bullfinch Press, 1992.

Gehr, Herbert, ed. *Optische Poesie: Oskar Fischinger, Leben und Werk*. Frankfurt am Main: Deutsches Filmmuseum, 1993. [Contains factual errors]

Moritz, William. "Visuelle Musik: Höhlenmalereien für MTV? (Visual Music: Cave Painting to MTV?)." In *Sound & Vision*, exhibition catalog, edited by Walter Schobert, 132–45. Frankfurt: Deutsches Filmmuseum, 1993. English version online at www.centerforvisualmusic.org/library/WMCavePtgs.htm

Moritz, William. "Musique chromatique - Cinéma intégral." In *Poétique de la Couleur, une Histoire du Cinéma Expérimental*, edited by Nicole Brenez and Miles McKane. Paris: Musée du Louvre, 1995. English version online at www.centerforvisualmusic.org/WMCM_IC.htm

Moritz, William. "Visual Music and Film-As-An-Art Before 1950." In *On the Edge of America – California Modernist Art 1900–1950*, edited by Paul J. Karlstrom. Berkeley: University of California Press, 1996.

Moritz, William. "Oskar Fischinger." In *L'Art du Movement*, edited by Jean-Michel Bouhours, 154–58. Paris: Centre Pompidou, 1996.

Moritz, William. "Gasparcolor: Perfect Hues for Animation." *Animation Journal* 5, edited by Maureen Furniss (1996): 52–57. Available online at www.oskarfischinger.org/GasparColor.htm

Moritz, William. "The Dream of Color Music, and Machines that Made it Possible," *Animation World Magazine* 2, no. 1 (1997). Available online at www.awn.com/magissue2.1/articles/moritz2.1.html [Contains factual errors]

Allan, Robin. *Walt Disney and Europe: European Influences on the Animated Feature Films of Walt Disney*. London: John Libbey & Co. Ltd. and Bloomington, IN: Indiana University Press, 1999.

Moritz, William. "Oskar Fischinger: Artist of the Century." *Animac Magazine*. Catalog to the Mostra Internacional de Cinema d'Animació, Lleida, Spain, 2001.

Haller, Robert. *Galaxy: Avant-garde Filmmakers Look Across Space and Time*. New York: Anthology Film Archives, 2001.

Leslie, Esther. *Hollywood Flatlands: Animation, Critical Theory and the Avant-Garde*. London and New York: Verso, 2002.

Levin, Thomas Y. "Tones from out of Nowhere: Rudolph Pfenninger and the Archaeology of Synthetic Sound." *Grey Room*, no. 12 (Summer 2003): 32–79, 50–59. Reprinted in *New Media, Old Media: A History and Theory Reader*, edited by Wendy Hui Chun and Thomas W. Keenan. New York: Routledge, 2005.

Moritz, William. *Optical Poetry: The Life and Work of Oskar Fischinger*. London, UK: John Libbey Publishing, 2004.

Duplaix, Sophie and Marcella Lista, eds. *Sons & Lumieres: Une histoire du son dans l'art du XXe siecle*. Exhibition catalog. Paris: Editions du Centre Pompidou, 2004.

James, David. *The Most Typical Avant-Garde: History and Geography of Minor Cinemas in Los Angeles*. Berkeley: University of California Press, 2005.

Keefer, Cindy. "'Space Light Art:' Early Abstract Cinema and Multimedia, 1900–1959," in *White Noise*, edited by Ernest Edmonds and Mike Stubbs, 21-28, 30-31, 33. Exhibition catalog. Melbourne: Australian Centre for the Moving Image, 2005. Online at www.centerforvisualmusic.org/CKSLAexc.htm

Brougher, Kerry and Judith Zilczer, et al. *Visual Music: Synaesthesia in Art and Music Since 1900*. Exhibition catalog. London: Thames & Hudson and Hirshhorn Museum (Washington DC) and Museum of Contemporary Art, Los Angeles. 2005.

Cox, Christoph. "Lost in Translation: Christoph Cox on Sound in the Discourse of Synesthesia." *Artforum* (October 2005).

Jewanski, Jörg and Natalia Sidler, eds. *Farbe - Licht - Musik: Synästhesie und Farblichtmusik*. Bern: Peter Lang, 2006.

Vail, Karole, ed. *The Museum of Non-Objective Painting: Hilla Rebay and the Origins of the Solomon R. Guggenheim Museum*. New York: Solomon R. Guggenheim Museum, 2009.

Bock, Hans-Michael and Tim Bergfelder, eds. *The Concise Cinegraph: Encyclopaedia of German Cinema*. Oxford, UK and New York: Berghahn Books, 2009.

Keefer, Cindy. "'Raumlichtmusik' – Early 20th Century Abstract Cinema Immersive Environments," *Leonardo Electronic Almanac* 16, no. 6–7 (October 2009): 1–5. Available online at www.leonardo.info/LEA/CreativeData/CD_Keefer.pdf

Melchior, Ib. *Six Cult Films from the Sixties*. Albany, GA: BearManor Media, 2009. See Chapter 3, about the film *Time Travelers*, 74–75.

Tobias, James. *Sync: Stylistics of Hieroglyphic Time*. Philadelphia: Temple University Press, 2010. See Chapter 3, "For Love of Music: Oskar Fischinger's Modal, Musical Diagram," 76–108.

Brown, Richard H. "The Spirit inside Each Object: John Cage, Oskar Fischinger, and The Future of Music." *The Journal of the Society of American Music* 6, no. 1 (February 2012).

Kiening, Christian and Heinrich Adolf, eds. *Der absolute Film. Dokumente der Medienavantgarde (1912–1936)*. Zurich: Chronos, 2012.

Evers, Frans. *The Academy of the Senses: Synesthetics in Science, Art and Education*. The Hague: ArtScience Interfaculty Press, 2012.

Zinman, Gregory. "Man out of Time" In *Moving Image Source*. Astoria, NY: The Museum of The Moving Image, August 2012. Online Resource Guide.

Johnson, Ken. "The Lines and Shapes of a Mystical Stenography: Signs and Symbols and Oskar Fischinger at The Whitney Museum," *New York Times*. July 26, 2012 (online), July 27, 2012 (print).

Buchan, Suzanne. "Three's Company." *Artforum* (September 25, 2012).

This bibliography represents selections. Some texts with numerous factual errors have not been included. An extensive bibliography to the year 2004, including many early German texts, can be found in Moritz's *Optical Poetry* (2004).

Please also see the Center for Visual Music's Fischinger Resources website for an updated bibliography and Fischinger's statements, correspondence, and texts: www.centerforvisualmusic.org/Fischinger

Sources for Fischinger's Films

Light Cone, 16mm and selected 35mm prints
Postal address: 41 bis, Quai de Loire, 75019 Paris, France
Phone: +33 1 46 59 01 53
Website: www.lightcone.org

Canyon Cinema, 16mm prints only
1777 Yosemite Ave Suite #210, San Francisco, CA 94124, US
Phone: +1 415-626-2255.
Email: info@canyoncinema.com
Website: www.canyoncinema.com

For digital licensing for exhibitions, and all other film requests, contact Center for Visual Music in Los Angeles
Phone: +1 213-683-1514
Email: cvmaccess@gmail.com

For updated information, see the websites for The Fischinger Trust (www.oskarfischinger.org) and Center for Visual Music (www.centerforvisualmusic.org).

Rental package programs

Two retrospective programs featuring many restored 35mm prints are available from Center for Visual Music in association with The Fischinger Trust.
For booking information contact Center for Visual Music.
Email: cvmaccess@gmail.com
Phone: +1 213-683-1514
Website: www.centerforvisualmusic.org

DVDs

The DVD *Oskar Fischinger: Ten Films DVD* (region-free) features selected Fischinger films. Available through Center for Visual Music (CVM, www.centerforvisualmusic.org) and selected shops.
For future releases, check the websites of CVM or The Fischinger Trust (www.oskarfischinger.org).

Paintings and art

The art dealer for the Fischinger Trust is the Peyton-Wright Gallery.
237 East Palace Avenue, Santa Fe, New Mexico 87501, US
Phone: +1 505-989-9888
Email: info@peytonwright.com
Website: www.peytonwright.com

The Fischinger Trust, Long Beach, California, US, holds many of Fischinger's paintings and drawings.
Email: info@oskarfischinger.org and/or ofischingerinfo@gmail.com
Website: www.oskarfischinger.org

Research and other materials

Center for Visual Music (CVM), Los Angeles, has an extensive collection of Fischinger's papers, films, animation drawings, process material, paintings and related material. CVM also handles requests for photographic reproductions and other materials.
Email: cvmaccess@gmail.com
Website: www.centerforvisualmusic.org/Fischinger/

The Fischinger Trust, Long Beach, CA also has 2 Lumigraphs, some of Fischinger's equipment and various artifacts.

The Deutsches Filmmuseum, Frankfurt, Germany, holds a small collection of Fischinger's early German language business-related papers, one of his Lumigraphs, and a few paintings including the original *Motion Painting No. 1* Plexiglass panels.
Website: www.deutsches-filminstitut.de/filmmuseum/

For all other information contact CVM (cvmaccess@gmail.com) or The Fischinger Trust, (info@oskarfischinger.org and/or ofischingerinfo@gmail.com)

Images

p. 13–14
Autobiography of Oskar Fischinger, c. 1952
Collection Center for Visual Music
© The Fischinger Trust, Long Beach, CA , courtesy Center for Visual Music

I

p. 17
Film still from Oskar Fischinger's very early tinted liquid experiments, c. 1920
35mm, tinted
© Center for Visual Music

p. 18
Stills from *Wachsexperimente* (*Wax Experiments*), 1921–26
35mm, b/w and tinted, silent
© Center for Visual Music

p. 19
Example of Oskar Fischinger's very early film experiments, film still, c. 1923
35mm, b/w, silent
Collection Center for Visual Music
© Center for Visual Music

p. 20
Stills from *Pierrette 1* (from *Münchener Bilderbogen* series), 1924–26
35mm, b/w, silent
© Center for Visual Music

p. 21
Early animation drawings, c. 1920–21
Charcoal on paper, 8.8 x 11.2 in. / 22.5 x 28.5 cm
Collection Center for Visual Music
© The Fischinger Trust, Long Beach, CA, courtesy Center for Visual Music

pp. 22–25
Stills from *Spiralen* (*Spirals*), c. 1926
35mm, b/w, silent
© Center for Visual Music

p. 26
Example of Oskar Fischinger's very early film experiments, film still, early 1930s
Collection Center for Visual Music
© Center for Visual Music

pp. 27–29
Stills from *Seelische Konstruktionen* (*Spiritual Constructions*), c. 1927
35mm, b/w, silent
© Center for Visual Music

p. 30
Stills from *München–Berlin Wanderung* (*Walking from Munich to Berlin*), 1927
35mm, b/w, silent
© Center for Visual Music

II

p. 63
Still from the set of Fritz Lang's *Frau im Mond* (*Woman in the Moon*), showing the special effects rocket by Fischinger, 1929
35mm, b/w, sound
Collection Center for Visual Music
© The Fischinger Trust, Long Beach, CA, courtesy Center for Visual Music

p. 64
Animation drawing with "Krieg" (War), from a sequence, c. 1927, possibly for a UFA film
Charcoal on paper, 8.8 x 11.2 in. / 22.5 x 28.5 cm
Collection Center for Visual Music
© The Fischinger Trust, Long Beach, CA, courtesy Center for Visual Music

pp. 65–67
Stills from *Studie Nr. 3* (*Study No. 3*), 1930
35mm, b/w, soundtrack lost
© The Fischinger Trust, Long Beach, CA
Photographed by Mark-Paul Meyer

p. 68
Animation drawings for *Studie Nr. 5* (*Study No. 5*), 1930
Charcoal on paper, 8.8 x 11.1 in. / 22.5 x 28 cm
Collection Center for Visual Music
© The Fischinger Trust, Long Beach, CA, courtesy Center for Visual Music

pp. 69–72 and back flap
Stills from *Studie Nr. 5* (*Study No. 5*), 1930
35mm, b/w, sound
© Center for Visual Music

pp. 73–77
Still from *Studie Nr. 6* (*Study No. 6*), 1930
35mm, b/w, sound
© Center for Visual Music

pp. 78–79
Still from *Studie Nr. 7* (*Study No. 7*), 1931
35mm, b/w, sound
© Center for Visual Music

pp. 80–81
Animation drawings for *Studie Nr. 8* (*Study No. 8*), 1931
Charcoal on paper, 8.8 x 11.1 in. / 22.5 x 28 cm
Collection Center for Visual Music
© The Fischinger Trust Long Beach, CA, courtesy Center for Visual Music

p. 82
Still from *Studie Nr. 6* (*Study No. 6*), 1930
35mm, b/w, sound
© Center for Visual Music

pp. 83–84
Stills from *Studie Nr. 8* (*Study No. 8*), 1931
35mm, b/w, sound
© Center for Visual Music

p. 85
Still from *Koloraturen* (*Coloratura*), 1932
35mm, b/w, sound
© Center for Visual Music

p. 86
Still from *Swiss Trip (Rivers and Landscapes)*, 1934
35mm, b/w, sound
© Center for Visual Music

III

p. 117
Animation plans for *Kreise* (*Circles*), 1933–34
Pencil on paper, 11.5 x 12 in. / 29.5 x 30.5 cm
Collection Center for Visual Music
© The Fischinger Trust, Long Beach, CA, courtesy Center for Visual Music

pp. 118–19 and cover
Stills from *Kreise* (*Circles*, Tolirag commercial version), 1933–34
35mm, color, sound
© Center for Visual Music

pp. 120-21
Stills from *Kreise* (*Circles*), 1933–34
35mm, color, sound
Collection Center for Visual Music
© The Fischinger Trust, Long Beach, CA, courtesy Center for Visual Music

pp. 122–23
Animation designs for *Kreise* (*Circles*), 1933–34
Gouache on paper, 11.5 x 12 in. / 29.5 x 30.5 cm
Collection Oskar Fischinger / Deutsches Filminstitut — DIF, Frankfurt am Main (Germany)
© The Fischinger Trust, Long Beach, CA

p. 124
Animation gouaches for *Quadrate* (*Squares*), 1934
Gouache on paper, 11.5 x 12 in. / 29.5 x 30.5 cm
Collection Oskar Fischinger / Deutsches Filminstitut — DIF, Frankfurt am Main (Germany)
© The Fischinger Trust, Long Beach, CA

p. 125
Animation gouaches for *Quadrate* (*Squares*), 1934
Gouache on paper, 11.5 x 12 in. / 28 x 30.5 cm
Collection The Fischinger Trust, Long Beach, CA
© The Fischinger Trust, Long Beach, CA
Photograph by Peter Brenner

pp. 126–27
Stills from *Muratti Greift Ein* (*Muratti Gets in the Act*) Commercial, 1934
35mm, color, sound
© Center for Visual Music

pp. 128–31
Stills from *Komposition In Blau* (*Composition in Blue*), 1935
35mm, color, sound
© Center for Visual Music

p. 129 (bottom)
© The Fischinger Trust, Long Beach, CA, courtesy Center for Visual Music

p. 132
Four painted circles from animation sequence; likely unfilmed, no date, likely 1930s
(bottom) Reverse of painted animation, showing plans for the sequence
Tempera and pencil on paper, 7.9 x 9 in. / 20 x 22.9 cm
Collection Center for Visual Music
© The Fischinger Trust, Long Beach, CA, courtesy Center for Visual Music

IV

p. 169
Animation drawings for *Allegretto*, 1936–43
Pencil on paper, 8.8 x 11.1 in. / 22.35 x 28.1 cm
These were used as a guide under transparent animation cels, which were painted according to the pencil drawings and notes
Collection Center for Visual Music, gift of The Fischinger Trust
© The Fischinger Trust, Long Beach, CA, courtesy Center for Visual Music

p. 170 (top, left)
Still from *Allegretto*, 1936–43
35mm, color, sound
© The Fischinger Trust, Long Beach, CA, courtesy Center for Visual Music

pp. 170–71 and front flap
Stills from *Allegretto*, 1936–43
35mm, color, sound
© Center for Visual Music

p. 172
Sketch for *Fantasia*, 1939, not used in the film
Pastel and pencil on paper, 5.4 x 7 in. / 12.7 x 17.8 cm
Collection The Fischinger Trust, Long Beach, CA
Courtesy Center for Visual Music

p. 172
Sketch for *Fantasia*, 1939, not used in the film
Tempera on animation paper, 8.3 x 8.8 in. / 21 x 22.5 cm
Collection The Fischinger Trust, Long Beach, CA
Courtesy Center for Visual Music

p. 173
An Optical Poem, 1938
Oil on plywood, 36 x 25 in. / 91.4 x 63.5 cm
Collection The Fischinger Trust, Long Beach, CA, promised gift to Center for Visual Music
This is part of a background used in the making of the film of the same name.
© The Fischinger Trust, Long Beach, CA

pp. 174–75
Animation designs for an unrealized film, from a series, no date, likely 1940s
Gouache on paper, 4.5 x 5 in. / 11.4 x 12.7 cm (image); 8.6 x 8.75 in. / 21.8 x 22.2 cm (animation paper)
Collection The Fischinger Trust, Long Beach, CA
© The Fischinger Trust, Long Beach, CA, courtesy Center for Visual Music

p. 176
Experiment, 1936
Oil on canvas, 60 x 40 in. / 152.5 x 101.5 cm
The Buck Collection, Laguna Hills, CA
© The Fischinger Trust, Long Beach, CA

p. 177
Abstraction, 1936
Gouache and watercolor on paper 17.8 x 11.8 in. / 45.5 x 30 cm
Yale University Art Gallery, New Haven, Connecticut, gift of Collection Société Anonyme

pp. 178–79
Stills from *An American March*, 1941
35mm, color, sound
© Center for Visual Music

pp. 180–81
Unshot animation drawings, from a sequence, no date
Tempera on paper, 7.9 x 9.8 in. / 20 x 25cm
Collection Center for Visual Music
© The Fischinger Trust, Long Beach, CA, courtesy Center for Visual Music

pp. 182–85
Stills from *Radio Dynamics*, 1942
35mm, color, silent
© Center for Visual Music

p. 184 (bottom, left)
Still from *Radio Dynamics*, 1942
35mm, color, silent
© The Fischinger Trust, Long Beach, CA, courtesy Center for Visual Music

pp. 186–87
Stills from *Motion Painting No.1*, 1947
35mm, color, sound
© Center for Visual Music

p. 188 (left)
Stills from *Sugar Pops Cereal Commercial*, early 1950s
35mm, b/w, unfinished
© Center for Visual Music

p. 188 (right)
Stills from *Oklahoma Gas Commercial*, c. 1952
35mm, b/w, sound
© Center for Visual Music

p. 189 (left)
Stills from Fischinger's special effects rocket for the title sequence of *Space Patrol*, a 1950s children's television program
Collection Center for Visual Music
© Center for Visual Music

p. 189 (right)
Stills from *Muntz TV Commercial*, 1952
35mm, b/w, sound
© Center for Visual Music

p. 190 (top)
Possible sketch for animation, post-1936 done in Los Angeles
Collection Center for Visual Music
© The Fischinger Trust, Long Beach, CA , courtesy Center for Visual Music

p. 190 (bottom)
Design sketch, 1944, title sequence for *Jane Eyre* feature film starring Orson Welles (not used in film)

Collection Center for Visual Music
© The Fischinger Trust, Long Beach, CA, courtesy Center for Visual Music

V

p. 203
Layers of Sounds, 1947
Oil on canvas, 12.9 x 19 in. / 33 x 48 cm
Collection The Fischinger Trust, Long Beach, CA
© The Fischinger Trust, Long Beach, courtesy Peyton-Wright Gallery, Santa Fe, NM
Photograph by Peter Brenner

p. 204
Triangular Planes (Stereo painting), 1949
Oil on wood, 9.8 x 14.9 in. / 25 x 38 cm
Collection of John Gunn, Sante Fe, NM
Photo courtesy Peyton-Wright Gallery, Santa Fe, NM
© The Fischinger Trust, Long Beach, CA

p. 205
Circles in Circle (Stereo painting), 1949
Oil on Masonite, (2x) 12 x 12 in. / (2x) 30 5 x 30.5 cm
Collection The Fischinger Trust, Long Beach, CA
© The Fischinger Trust, Long Beach, CA
Photograph by Peter Brenner

p. 206
Untitled (Stereo film panels), 1957
Oil on acrylic and board
15.4 x 38.8 in. / 39 x 98.5 cm
Collection The Fischinger Trust, Long Beach, CA
© The Fischinger Trust, Long Beach, CA
photograph by Peter Brenner

p. 207
Sound Painting, 1951
Oil on canvas, 44 x 52 in. / 112 x 132 cm
Collection Center for Visual Music, gift from Dian Iversen
© The Fischinger Trust, Long Beach, CA
Photograph by Peter Brenner

p. 208
Red and Green Concentric, 1952
Oil on canvas board, 30 x 25 in. / 76 x 63.5 cm
Collection The Fischinger Trust, Long Beach, CA
© The Fischinger Trust, Long Beach, CA
Photo courtesy of Jack Rutberg Fine Arts and Center for Visual Music

p. 209
Fugue, 1959
Oil on canvas, 40 x 33 in. / 102 x 84 cm
Collection The Fischinger Trust, Long Beach, CA
© The Fischinger Trust, Long Beach, CA
photograph by Peter Brenner

p. 210
Pulsation, 1964
Oil on canvas panel, 18 x 24 in. / 46 x 61 cm
Collection The Fischinger Trust, Long Beach, CA
© The Fischinger Trust, Long Beach, CA
Photograph by Peter Brenner

p. 211
Molecular Study, 1965
Oil on canvas, 36 x 48 in. / 91.5 x 122 cm
Collection The Fischinger Trust, Long Beach, CA
© The Fischinger Trust, Long Beach, CA
Photo courtesy of Peyton-Wright Gallery, Santa Fe, NM

p. 212
Space Abstraction No. 3, 1966
Oil on canvas, 48 x 35 in. /122 x 89 cm
Collection Center for Visual Music
Photo courtesy Center for Visual Music and Jack Rutberg Fine Arts
© The Fischinger Trust, Long Beach, CA

p. 213
Stills from Fischinger's later experiments with his motion painting techniques, 1957–60
35mm and 16mm fragments, color, silent
Collection Center for Visual Music
© Center for Visual Music

p. 214–15
Raumlichtkunst, c. 1926/2012 (restoration/re-creation from Fischinger's 1920s originals)
Three-screen projection: three 35mm films transferred to high-definition video, b/w and color, accompanying sound
Installation views: Whitney Museum of American Art, New York, 2012
Collection Center for Visual Music
© Center for Visual Music

p. 216
Raumlichtkunst, c. 1926/2012 (restoration/re-creation from Fischinger's 1920s originals)
Three-screen projection: three 35mm films transferred to high-definition video, b/w and color, accompanying sound
Collection Center for Visual Music
© Center for Visual Music

Illustrations in the essays

p. 34, fig. 1
Léopold Survage, *Colored Rhythm: Study for the Film*, 1913
Watercolor and ink on paper on paper-faced board, 14.2 x 10.5 in. / 36 x 26.6 cm
Collection Museum of Modern Art, New York
© 2012 Léopold Survage / Artists Rights Society (ARS), New York / ADAGP, Paris

p. 34, fig. 2
Still from *Spiralen* (*Spirals*), c. 1926
35mm, b/w, silent
© Center for Visual Music

p. 34, fig. 3
Example of Gasparcolor test, 1930's
Collection Center for Visual Music
© Center for Visual Music

p. 36, fig. 4
Len Lye, stills from *Rainbow Dance*, 1936
35mm, color, sound; Gasparcolor
Reproduced with permission of the the British Postal Museum and Archive and the Len Lye Foundation and with the assistance of the Govett Brewster Art Gallery and the New Zealand Film Archive Nga Kaitiaki O Nga Taonga Whitiahua

p. 37, fig. 5
Still from *Staffs*, 1923–27
35mm, b/w and tinted, silent
© Center for Visual Music

p. 37, fig. 6
Paul Klee, *Fugue in Red*, 1921
Watercolor and pencil on paper on board, 9.65 x 12.4 in. / 24,5 x 31.5 cm
Private collection Switzerland, deposit at Zentrum Paul Klee, Bern (Switzerland)
© Zentrum Paul Klee, Bern (Switzerland)

p. 37, fig. 7
Still from *Radio Dynamics*, 1942
35mm, color, silent
© Center for Visual Music

p. 38, fig. 8
Still from *Studie Nr. 7* (*Study No. 7*), 1931
35mm, b/w, sound
© Center for Visual Music

p. 38, fig. 9
Still from *Komposition In Blau* (*Composition in Blue*), 1935
35mm, color, sound
© The Fischinger Trust, Long Beach, CA, courtesy Center for Visual Music

p. 38, fig. 10
Still from *Allegretto*, 1936–43
35mm, color, sound
© Center for Visual Music

p. 40
Letter written by Walter Ruttman to Oskar Fischinger, 1922
Thermal copy in Collection Center for Visual Music
Courtesy Center for Visual Music

p. 41
Technical drawing related to the Wax Slicing Machine, likely prepared for a patent application, 1921
Collection Center for Visual Music
© The Fischinger Trust, Long Beach, CA, courtesy Center for Visual Music

p. 41
Still from Wachsexperimente (*Wax Experiments*), 1921–26
35mm, b/w and tinted, silent
© Center for Visual Music

p. 41
Wax Slicing Machine by Oskar Fischinger, c. 1922
Collection Center for Visual Music
© The Fischinger Trust, Long Beach, CA, courtesy Center for Visual Music

p. 48, fig. 1
Certificate for Venice Biennale, 1935
Special mention given to Oskar Fischinger (not a juried award), for his "Tontrick Film Atelier" (sound animation film studio).The award is signed "Volpi," for Count Volpi di Misurata, the festival's founder.
Collection Center for Visual Music
Courtesy Center for Visual Music

p. 51, fig. 1
Oskar Fischinger in his Los Angeles studio, c. 1949
Collection Center for Visual Music
© The Fischinger Trust, Long Beach, CA, courtesy Center for Visual Music
Photograph by Lou Jacobs, Jr.

p. 51, fig. 2
Animation gouache for *Quadrate* (*Squares*), 1934
Gouache on paper, 11.5 x 12 in. / 28 x 30.5 cm
Collection The Fischinger Trust, Long Beach, CA
© The Fischinger Trust, Long Beach, CA
Photograph by Peter Brenner

p. 52, fig. 3
An Optical Poem, 1938
Oil on plywood, 36 x 25 in. / 91.4 x 63.5 cm
Collection The Fischinger Trust, Long Beach, CA, promised gift to Center for Visual Music
© The Fischinger Trust, Long Beach, CA

p. 52, fig. 4
Sound Painting, 1951
Oil on canvas, 44 x 52 in. / 112 x 132 cm
Collection Center for Visual Music, gift from Dian Iversen
© The Fischinger Trust, Long Beach, CA
Photograph by Peter Brenner

p. 55, fig. 5
Space Abstraction No. 3, 1966
Oil on canvas, 48 x 35 in. / 122 x 89 cm
Collection The Fischinger Trust, Long Beach, CA
Photo courtesy Center for Visual Music and Jack Rutberg Fine Arts
© The Fischinger Trust, Long Beach, CA

p. 55, fig. 6
Abstraction, 1936
Gouache and watercolor on paper 17.8 x 11.8 in. / 45.5 x 30 cm
Yale University Art Gallery, New Haven, Connecticut, gift of Collection Société Anonyme

p. 56, fig. 7
Bird in Flight, 1946
Oil on canvas, 18 x 24 in. / 46 x 61 cm
Collection Norton Simon Museum of Art, Pasadena, CA
© The Fischinger Trust, Long Beach, CA
Photograph by The Fischinger Trust, Long Beach, CA

p. 56, fig. 8
Experiment, 1936
Oil on canvas, 60 x 40 in. / 152.5 x 101.5 cm
The Buck Collection, Laguna Hills, CA
© The Fischinger Trust, Long Beach, CA

p. 57, fig. 9
Paul Klee, *Memory of a Bird*, 1932
Watercolor and pencil on laid paper, 12.4 x 18.9 in. / 31.5 x 48 cm
Collection Norton Simon Museum, The Blue Four Galka Scheyer Collection, Pasadena, CA

p. 57, fig. 10
Circles in Circle (Stereo painting), 1949
Oil on Masonite, (2x) 12 x 12 in. / (2x) 30.5 x 30.5 cm
Collection The Fischinger Trust, Long Beach, CA
© The Fischinger Trust, Long Beach, CA
Photograph by Peter Brenner

p. 58, fig. 11
Entrance to Oskar Fischinger exhibition at San Francisco Museum of Art, 1953
Collection Center for Visual Music
© The Fischinger Trust, Long Beach, CA, courtesy Center for Visual Music

p. 60, fig. 12
Oskar Fischinger in his Hollywood studio with panels from *Motion Painting No.1*, 1949
Collection Center for Visual Music
© The Fischinger Trust, Long Beach, CA, courtesy Center for Visual Music

p. 90, fig. 1
Kandinsky/Mickey Mouse Collage, c. 1940
Collage on paper, 8.5 x 11 in. / 22.5 x 28 cm
Collection The Fischinger Trust, Long Beach, CA
Photo courtesy Center for Visual Music

p. 92, fig. 2
Animation setup for Muratti cigarette commercial, in Fischinger's Berlin studio, 1934
Collection Center for Visual Music
© The Fischinger Trust, Long Beach, CA, courtesy Center for Visual Music

p. 92, fig. 3
Oskar Fischinger working at Disney Studio on *Fantasia*, 1939
Collection Center for Visual Music
© The Fischinger Trust, Long Beach, CA, courtesy Center for Visual Music

p. 95 and back cover
Elfriede and Oskar Fischinger, stills from *Berlin Home Movies* footage, shot in studio of Oskar Fischinger, early 1930s
35mm, b/w, silent
© Center for Visual Music

pp. 98–101
Unshot animation related to the ornament sound experiments, c. 1932–33.
Paint on paper, 11.6 x 12 in. / 28 x 30.5 cm
Collection Center for Visual Music, gift from The Fischinger Trust
© The Fischinger Trust, Long Beach, CA, courtesy Center for Visual Music

p. 102
Display card with examples of Fischinger's ornament sound, no date
Collection Center for Visual Music, gift from The Fischinger Trust
© The Fischinger Trust, Long Beach, CA, courtesy Center for Visual Music

p. 103
Stills from *Ornament Sound*, 1932
b/w, sound (re-creation by William Moritz)
© Center for Visual Music

p. 104
Examples of strips of ornaments used in Oskar Fischinger's c. 1932 experiments.
Collection Center for Visual Music
© The Fischinger Trust, Long Beach, CA, courtesy Center for Visual Music

p. 104
Oskar Fischinger with fake rolls of *Ornament Sound* experiments, in his Berlin studio, c. 1932
Collection Center for Visual Music
© The Fischinger Trust, Long Beach, CA, courtesy Center for Visual Music

p. 105
"Klingende Ornamente." *Deutsche Allgemeine Zeitung, Kraft Und Stoff* no. 30, 28 July 1932
Syndicated worldwide. Original newspaper
Collection Center for Visual Music
Courtesy Center for Visual Music

p. 109
Example of Gasparcolor tests, c. 1933
35mm. color, silent; Gasparcolor
Collection Center for Visual Music
© Center for Visual Music

p. 110
Two examples of Fischinger's tinting tests, using some of his black and white Studies footage, on Agfa nitrate stock, early 1930s. He also tested pink, blue, and amber tints in this reel
Collection Center for Visual Music
© Center for Visual Music

p. 111
Two examples of Fischinger's hand-painted tests using some of his black and white Studies footage, early 1930s.
Collection Center for Visual Music
© Center for Visual Music

p. 114
About "Motion Painting Nr. 1"
Collection Center for Visual Music
© Center for Visual Music

p. 136, fig. 1
Alexander László, c. 1925
Collection Jörg Jewanski
Courtesy Jörg Jewanski and The Fischinger Trust, Long Beach, CA

p. 136, fig. 2
Postcard *Ein Farblichtkonzert* (A color–light music concert) by Alexander László, c. 1925
Collection Jörg Jewanski
Courtesy Jörg Jewanski, private archive

p. 139
Oskar Fischinger in his Los Angeles studio working with strips for one of his later experiments with synthetic sound, c. 1948
Collection Center for Visual Music
© The Fischinger Trust, Long Beach, CA , courtesy Center for Visual Music

p. 139
Three strips from the synthetic sound experiments, c. 1948
Paper, each 1.5 x 19 in. / 2.5 x 48.3 cm
Collection Center for Visual Music
© The Fischinger Trust, Long Beach, CA , courtesy Center for Visual Music

p. 141
John Cage, postcard invitation to Oskar Fischinger, 1937
Collection Center for Visual Music
Courtesy Center for Visual Music

p. 142
Graphic notation for *An Optical Poem*, c. 1937
Collection Center for Visual Music
© The Fischinger Trust, Long Beach, CA, courtesy Center for Visual Music

p. 144
Oskar Fischinger working at MGM studios on *An Optical Poem*, 1937
Collection Center for Visual Music
© The Fischinger Trust, Long Beach, CA, courtesy Center for Visual Music

p. 146, fig. 1
Photograph of main part of Synthetic Sound Machine
Collection Center for Visual Music, gift of The Fischinger Trust
© Center for Visual Music, courtesy Joseph Hyde

p. 146, fig. 2
Template score, page 3 of 5, titled "Bolero" (segment)
Collection Center for Visual Music
© The Fischinger Trust, Long Beach, CA, courtesy Center for Visual Music

p. 147, fig. 3
Diagram for Synthetic Sound patent application (never filed), page 1 of 2, c. 1948
Collection Center for Visual Music
© The Fischinger Trust, Long Beach, CA, courtesy Center for Visual Music

p. 149, fig. 1
Cut up score, fragments taken from piano reduction to Souza's "Stars and Stripes" march (excerpt), no date
Collection Center for Visual Music, gift from The Fischinger Trust, Long Beach, CA
© The Fischinger Trust, Long Beach, CA, courtesy Center for Visual Music

p. 149, fig. 2
Graph paper score, page 3 of 3, titled "Die Lustigen Weiber," believed connected to *Komposition In Blau* (*Composition in Blue*, excerpt)
Collection Center for Visual Music
© The Fischinger Trust, Long Beach, CA, courtesy Center for Visual Music

p. 150, fig. 3
Graph paper fragment, untitled, believed connected to *An American March*
Collection Center for Visual Music, gift of Fischinger Trust, Long Beach, CA
© The Fischinger Trust, Long Beach, CA, courtesy Center for Visual Music

pp. 153–56, fig. 1–4
Still from *Motion Painting No.1*, 1947
35mm, color, sound
© Center for Visual Music

p. 156, fig. 5
Award from *Festival Mondial du Film et des Beaux-arts de Belgique*, Knokke–Le Zoute, 1949
During this period Fischinger used both the Americanized "Oscar" and the German "Oskar," though he settled on "Oskar," as used on his film head credits
Collection Center for Visual Music
Courtesy Center for Visual Music

p. 158, fig. 6
Oskar Fischinger in his Hollywood studio with panels from *Motion Painting No.1*, 1949
Collection Center for Visual Music
© The Fischinger Trust, Long Beach, CA, courtesy Center for Visual Music
Photograph by Lou Jacobs, Jr

p. 163
Oskar Fischinger, Berlin, early 1930s
Collection Center for Visual Music
© The Fischinger Trust, Long Beach, CA, courtesy Center for Visual Music

p. 194, fig. 1
Drawing for the Lumigraph, on Fischinger's letterhead, likely late 1940's
Collection Center for Visual Music
© The Fischinger Trust, Long Beach, CA, courtesy Center for Visual Music

p. 195, fig. 2
Drawing for patent application for the Lumigraph, 1950
Collection Center for Visual Music
© Fischinger Trust, Long Beach, CA, courtesy Center for Visual Music

p. 196, fig. 3
Elfriede Fischinger, stills from *Lumigraph Film*, 1969
16mm, color, silent
© Center for Visual Music

p. 198, fig. 4
Invitation card, San Francisco Museum of Art, 1953
Collection of Center for Visual Music
© Center for Visual Music

p. 198, fig. 5
L–R: Elfriede Fischinger, Barbara Fischinger, and William Moritz with the Lumigraph in Goethe Institut, Los Angeles, c. 1995
Collection Center for Visual Music
© Fischinger Trust, Long Beach, CA
Photograph by Conrad Fischinger

Contributors to this publication

Cindy Keefer is an archivist and curator, and Director of Center for Visual Music. She curates, lectures, teaches, and publishes on Fischinger and visual music internationally. She has preserved dozens of films by artists including Fischinger, Jordan Belson, Jules Engel, Jud Yalkut, John and James Whitney, and she produced the Fischinger *Raumlichtkunst* restoration/re-creation project, Belson's last film *Epilogue* (2005), and the Fischinger and Belson DVDs. Keefer curates and presents film and media programs at museums, festivals, and venues worldwide, and has recently served as consultant to The Guggenheim Museum, LACMA, The John Cage Trust, and Terrence Malick (*Tree of Life*). She has a degree in Film from New York University and received a Peabody Award for her work. She has worked with Fischinger's estate since 1997. She is currently working on a book about Jordan Belson's Vortex Concerts.

Jaap Guldemond is Director of Exhibitions at EYE Filmmuseum. Prior to this he was a senior curator at Museum Boijmans Van Beuningen in Rotterdam, Head of Collections and Presentations at the Kröller-Müller Museum in Otterlo, and a curator at the Van Abbemuseum in Eindhoven, where he organized the exhibition *Cinéma Cinéma. Contemporary Art and the Cinematic Experience* in 1999. Guldemond has worked with many film-related artists, including Douglas Gordon, Pierre Huyghe, Eija-Liisa Ahtilla, Mark Lewis, Anri Sala, Isaac Julien, and Yang Fudong. At Museum Boijmans Van Beuningen, he organized the Artist in Focus series for the International Film Festival Rotterdam (IFFR).

Sandra den Hamer studied Film and Theatre Sciences at the University of Utrecht. She began her long-time association with the International Film Festival Rotterdam (IFFR) in 1986, while still studying. She started as coordinator at the CineMart and Hubert Bals Fund and as festival producer, before becoming its deputy director in 1991. In 2000 she was appointed as director of the festival, first together with Simon Field and since 2004 as sole director. Over the last twenty-five years Den Hamer has actively participated in various international juries, panels, seminars and co-production work-shops. She was appointed in 2007 as Director of the Netherlands Filmmuseum in Amsterdam, and in 2010 as the director of the newly founded EYE Filmmuseum (a merger between the Filmmuseum, Holland Film, the Netherlands Institute for Film Education, and the Filmbank).

Authors

Jean-Michel Bouhours was head of the film department of the Centre Georges Pompidou from 1992 to 2003. From 2003 to 2008 he was Director of the Nouveau Musée National de Monaco (NMNM), and from 2008 to 2011 he was Head Curator of Modern Collections at the Musée National d'Art Moderne (MNAM). He has published and edited numerous works and exhibition catalogs, including *L'âge d'or*, a special issue of the *Cahiers du MNAM* (1994), *L'art du mouvement* (1997), *Man Ray, directeur du mauvais movies* (1997), and more recently, *Quel cinéma* (2010) at the Presses du Réel. Bouhours has curated numerous exhibitions centering on cinema: *Len Lye* (Centre Pompidou, 2000), *Les Années Pop* (Centre Pompidou, 2001), *Michael Snow* (Centre Pompidou, 2002), *Lumière, Transparence, Opacité* (Monaco, 2005), *José Antonio Sistiaga* (Koldo Mitxelena, San Sebastían, Spain, 2011). He is currently preparing an exhibition dedicated to Salvador Dalí at the Centre Pompidou and the Museo Nacional Reina Sofia in Madrid, as well as a monograph on the artist.

Richard H. Brown received his PhD in Musicology at the University of Southern California in 2012, and currently lectures at the University of Southern California, California State University, Northridge, and at Chapman University. He has presented research on John Cage, visual music, and experimental film to the national meetings of the American Musicological Society, the "Music and Media" study group of the International Musicological Society, as well as the Society for Music Theory, and has published articles in the *Journal of the Society for American Music*, *Contemporary Music Review*, and *Leonardo Electronic Almanac*. Brown is currently working on a monograph publication, *Through the Looking Glass: John Cage and Avant-Garde Cinema*.

Dr. Ilene Susan Fort is Senior Curator and The Gail and John Liebes Curator of American Art at the Los Angeles County Museum of Art. An authority in historical American painting and sculpture and its intersections with European and Mexican arts, she has organized many landmark exhibitions and published numerous books, catalogue, articles and reviews, the most recent being *In Wonderland: The Surrealist Adventures of Women Artists in Mexico and the United States*.

Jean-Paul Goergen is a film historian, author, and curator of film programs. Born in 1951 in Esch/Alzette, Luxembourg, he studied political science and journalism at the Free University of Berlin. His research focus is on the unknown German film heritage, early cinema, avant-garde film, animation, culture, advertising, and documentary, and he has published on radio history and Dada. Goergen's research on German animation and documentary focuses on Viking Eggeling, Werner Graeff, George Grosz, John Heartfield, László Moholy-Nagy, Henny Porten, Hans Richter, Walter Ruttmann, Erwin Schulhoff and Viktor Trivas.

Paul Hertz is an independent artist and curator who lectures in Art History and Theory, and Art and Technology Studies at the School of the Art Institute of Chicago. He was Co-Director of the Center for Art and Technology at Northwestern University from 2003 to 2004. His curatorial work includes *Imaging by Numbers* at Block Museum, Northwestern University, 2008. His work has been exhibited at many international media festivals and symposia.

Dr. Joseph Hyde is a musician and sound artist, with a particular interest in visual music. As well as making his own visual music works, he is engaged in research on the work of pioneers in the field, in particular Oskar Fischinger. He is a Professor at Bath Spa University, UK, where he runs the biennial visual music symposium "Seeing Sound."

Jörg Jewanski was born in 1959 in Herne, Germany, and he obtained his PhD in musicology in 1996. He specializes in synesthesia and in the relation between music and visual arts, and has published several books, including *Ist C = Rot?* (1999), *Farbe – Licht – Musik* (2006), and *Musik und Bildende Kunst* (2009). From 1995 to 2008 he was an assistant of the editorial board of the music encyclopedia *Die Musik in Geschichte und Gegenwart*, and he currently teaches musicology at the University of Münster.

Dr. Esther Leslie is Professor of Political Aesthetics at Birkbeck, University of London. She has written two books on Walter Benjamin, published by Pluto and Reaktion, a study of animation and critical theory, titled *Hollywood Flatlands* (Verso, 2002), and *Synthetic Worlds: Nature, Art and the Chemical Industry* (Reaktion, 2005). She runs the website www.militantesthetix.co.uk together with Ben Watson.

Dr. James Tobias is an Associate Professor of media studies and is currently Director of Graduate Studies in the English Department of the University of California, Riverside. Among other publications, he is the author of *Sync: Stylistics of Hieroglyphic Time* (Temple University Press, 2010), a study of musicality across twentieth and early twenty-first century audio-visual media art.

Production and design

Marente Bloemheuvel is an art historian and curator of contemporary and modern art. She is a former curator at the Van Abbemuseum in Eindhoven and at the Kröller-Müller Museum in Otterlo. Since 2001 she has been involved with the official Dutch entry for the Venice Biennale. She organizes exhibitions and has worked as an editor, compiler, and writer for numerous publications and artist's books. Artists Marente Bloemheuvel has worked with include Marlene Dumas, Douglas Gordon, Claes Oldenburg, Willem de Rooij, Ger van Elk, Lothar Baumgarten, and Jason Rhoades. She is currently associate curator at EYE Filmmuseum.

Joseph Plateau graphic designers is located in Amsterdam. Since its founding in 1989, the company has consisted of Eliane Beyer, Wouter van Eyck, Peter Kingma, and Rolf Toxopeus. Joseph Plateau graphic designers works for a wide range of clients, the majority of whom focus specifically on art, culture, and policy.

This book was published on the occasion
of the exhibition
Oskar Fischinger (1900-1967)
Experiments in Cinematic Abstraction
December 16, 2012 – March 17, 2013
EYE Filmmuseum
IJpromenade 1
1013 KT Amsterdam, the Netherlands
+31-20-5891400
info@eyefilm.nl
www.eyefilm.nl

Exhibition

This exhibition is co-organized by EYE Filmmuseum and Center for Visual Music, and co-curated by EYE's Director of Exhibitions Jaap Guldemond and Cindy Keefer of Center for Visual Music

EYE Filmmuseum
Director: Sandra den Hamer
Director of Exhibitions: Jaap Guldemond
Associate Curator: Marente Bloemheuvel
Project Coordinators: Sanne Baar; Claartje Opdam
Film Programmers: Jan van den Brink; Anna Abrahams
Debate and Reflection: Gerlinda Heywegen
Director of Presentation and Communication: Ido Abram
Publicity and Marketing: Inge Scheijde; Marnix van Wijk
Education: Florine Wiebenga
Technical Production: Rembrandt Boswijk; Martin Schrevelius
Audiovisual Equipment: BeamSystems
Installation: Landstra & De Vries

Center for Visual Music
Cindy Keefer
With Barbara Fischinger and James Tobias
Exhibition Interns: Stella Ahn, Katerina Gill
www.centerforvisualmusic.org

Films

Films screened in the exhibition were restored by Center for Visual Music, Academy Film Archive, EYE Filmmuseum and The Fischinger Trust. All films are from the Collection of Center for Visual Music, except *Studie Nr. 8*, from the Collection of EYE Filmmuseum, and *An Optical Poem*, from Warner Bros. Center for Visual Music thanks The National Film Preservation Foundation and The Film Foundation.
Restoration and Digitization EYE Filmmuseum:
Senior Curator: Mark-Paul Meyer
Collection Specialist: Simona Monizza
Film Restorers: Annike Kross; Jan Scholten

Publication

The texts for this publication were compiled by Cindy Keefer, and edited by Cindy Keefer and Jaap Guldemond

EYE Filmmuseum
Editing: Marente Bloemheuvel, Jaap Guldemond
Project Coordinators: Sanne Baar; Claartje Opdam
Translations: Fiona Elliott, Steve Green, Mike Ritchie, Walter van der Star
Graphic Design: Joseph Plateau, Amsterdam
Paper: Arctic Volume highwhite
Fonts: Geometric 415, FF Letter Gothic
Printing and lithography: Die Keure, Bruges (Belgium)

Center for Visual Music
Editing: Cindy Keefer
With James Tobias and Barbara Fischinger
Additional scans, photos and photo preparation: Stella Ahn, Liza Simone, Jan Thoben, Joseph Hyde, Richard Brown, Cinemaculture, The Fischinger Trust, Peter Brenner, Deluxe Archival Services
Research intern: Rachel Wilson
Translations: James Tobias, Barbara Fischinger, William Moritz, Amy Hough

Acknowledgements
The Fischinger Trust, Long Beach, CA;
Barbara Honrath; Helga Marx

Publishers: EYE Filmmuseum, Amsterdam, and Center for Visual Music, Los Angeles

Generous support for the exhibition has been provided by the VSBfonds, Goethe-Institut Nederland and the German Embassy in the Netherlands.

Distributed in the United States of America
by Thames & Hudson Inc.,
500 Fifth Avenue, New York, New York 10110

thamesandhudsonusa.com

ISBN: 978-0-500-97051-5
Library of Congress Catalog Card Number:
2012954144

Distributed in all other countries,
by Thames & Hudson Ltd,
181A High Holborn, London WC1V 7QX

www.thamesandhudson.com

ISBN: 978-90-71338-00-7
NUR: 644

Printed and bound in Belgium.